PH $4 50

PELICAN BOOKS

A HISTORY OF ECONOMIC THOUGHT

William J. Barber is Professor of Economics at Wesleyan University, Middletown, Connecticut. Born in 1925, he was educated at Harvard and then at Oxford, where he was a Rhodes Scholar at Balliol College. After graduating with First Class Honours in Philosophy, Politics and Economics, he studied at Nuffield College, Oxford, and in 1956 he became a lecturer in economics at Balliol. He was awarded his Ph.D. in 1957, and since then he has taught at Wesleyan University.

Professor Barber has a long-standing interest in economic theory, the history of economic thought, and the application of economic analysis to policy making. His writings include *The Economy of British Central Africa* (1961), *British Economic Thought and India, 1800–1858* (1975), and contributions to *Asian Drama: An Inquiry into the Poverty of Nations* (directed by Gunnar Myrdal) and to the Brookings Institution's studies of wage–price policy in the United States.

A HISTORY OF
ECONOMIC THOUGHT

WILLIAM J. BARBER

PENGUIN BOOKS

Penguin Books Ltd, Harmondsworth, Middlesex, England
Penguin Books, 625 Madison Avenue, New York, New York 10022, U.S.A.
Penguin Books Australia Ltd, Ringwood, Victoria, Australia
Penguin Books Canada Ltd, 41 Steelcase Road West, Markham, Ontario, Canada
Penguin Books (N.Z.) Ltd, 182–190 Wairau Road, Auckland 10, New Zealand

—

First published 1967
Reprinted 1970, 1972, 1977

—

Copyright © William J. Barber, 1967
All rights reserved

—

Printed in the United States of America by
Offset Paperback Mfrs., Inc., Dallas, Pennsylvania
Set in Linotype Baskerville

Contents

Contents

Acknowledgements

My intellectual debts to those who have contributed, some of them unknowingly, to the shaping of this book are too heavy to enumerate in full. I wish particularly, however, to record obligations which date from student days in Oxford to a remarkable group of Balliol tutors: Paul Streeten, Thomas Balogh and Patrick Corbett. I should also like to express my thanks to three colleagues in Wesleyan University's College of Social Studies: E. O. Golob, L. O. Mink and E. J. Nell, who have read and commented on portions of the manuscript. None of the above should be incriminated for the shortcomings of the final product.

I wish to thank the following: Macmillan & Co Ltd, London, Harcourt, Brace and World, Inc, New York, and the trustees of the estate of the late Lord Keynes for permission to quote from John Maynard Keynes *The General Theory of Employment, Interest and Money*: Macmillan & Co Ltd, London, and Crowell-Collier and Macmillan Inc, New York, for permission to quote from Alfred Marshall's *Principles of Economics and Money, Credit and Commerce.*

W. J. B.

Prefatory Note

THIS study deals with the development of systematic economic ideas. It is not, however, intended as an inventory of the noteworthy contributions to economic discourse recorded throughout history. Nor, for that matter, does it purport to deal exhaustively with the thought of those writers whose works are discussed. Its objective is at once more limited and more ambitious: to inspect the properties of four distinct modes of economic reasoning developed in the past two centuries by considering the writings of representative contributors to these traditions.

Despite its ruthless selectivity, this procedure has much to recommend it. Each of the intellectual systems to be examined – i.e., those of classical, Marxian, neo-classical, and Keynesian thought – yield different insights into the nature of the economic universe and into the ways in which men can most effectively come to grips with it. The ideas they contain have long outlived their authors and have been adapted to deal with problems quite different from the ones which first prompted their formulation. Investigation of the properties of the major theoretical systems devised in the past thus has a perpetual relevance. Few things on this earth approach immortality so closely as a logically taut set of economic ideas.

The programme sketched above will, it is hoped, make a useful contribution to the reader's appreciation of the nature and significance of the main analytical systems offered by the rich literature of economic theory. But it can provide no more than a beginning. Those who seek a fully satisfying grasp of economic analysis should grapple with its great minds at first hand. If this study can spur some of its readers to explore the classic works of economic theory in depth, its author will have been well rewarded.

9

Prologue

WHY should the history of economics be studied? A sceptic could marshal at least a superficially impressive array of arguments for assigning to any work of economic theory on which the copyright had expired the treatment Hume recommended for treatises on metaphysics: that they be 'consigned to the flames'. Indeed, supporters of this position might be prepared to argue that the writings of dead economists are the repositories of outmoded doctrine, best forgotten lest error be perpetuated.

This line of challenge to historical studies is not limited to the discipline of economics. James Bryant Conant dealt with a similar problem when, as President of Harvard, he taught a course in the history of science. He did so, he confessed, with certain misgivings. If he succeeded in conveying to students how intelligent men could once support the theory of phlogiston with conviction, he might be doing a disservice to budding scientists. In this case he judged the gains from alerting the younger generation to their intellectual heritage to be more than sufficient to offset such risks.

A less militant challenge to the serious study of the past is now perhaps more pervasive. It can be plausibly argued that the concerns of the present call for all our intellectual energies and more. Resuscitating old works, though not necessarily harmful in itself, can be regarded as an expensive luxury. Whatever the intrinsic interest of the subject matter, it can be maintained that its systematic pursuit constitutes a misallocation of resources. It does not necessarily follow from this view that complete neglect of older theories is recommended. Certain proponents of this position would justify a place for the

11

history of economic theory on the grounds that promising students can cut their teeth by exposing the errors of their ancestors.

One need neither venerate earlier economists nor be blind to their shortcomings to feel less than satisfied with this rationale for re-reading them. Such an attitude toward their work easily lends itself to caricatures of their thought and does less than justice to the analytical subtlety of the pioneers. And it may have another unfortunate effect. By implication, modern theories are treated as superior for all purposes to those worked out earlier. Economic analysis, to be sure, has made striking advances in the course of its evolution, particularly over the past two centuries. But to approach the literature that has contributed to this progress in a mood of self-congratulation imputes to current wisdom a quality of universal truth that does not augur well for the prospects for continued theoretical progress.

A strong case for perpetuating the historical study of economic thought can be made on humanistic grounds. Contact with the intellectual giants of the past yields its own rewards. The pure intellectual enjoyment it affords – as well as its capacity to liberate the imagination from the parochialism of our own time and place – requires no justification. This argument may be unanswerable. But, to a pragmatically-minded age, it is unlikely to be entirely convincing. Happily, explorations of older theoretical systems have more to offer to those for whom relevance to the present is an over-riding consideration. Many ideas of the past, for good or ill, live on and with consequences that touch the lives of all of us. The most distinguished economist of this century had this point in mind when he wrote:

... the ideas of economists and political philosophers, both when they are right and when they are wrong, are more powerful than is commonly understood. Indeed the world is ruled by little else. Practical men, who believe themselves to be quite exempt from any intellectual influences, are usually

Prologue

the slaves of some defunct economist. Madmen in authority, who hear voices in the air, are distilling their frenzy from some academic scribbler of a few years back. I am sure that the power of vested interests is vastly exaggerated compared with the gradual encroachment of ideas.*

A fuller appreciation of the modern world and of the ideas that have contributed to its shaping is not, however, the only practical dividend accruing from reflection on theoretical systems of the past. Anyone who seeks to penetrate beneath the surface of complex economic events requires a frame of reference within which the flux of economic life can be reduced to manageable proportions. Only with the aid of such an organizing framework can the world we observe be made intelligible. Otherwise, we lack a criterion for isolating the important from the unimportant influences on economic events.

The way in which this essential operation is usually performed draws on the technique of building up an abstract picture of an economic system – or a 'model' – designed to indicate the inter-relationships between its various components. In the present division of labour, this job usually falls to professional economists. It can be done by others, and at earlier moments in history the concerned amateur often undertook it. Not all of the 'models' guiding thought are, of course, explicitly articulated. Many widely held views on the nature of the economic system and its potentialities and limitations are shaped by less self-conscious and more implicit processes. Nevertheless, it is helpful to all concerned when the organizing theoretical framework is clearly articulated. The findings can then most readily be tested and debated and in this form they can be most easily communicated. At least in democratic societies, the social significance of theoretical inquiries largely depends upon the extent to which their insights can be transmitted to a public audience. For this reason, the more we all know

*John Maynard Keynes, *The General Theory of Employment, Interest and Money* (Macmillan, London, 1949), p. 383.

about the properties of analytical systems employed by economists, the more intelligent our judgements on matters of policy are likely to be.

While economists – both of the past and the present – have been engaged in a common venture in which the public also participates, their efforts have produced a variety of analytical systems. In part the differences between these systems are related to the diversity of institutional conditions to which their formulators addressed themselves. But another matter deserves a prominent place in an interpretation of the various types of analytical structures – the differing purposes each of the major systems was constructed to serve. One should not expect theoretical systems designed primarily to throw light on the causes and consequences of economic growth over a prolonged period, or on the short-period allocative properties of a market system, or on problems of unemployment and inflation, to yield identical perspectives. And indeed they do not. One of the fundamental sources of differentiation between the main families of ideas in economics is to be found in the differing themes around which they were originally organized and which, in turn, moulded the categories used to fill out the analytical structure.

Two analogies may be helpful in conveying the significance of this point. The theoretical constructs supplied by economic theorists are often characterized as sets of tools. But the tools contained in these conceptual kits – like those in tool boxes of the tangible variety – are not cut to identical specifications. Instead, their shaping is influenced by the dimensions of the job they are expected to perform. Tools useful for dealing with certain problems often fail to provide the leverage needed for others.

The operations of an economic theorist may also be likened, in an important respect, to those of a professional photographer. Both are engaged in producing images of reality, but neither can depict reality in its full complexity. Nor would they be doing their job if they did so.

Their task is to capture the essential quality of their subject and thereby to offer insights that the casual observer might otherwise miss. Moreover, in both cases the images conveyed depend on the observer as well as his field of observation. What a camera records, for example, is determined by the direction in which it is aimed, by the focal length setting and by the lens opening. In similar fashion analytical systems in economics sharpen our insights into certain features of the real world, but blur others that lie beyond their central focus. No single system, in other words, can do everything. Indeed, its strengths and weaknesses are the reverse sides of the same coin.

This attribute of theoretical constructions in economics provides a further justification for revisiting the literature of the past. If economists had always aimed at identical targets we would probably be justified – for all practical purposes – in restricting our attention to their most recent findings. But, in fact, this has not been the case. At different moments in time, economists have forged their tools with quite different ends in view.

In the history of economic ideas four major analytical traditions – the classical, Marxian, neo-classical, and Keynesian – stand out. Each was organized around a different set of questions. The circumstances that spurred their formulation have been considerably altered by subsequent events. Nevertheless, many of the central questions on which the pioneer formulators of these 'master models' focused are re-asked at later moments in time. When this occurs, we again encounter the theoretical problems with which they wrestled. The study of these systems thus has a perpetual relevance. The more we know about their capabilities and their limitations, the better equipped we are to deal with similar questions when we re-open them.

PART ONE

CLASSICAL ECONOMICS

Introduction

IT has become commonplace to describe the discipline of economics as beginning with an Adam, whose surname was Smith. While it is true that his great work – published in that revolutionary year, 1776 – launched the classical tradition in economic thought, a larger claim for his innovating role would not be justified.

Long before the eighteenth century, men had speculated about the nature of the economic process and recorded their judgements of its significance. Nevertheless, the questions raised by the classical approach – and the manner in which its practitioners handled them – were recognizably modern. In the main, pre-classical literature had been more disposed to judge economic performance than to analyse it. Medieval economic debates, for example, were largely preoccupied with such ethical questions as: what constitutes the just price? and is usury (i.e. lending at interest) morally defensible? Even after these considerations shaded towards the background, as they had by the seventeenth century, explicit economic analysis on a comprehensive scale was yet to flourish. Though a lively debate was carried on in tracts produced in England at this time, most of its participants took only a piecemeal view of the workings of the economic system and few of them made a conscious effort to detach their arguments from their interest in promoting the advantage of particular groups.

The classical perspective gave a fresh orientation to economic discussion. Yet in at least one respect the classical outlook can be understood as an extension of inquiries initiated by its immediate forerunners. The mercantilist

tradition in England and the Physiocratic School in
France had, in quite different ways, directed attention
to the importance of an economic 'surplus'. The classical
economists sustained the exploration of this issue, but
gave it another interpretation.

Mercantilist pamphleteers in the seventeenth and early
eighteenth centuries, though they did not speak with one
voice on many important subjects, were virtually unani-
mous on one point: the importance of a surplus of
exports over imports (i.e. a favourable balance of trade).
As a practical matter, the generation of a 'surplus' in this
form was also favourable to the earnings of firms engaged
in foreign trade, in whose fortunes a fair number of the
pamphleteers had a personal stake. But the case for a
'surplus' through trade could be and was argued on
grounds of national benefit. A favourable international
balance was alleged to promise power, plenty, or both.
The mechanism through which these happy results were
to be achieved, however, was seldom explicitly articulated.

Circumstances of the times provided several plausible
links between export surpluses and the national interest.
In an age in which the circulating medium consisted
almost exclusively of precious metals, countries (of which
England was one) lacking sizeable and exploitable deposits
of gold or silver were obliged to draw on foreign supplies.
A favourable balance in the international accounts was
thus a pre-condition for substantial enlargements of the
money supply called for by a prospering and expanding
economy. Similarly the accumulation of monetary reserves might promote the interests of the state in either
or both of two ways. The sovereign's ability to command
men and arms was thereby enhanced. In addition, the
acquisition of gold and silver through foreign trade might
deplete the reserves of other states, thus improving the
relative – as well as the absolute – position of the surplus
country. In an era of intense national rivalries few statesmen were indifferent to these considerations.

The pursuit of mercantilist objectives implied a considerable degree of state intervention in economic activity. In the interests of curtailing expenditures on imports most European states of that era encouraged steps toward national self-sufficiency, and on these grounds governments attempted to nurture and protect home enterprises. In England agriculture was sheltered from foreign competition through the sliding scale tariff provided by the Corn Laws (which in years of good harvests virtually excluded grain imports, though when home supplies were low and prices high, imported grain could then bear the cost of the lowered protective duties). Meanwhile, in the France of Colbert, manufacturing establishments were launched and subsidized by government. In addition governments sought to earn as well as to save foreign exchange by stimulating their export trades. This consideration appeared to recommend the award of monopolistic trading privileges to companies prepared to develop new markets – particularly, though not exclusively, in the trade beyond Europe. Moreover, it was held to be important to both the strategies of import restriction and export promotion to hold down costs of production – especially labour costs – at home.

The approach to economic policy adopted by French mercantilism provided the background for the intellectual protests of the Physiocratic School. In the history of economic ideas, however, writers of this persuasion are better remembered for the fundamentally different account they offered of an economy's crucial surplus. In this doctrine agriculture was the only genuinely productive sector of the economy, and the generator of a 'surplus' upon which all else depended. Agricultural production was alleged to be unique; a farmer could plant one seed and, in due course, reap twenty. A manufacturer, on the other hand, could register no similar multiplication in the physical product; he simply altered the shape of the material inputs on which he worked. The Physiocrats drove this point home by describing manufacturing as 'sterile' and reserving the term 'productive' for agriculturalists. One prominent Physiocrat – Dr François Quesnay, a physician in the court of Louis XV, whose duties included attendance on Mme de Pompadour – produced an ingenious diagram, labelled the 'Tableau Economique', to communicate this finding. His intention was to demonstrate how the fate of the economy was regulated by productivity in agriculture and how its surplus was diffused throughout the system in a network of transactions. With this scheme French economic policy could be attacked with the argument that it discriminated against 'productive' agriculture in favour of 'sterile' manufacturing enterprise. This assault on mercantilist policies anticipated Smith's criticism. But the 'Economistes' of the Physiocratic School were also pioneers in another respect: they demonstrated, with a degree of sophistication then unprecedented, how deductive reasoning could be employed to convey a picture of the functioning of an economic system.

The English classical school sustained interest in the origins and nature of an economic surplus and enlarged the assault on the restrictive policies of mercantilism. Like the Physiocrats (but unlike mercantilist writers) its members were to argue that the surplus arose not from trade but from production. Beyond this point the classicists and Physiocrats parted company. In the view of classical writers agriculture was no longer the only productive activity; manufacturing could also generate a surplus. The further probing into the character of the surplus and into the factors influencing its magnitude became, in fact, one of the central themes of classical analysis.

This line of argument was readily compatible with the requirements of emerging industrialism. The availability of a surplus from which capital could be accumulated was clearly a vital concern. No less important to the successful fostering of economic expansion was the efficient utilization of this potential. In the diagnosis provided by classical writers, the institutional arrangements of mercantilism were ill-suited to this assignment. As they saw matters, regulations and restrictions on the movement of men and goods were shackles to efficiency and to growth. They called for a world in which the energies of enterprising individuals would be liberated and in which market privileges accorded to those in official favour would be stripped away.

As has been true both before and since, the technique of inquiry in the classical era – no less than the choice of problems to be addressed – was influenced by the intellectual climate of the times. Most of the main contributors to the classical tradition – and all of its founding fathers – viewed the economic order as analogous to the physical universe depicted by Newtonian mechanics. Economic affairs were regarded as governed by laws which, though ascertainable by man, lay beyond his direct control. In their day-to-day business, men were still well advised to understand the properties of these laws in order to guide their actions intelligently. It was indeed an important objective of economic studies to propagate an understanding of the significance of these laws.

Such a view of the world was to have a formidable influence on the development of classical analysis and on the policy recommendations of its practitioners. Classical economists, like political theorists before them, were disposed to idealize the state of nature. Locke and Rousseau, each in quite different ways, had argued that the conditions of nature provided an appropriate standard against which to measure existing social institutions, and their doctrines could be used to support revolutionary causes. In the hands of classical economists the 'natural order' became a weapon with which to attack the state regulation and protection associated with the mercantilist era. The term 'mercantilism' was actually coined by the English classicists and Physiocrats who used it as a label of abuse. This polemical device has done less than ideal service to historical accuracy. Expressions like Smith's 'the mercantile system' imputed more coherence to the thought of that era than it, in fact, possessed.

These ingredients of the classical mentality were forcefully brought to bear on one central question – the analysis of economic growth over extended time periods. Though the theoretical literature of classicism was to deal with a variety of issues, an overriding concern with the theme of economic growth took precedence in the moulding of its analytical categories.

This choice of focal point was clearly pertinent to the concerns of the time. By all the measurable indices, eighteenth-century Britain had enjoyed a considerable expansion in real output. At least in embryonic form, industrialism was well under way. The tempo of economic life was changing, and at a pace more rapid than most of the classical writers themselves perceived. But if economic expansion had already occurred, it was also clear that much remained to be done.

CHAPTER 1

Adam Smith and the Framework of Classical Analysis

The Wealth of Nations has suffered the fate accorded to most classics: it is more talked about than read. To the popular mind in the mid-twentieth century, Smith's work is now commonly associated – not always accurately – with observations on economic policy. Though Smith was clearly an opponent of 'the mercantile system' and of the apparatus of privilege and state protection supporting it, one may reasonably doubt whether those who pigeon-hole the man solely as an apologist for unregulated business enterprise have fully appreciated such passages as the following:

People of the same trade seldom meet together, even for merriment and diversion, but the conversation ends in a conspiracy against the public, or in some contrivance to raise prices. . . .[1]

The interest of dealers . . . in any particular branch of trade or manufactures, is always in some respects different from, and even opposite to, that of the public. . . . The proposal of any new law or regulation of commerce which comes from this order, ought always to be listened to with great precaution, and ought never to be adopted till after having been long and carefully examined, not only with the most scrupulous, but with the most suspicious attention. It comes from an order of men, whose interest is never exactly the same with that of the public, who have generally an interest to deceive and even to oppress the public, and who accordingly have, upon many occasions, both deceived and oppressed it.[2]

At the same time, Smith saw manufacturers and 'projectors' as the carriers of progress and he urged that they be afforded more space in which to manoeuvre. Much of his practical message was that institutional restrictions (whether legislated by governments or rooted in parochial traditions) were unhealthy. They cramped the rate at which a new and more productive industrial era could mature. Smith's vision of the 'industrial revolution', however, was still remarkably circumscribed. He wrote more about pin factories than about iron fabrication and failed to appreciate fully the pace at which technological change was occurring during his lifetime.

Despite its impressive impact on popular attitudes (and thus, indirectly, on economic policies) Smith's work deserves to be remembered primarily as a highly ingenious contribution to economic theory. *The Wealth of Nations* brought to the foreground the issues that were to dominate the attention of economists for the next three quarters of a century and which, for that matter, have never lost their pertinence. This aspect of his thought, set out most fully in the first two of the five books into which his treatise is divided, calls for careful inspection. With a degree of comprehensiveness unrivalled by his predecessors he here formulated the grand design of an economic order in which all the parts could be seen in relation to one another. His views on policy, however, were derivative and cannot be adequately understood if detached from their theoretical moorings.

1. ADAM SMITH (1723–90)

Smith was born to a Lowland Scots family of modest circumstances and reared by a mother who was widowed a few months before his birth. He early distinguished himself as a student and, at the age of fourteen, entered the University of Glasgow. While there, he studied under the colourful Professor Hutcheson, the man credited with coining the phrase 'the greatest happiness for the greatest number', whose naturalistic approach to moral questions and espousal of religious and political liberty clashed with prevailing theological doctrine. Smith was later to count Hutcheson among his important intellectual creditors.

In 1740 Smith was elected to the Snell Exhibition, a scholarship awarded to promising Scotsmen for continued study at Balliol College, Oxford. He was to spend the next six years of his life there. Despite the duration of his stay he found the Oxford academic atmosphere far from congenial. He was not a popular figure and did not get on well with fellow students or with his teachers. He found space in *The Wealth of Nations* to record his judgement on the latter: 'In the University of Oxford, the greater part of the public professors have, for these many years, given up altogether even the pretence of teaching.'[3] This state of affairs, in his view, was but a manifestation of a general economic principle: that when financial rewards were divorced from criteria of performance, neglect of duties was likely to result.[4]

Smith had originally been sent to Oxford with the expectation that he would enter holy orders. His sceptical turn of mind and sympathy for the works of David Hume (an attachment that strained his relationship with the Balliol tutors) ruled out this career. Upon his return to Scotland in 1746 he sought a teaching position – a search fulfilled five years later when his old university, Glasgow, called him to fill the chair of Logic. In the following year, he shifted to the chair Hutcheson had once held as Professor of Moral Philosophy.

The major fruit of this period in his life was *The Theory of Moral Sentiments*, published in 1759. This work, which has little distinction as a contribution to philosophy, was a preliminary attempt on Smith's part to formulate the character of a 'natural order' of society. Human conduct was analysed in terms of three pairs of motives: self-love and sympathy; the desire to be free and a sense of propriety; the habit of labour and the propensity to exchange. In Smith's view these natural sentiments acted as checks and balances on one another and

supported a social order of natural harmonies in which
each man, when left to pursue his own interests, uncon-
sciously promoted the common good. Other themes, later
to be worked out more fully in *The Wealth of Nations,*
emerged in his Glasgow lectures. Already he was arguing
that 'the division of labour is the great cause of the increase of public opulence, which is always proportioned
to the industry of the people, and not to the quantity
of gold and silver, as is foolishly imagined.'[5]

In 1762 Smith resigned his professorship to accept a
position as tutor to the son of the Duke of Buccleuch.
Quite apart from its financial attractions this appointment brought opportunities for continental travel and
made few demands on his energies. He wrote from France
to his friend, David Hume, on 5 July 1764: 'I have begun
to write a book in order to pass away the time. You may
believe I have very little to do.'[6]

The incubation period of *The Wealth of Nations* was
extended. Writing from Edinburgh in 1772, Hume, who
had been led to believe that the work was near completion in 1769, upbraided Smith:

I should agree to your Reasoning if I could trust your
Resolution. Come hither for some weeks about Christmas;
dissipate yourself a little; return to Kirkaldy; finish your
work before autumn; go to London, print it, return and settle
in this town, which suits your studious independent turn
even better than London. Execute this plan faithfully, and I
forgive you. . . .[7]

Ultimately, *The Wealth of Nations* appeared in 1776.

Smith spent the last thirteen years of his life as His
Majesty's Commissioner of Customs for Scotland. He is
reported to have discharged his administrative duties
competently. It is one of those ironies of the times that a
man who had devoted a substantial part of his intellectual activity to producing arguments favouring the
promotion of free trade and the minimization of governmental interference in economic affairs should have
ended his days as the beneficiary of such patronage.

2. THE DEFINITIONAL BASIS OF
THE WEALTH OF NATIONS

The central focus of Smith's analysis was stated clearly in the full title of his work – *An Inquiry into the Nature and Causes of the Wealth of Nations*. Put in more modern terms, he was concerned with developing a theory of economic growth.

Smith announced his major explanation for economic growth in the early pages of his work with a phrase that has since become the stock-in-trade of economists – 'the division of labour'. This expression has a deceptive simplicity. Smith employed it in two quite distinct senses. The first referred to the specialization of the labour force accompanying economic advance that brought with it the 'greatest improvement in the productive powers of labour, and the greater part of the skill, dexterity, and judgement with which it is any where directed, or applied. . . .'[8] The full benefits of the progressive sub-division of tasks were available, however, only to a society in which production for exchange could take place. The capacity of a subsistence economy to generate these output-raising innovations and adaptations was severely restricted. From these considerations it followed that the division of labour was limited by the 'extent of the market'[9] and that measures widening the market – whether geographically (e.g. through improvements in transport and communication) or economically (e.g. through the removal of restraints on trade) – were in the general interest.

Smith's interpretation of 'the division of labour' was not confined to job specialization. It also referred to the division of the labour force between those 'employed in useful labour . . . and those not so employed'.[10] The 'division of labour' in this second sense – which referred to the allocation of the labour force between various lines of employment – played an important role in his analysis of capital accumulation and of the 'progress of improvement' (as Smith was often to describe economic growth). The distinction he had in mind is one which modern readers are likely to find perplexing. Nowadays economists are reluctant to stand in judgement over particular types of jobs, declaring some to be 'productive' and others to be 'unproductive'. They prefer to follow the market's guidelines by regarding labour as productively employed whenever there is a buyer for its services; in short, the gainfully employed population is by definition productive.

Smith, on the other hand, was prepared to divide the working population into two distinct categories. The basis for this segregation can only be understood in relation to his preoccupation with the process of economic expansion over a prolonged period of time. From such a perspective it can be argued – though it is by no means as self-evident as Smith appeared to believe – that differing allocations of the labour force have quite different implications for economic expansion. As he viewed the matter, workers engaged in certain occupations were more likely to promote the advancement of output in the future than those employed in others. He developed the point by asserting that the 'productive' employments must meet two tests: (1) that they led to the production of tangible objects, a condition prerequisite to accumulation; and (2) that they gave rise to a 'surplus' that could be made available for future re-investment. For most practical purposes he equated the 'productive' employments with those in which labour worked with capital.

In Smith's scheme of things the line dividing 'productive' from 'unproductive' employments was not regarded as a value judgement but as an analytical distinction of fundamental importance to the study of long-period economic change. He was, in effect, giving a fresh twist to the distinction used by the Physiocrats before him who had maintained that agriculture was the only 'productive' (or surplus-generating) economic activity. It is worth noting that some modern economists, despite an uneasiness when doing so, have adopted a similar practice when examining the problems of underdeveloped economies. They often describe part of the working population in these areas (most particularly persons engaged in traditional agriculture, but often also in certain services) as 'disguisedly unemployed' – i.e., though working, they make no contribution to the social product.

The implications of Smith's definition of 'productive' also found their way into his interpretation of the national product. Concerned as he was with analysing the changes in an economy's output over extended time periods, he was obliged to operate with a concept that could serve the function now performed by calculations of the national income. In fact, Smith's usage of the term 'wealth' can, with one important qualification, be translated into modern terminology as 'national income'. The point at which Smith and today's national income accountants in Western countries part company turns on the definition of 'productive' activity. In Smith's view, only the outputs of the productive employments of labour should count in calculations of the social product. Virtually all 'service' activities were excluded, on the grounds that they failed to yield either tangible products or reinvestable surpluses.[11] This definition also reinforced Smith's general attitude towards a wide range of policy issues. It followed that all activities of governments were unproductive as well as:

. . . some both of the gravest and most important, and some of the most frivolous professions: churchmen, lawyers, physicians, men of letters of all kinds; players, buffoons, musicians, opera-singers, opera-dancers, etc.[12]

Smith would not deny these groups an income for services rendered. He merely wished to insist that their efforts did not help to make society richer tomorrow.

It would be tempting to dismiss this scheme of classification as nothing more than an expression of a misguided 'materialist' bias. This view, however, was not unique to Smith. All of the major figures of classicism worked with a similar notion. In the modern world it survives in Soviet bloc countries, where it influences the preparation of national income statistics – a phenomenon bearing witness to the classical mould of much of Marxian thought.

3. THE ANALYSIS OF VALUE

The emphasis Smith assigned to the market as a regulator of the division of labour called for further probing into the nature of the economic process and, in particular, into the manner in which economic value was determined. In this connexion, his opening move was to draw a sharp line of demarcation between 'value in use' and 'value in exchange'. He found only the latter economically interesting. Some items (his examples were water and air) have vast utility but are not exchanged, while others (e.g. diamonds) possessed in his view little utility though they clearly could command a great deal in exchange. Smith mapped out a three-stage programme for his investigation of the problems of economic value: (1) to identify the 'real' measure to value; (2) to isolate its component parts; and (3) to analyse the factors that might account for a deviation of the 'market price' from the 'natural price'.[13]

From his own characterization of his analytical targets it is readily apparent that Smith was raising questions some distance removed from those most economists would now consider pertinent. A mid-twentieth century economist, asked to state the 'value' of a particular commodity, would normally proceed by trying to establish the price the market was prepared to pay for it. Writers in the classical tradition, on the other hand, were at pains to insist that price and value could not be so readily collapsed into one another. 'Value' was viewed as independent of the market's whims. Nominal (or market) prices might fluctuate, but value remained constant and invariant.

Many later commentators have treated this approach as superfluous metaphysics. Yet most classical writers set great store on the distinction and, by their lights, with good reason. Smith expected his account of value to do two jobs. In the first place, he said that it provided at least a partial explanation of the behaviour of market prices; further (and more important to the general thrust of his reasoning), it promised to provide a basis for measuring aggregate economic change over an extended period. As market prices were too volatile to be satisfactory in measuring inter-temporal changes in output, a stable and invariant standard was sought. This point has caused considerable confusion, partly because the classical approach is quite alien to thought patterns now conventional and partly because classical writers were not themselves always careful to distinguish between the various uses to which they put their concepts of value.

If value was distinct from price, how then was the former established? Smith asserted that labour was 'the measure of value'. This was readily compatible with the themes he had already developed; moreover, it was in harmony with intellectual currents of his time. At least since Locke an influential strand of English thought had been disposed to regard labour as a 'basic' or 'original' contributor to the economic process.

The assertion that labour provided the 'measure of value' was not, however, free from ambiguity. At least two divergent interpretations of the relationship of labour to value are possible. The first might base the value of a commodity on the quantity of labour required for its production. Smith entertained this interpretation, but he chose to apply it only to the circumstances of a hypothetical 'early and rude' society preceding the appropriation of private property and the accumulation of capital. With this situation in mind, he wrote:

If among a nation of hunters, for example, it usually costs twice the labour to kill a beaver which it does to kill a deer, one beaver should naturally exchange for or be worth two

deer. It is natural that what is usually the produce of two days'
or two hours' labour, should be worth double of what is
usually the produce of one day's or one hour's labour.[14]

He shifted his ground when considering more complex
institutional settings. Value could then no longer be
reckoned simply in terms of direct labour inputs; other
factors – in particular, land and capital – now contributed
to the production process, and their contribution could
not so readily be reduced to labour units. At this point
Smith abandoned the 'labour content' view and asserted
that 'command over labour' was the appropriate measure
of value.

The significance of this measure can best be conveyed
in a hypothetical illustration. Let us suppose that 600
units of labour input[15] are required to produce a particular volume of output. Further, let it be assumed that
landowners and capitalists together require a remuneration equal to the wage bill before making available the
services of the factors of production they control (in other
words, profits plus rents must equal the wage bill as a
condition for production). By Smith's reasoning the value
of the total output would be 1200 labour units – 600
units of direct labour input plus 600 labour units that the
recipients of rents and profits could 'command'.

This circuitous procedure at least salvaged a measurement of output in terms of labour units. Moreover, in
Smith's view it yielded insights into the manner in which
prices were actually formed. The key to an understanding
of Smith's notion of this mechanism lies in his interpretation of the components of the 'natural price' (i.e. value).
The natural price of commodities, he argued, was compounded from three ingredients: wages, rents (the return
to owners of land), and profits (the return to the owners
of capital). The size of each of these shares also had a
natural level. Smith blended these concepts as follows:

When the price of any commodity is neither more nor less
than what is sufficient to pay the rent of the land, the wages

of the labour, and the profits of the stock employed in raising, preparing, and bringing it to market according to their natural rates, the commodity is then sold for what may be called its natural price.

The commodity is then sold precisely for what it is worth, or for what it really costs the person who brings it to market . . . [16]

The market price, however, might not conform to these specifications. Should it fail to do so, the forces of competition were expected to push the market price toward the natural price.[17] Without using the term, Smith was clearly groping for a concept later economists have described as 'equilibrium'. He came close to the crucial idea when describing the convergence of natural and actual prices as 'this centre of repose and continuance . . .'[18]

These formulations, though quite innocent in appearance, contained an important social message. If it was accepted that the natural price represented the real worth of a product, it followed that any practices – whether initiated by governments (in such forms, for example, as restrictions on trade or the award of privileges to chartered companies) or by private interests (in such forms as monopolies or statutes of apprenticeship) – tending to thwart the market's behaviour were socially reprehensible. The outcome would be far better, he maintained, if affairs were guided by the market's 'invisible hand'.

Useful as this by-product of Smith's handling of value was to his larger argument, it was by no means the major influence on the shape of his theoretical structure. Of greater importance was his interest in devising a technique for measuring changes in the national output. To an analyst concerned (as Smith was) with the problem of economic expansion over extended periods of time, it was obviously important to be able to establish whether or not growth had, in fact, occurred. This required a technique for eliminating the distorting effects of price variations. In more modern terminology: the problem called for an index number or its equivalent.

At first glance it appeared that Smith's 'command over labour' formulation provided a solution to this index number problem. It implied that comparative statements could be made about changes in aggregate output between two points in time by stating total output in terms of the number of labour units it could purchase. As a first approximation, this exercise could be performed by dividing the total output, expressed in money terms, by the basic wage. If the result in period 2 exceeded that for period 1, it could be asserted that growth had occurred; moreover, the amount of change in the economy's total output could be established.

But this procedure, on closer inspection, did not fully live up to its initial promise. If wage rates changed between periods 1 and 2, the results would no longer be comparable, unless it could also be assumed that all other prices and income shares had changed in the same proportion.[19] Otherwise conclusions derived from Smith's formula could be quite misleading; if, for example, wages fell while other prices and income shares remained the same, output (expressed as command-over-labour) would appear to have expanded even when no change in production had actually occurred. In parts of his argument Smith seemed to protect himself against this perplexity by taking the position that the natural wage rate tends to be stable for prolonged periods. This view, however, conflicted with notions advanced elsewhere in *The Wealth of Nations* on the course of wages during the progress of improvement.

Another difficulty also confronted this formulation. It could not conveniently deal with the case in which the productivity of labour increased (i.e. when the same amount of labour input produced a larger volume of output). In this situation the total wage bill required for the production of a targeted level of output would be smaller than had formerly been the case, even if wage rates were constant. Should a reduction in the price of outputs then follow (not unlikely in such circumstances), the command-over-labour measurement would convey the impression that total output had shrunk when, in fact, it had grown. Implicitly Smith protected himself against this objection by assuming that costs of production (and with them the income share-out between the various classes) would not vary with changes in the volume of output produced by individual firms. Thus, for example, the cost per pair of shoes would be the same in a plant equipped to produce 100 pairs of shoes per day as in a plant producing ten pairs per day.

This view has been invalidated by later experience. It has since been abundantly demonstrated that in many lines of production unit costs are substantially reduced when high technologies are applied in large concentrations. In the infancy of industrialism, when the economic universe was dominated by small-scale producers, it was not altogether implausible. Smith, while neglecting the influence on productivity of variations in the scale of operations of individual producers, was aware that expansion in the economy as a whole would generate important gains in productivity. As the scale of the economic system grew, the division of labour would be extended bringing benefits to all. Smith appears to have thought that the effects of this gain in productivity would be fairly uniformly distributed throughout all productive branches.

If Smith encountered some awkward stumbling blocks in his attempt to devise an invariant standard for measuring economic change, the problems he grappled with were still real and important. Similar issues persist in modern analyses of economic growth. For his part, Smith pursued the problem even further by trying to devise a procedure that would be convenient for statistical purposes. Though he consistently maintained that 'command over labour' was the conceptually correct approach, he recognized that it might be cumbersome to apply. He ultimately concluded that the availability of food grains – in his terms 'corn' – might, for most practical purposes, be regarded as a proxy. This matter could be more readily established empirically. Corn, in his view, was the main component of subsistence and its availability was a precondition for the effective exercise of a command over labour.

In Smith's hands the appeal to labour as a basic measure of value underwent one further variation. He announced the theme in the following passage:

> Equal quantities of labour, at all times and places, may be said to be of equal value *to the labourer* (italics added). In his ordinary state of health, strength and spirits; in the ordinary degree of his skill and dexterity, he must always lay down the same portion of his ease, his liberty, and his happiness. The price which he pays must always be the same, whatever may be the quantity of goods which he receives in return for it.[20]

The constancy referred to here implied a stability in the sacrifice workers underwent when foregoing leisure for the toil and trouble of work. The realism of this assumption over prolonged time periods may be open to challenge: an increasing specialization of jobs and growth in their variety in a changing economy, as well as the adjustments in wage scales, may well alter the irksomeness of work. Even so, Smith was drawing attention to a highly relevant point that now receives little direct attention in the analysis of long-period economic change: namely, that the extent of economic improvement should be judged not solely by changes in the size of the total bundle of goods but also by the effort required to produce the bundle. In this version of Smith's 'labour as the measure of value' economic improvement could be deemed to have occurred when a unit of labour input brought command over a larger quantity of goods.

Smith's labour approach to the analysis of value has been severely criticized by later schools of economists. To one group of writers its fatal shortcoming was that it did not offer a full account of the determination of prices, and, most particularly, that it neglected the demand side of market behaviour.[21] This criticism would carry more force had Smith sought to produce a systematic analysis of market price formation. But in fact this objective was peripheral to his main programme. He was more concerned with forging concepts that might provide leverage on the problem of measuring economic change over prolonged periods. The materials for developing a clearer analysis of the formation of short-term market prices were at his disposal. Concepts of utility and demand (which were to be used for their purpose by a later school of thought) had been part of the teaching he absorbed from Hutcheson. He chose to reject this orientation toward value theory, presumably because he regarded it as lacking relevance to his central purpose.

Another and more serious charge can be levelled against Smith's approach. It concerns an inconsistency in his treatment of labour units. The labour force, as he recognized, was not homogeneous;[22] some of its members were more skilled (and hence more productive) than others. How were these discrepancies to be reduced to a common denominator? Smith replied that an adjustment was provided 'not by any accurate measure, but by the higgling and bargaining of the market, according to that sort of rough equality which, though not exact, is sufficient for carrying on the business of common life'.[23] In other words, wage differentials established in the market place supplied the basis for reducing the various units of labour input to a common standard; an hour of unskilled labour might be taken as a standard unit while an hour's labour by a worker paid twice as much would be worth two units. It may well be asked: if the market test is sufficient for weighing the units in which value is measured, why cannot the same procedure be applied to the valuation of output? The whole problem of the distinction between value (natural prices) and actual prices would then vanish. Smith's *caveats* about approximations provided no escape from this logical trap.

Though it has become fashionable for modern economists to abuse any 'labour theory of value', a more charitable reading would be appropriate. After all, are

not intellectual operations of much the same sort performed nowadays when economists assume in their projections of growth-rates that prices will remain stable, or
when comparative statements about the economic health
of the U.S., the U.K. and the U.S.S.R. are made on the
basis of the number of working hours required in each
country before a typical worker can earn enough to buy a
specified package of goods – e.g. a pair of shoes, a radio,
or an automobile? Is not a device analogous to Smith's
distinction between natural and market price invoked by
some Western economists working in underdeveloped
areas? They argue that labour is priced too high, capital
too low, and that economic growth would be accelerated
if governments insisted that the decisions of businessmen
on combinations of labour and capital should be governed not by actual prices, but by 'accounting' prices that
more accurately reflect the 'real' scarcities of these productive agents.

4. THE ANALYSIS OF INCOME DISTRIBUTION

Smith's discussion of the 'natural price' had been developed around its three components: wages, profits and
rents. It was thus incumbent upon him to explain the
mechanisms governing the 'natural rates' of these shares
of income (or, in his terms, of 'revenue').

At this point, Smith's argument was constructed around
a tripartite division of society into 'orders', each of which
received a specified income share. Wages were paid to
members of the working class, profits accrued to capitalists
(or owners of stock), and rents were collected by landowners. These distinctions corresponded roughly to the
major social class divisions of his time, though some
blurring at the edges remained. The net receipts of the
smallholder in agriculture, for example, might be a com-
pound of three income shares: a wage return for his own
labour; a rent return from the land he owned; and a
profit on the capital he had invested in his farm. A similar

overlapping might occur in the case of the self-employed small manufacturer. Conceivably the large landowner, should he invest to improve his estate, could thereby receive a profit as well as a rent. While allowing for this possibility, Smith described large landowners as men who loved 'to reap where they never sowed',[24] and as given to 'indolence which is the natural effect of the ease and security of their situation'.[25] This characterization of the landlord class, which played a crucial role in his interpretation of society's prospects during the course of the 'progress of improvement', was not altogether just. As later historical research has demonstrated, much of the agricultural innovation of the period was initiated by progressive large landowners who exhibited the behavioural traits that Smith ascribed to capitalists.

It must be emphasized that Smith, while building his analysis of income distribution around 'three different orders of people', did not regard these divisions as closed compartments. He was too much a child of the Enlightenment to accept the view that a man's position in the social hierarchy was fixed at birth. Nevertheless, class distinctions should be recognized as a social fact, even though a man's membership in any particular group was not providentially ordained. 'The difference between the most dissimilar characters,' he maintained, 'between a philosopher and a common street porter, for example, seems to arise not so much from nature, as from habit, custom, and education.'[26]

At the same time, Smith's analytical categories contrast sharply with those widely used in much current economic analysis. A prevalent modern approach to income distribution is entirely 'functional' in orientation; that is to say, various income payments are treated as rewards to the 'factors' contributing to production. The wage share is the payment to human productive agents, without regard to their social status, including salaries as well as wages; moreover, part of the revenue Smith regarded as 'profit' would now be treated as a 'wage' to management.

Similarly, rent is now often treated as accruing to owners of the God-given productive factor, land; this procedure, though stripped of social class associations, is closer to Smith's approach. Interest (which Smith subsumed under profits) is treated as the return on capital, the inanimate but man-made factor of production. Though the treatment of profit is far from uniform, a venerable tradition supports the view that (apart from the case of monopoly) 'pure profit' over and above rewards necessary to retain the services of productive factors in their present uses can be realized only temporarily before being competed away. In such a 'functional' system all class lines are hidden. Smith, on the other hand, began with a social class division and built the greater part of his analytical structure around it. Though he did introduce some 'functional' considerations, they were intended primarily to cover the fuzzy cases.

How then was the national revenue divided between the various orders of society? Smith's answer was developed in two stages. In the first, he considered the special and peculiar features attached to the determination of wages, profits and rents with considerable attention to the influence of the institutional environment on variations in the level of each. But never far from view was a second and overriding influence: the 'general circumstances of society' – i.e. whether the economy as a whole was stationary, expanding, or declining.

Thus in the case of wages, prevailing scales at any particular moment were likely to be influenced by a variety of factors peculiar to individual jobs: their 'agreeableness or disagreeableness,' their geographical situation, expected duration, the worker's knowledge (or ignorance) of alternative employments and their terms, etc. But Smith also drew attention to another consideration – the relative bargaining strength of employers and employees – and he noted that the scales were often weighted to the disadvantage of workers.[27]

These variations, though important, could operate only

above a lower limit: the minimum wage level required to maintain the labour force in healthy and productive condition. After all, Smith argued, wages could not sink below subsistence requirements without shrinking the size of the labour force. Did it then follow that the 'subsistence' level of wage payments would also be the natural rate toward which actual wages, over the long period, would gravitate? Malthus was to argue this case at a later moment in the evolution of classical theory. At one point, Smith wrote as if in anticipation of the Malthusian position: '... the demand for men, like that for any other commodity, necessarily regulates the production of men'.[28] This assertion implied that a rise in wage rates above the minimum required for subsistence would soon be neutralized by an induced expansion in the size of the population and of the labour force. It would have been convenient for other parts of Smith's analysis had he consistently maintained this position. As noted above, his command-over-labour doctrine could yield intelligible results only when equal amounts of revenue could purchase the same quantity of labour at different times – i.e. when the natural price of labour was constant.

But, once having introduced this notion, Smith quickly moved away from it, arguing that the natural course of wages was closely related to 'the general circumstances' of the economy. An expanding economy was likely to be associated with rising wage rates, a declining one with falling wages, while in a stationary economy there would be little reason to expect wage levels to change.

This argument hinged on what Smith described as the volume of 'funds destined for the payment of wages'.[29] The notion he had in mind calls for a few words of elucidation, both because it is based on concepts now unfamiliar and because its central idea figured so prominently in the general classical outlook. In this view the process of production and exchange was regarded as beginning with 'advances' of funds by employers (capitalists and landlords) to acquire labour and the material inputs required in production. Workers, the recipients of these advances, later spent them on subsistence goods. The same transaction, however, involved the transfer of funds back to employers who could finance 'advances' to initiate the next round of production. Thus, whether the demand for labour in a subsequent period was greater or less than, or unchanged from, the preceding one depended in large measure on the size of the non-wage shares of income (profits and rents) and the proportion of the fund thus generated that was allocated as advances to labour. In a period of general economic expansion it was expected that the wage fund would be enlarged and the demand for labour augmented. This, in turn, would tend to bid wage levels beyond the subsistence minimum and to bring improved conditions to the 'servants, labourers and workmen of different kinds [who] make up the far greater part of every great political society'.[30] Population growth might then follow. But, at this point in the argument, Smith entertained no Malthusian fears:

> The liberal reward of labour, therefore, as it is the effect of increasing wealth, so it is the cause of increasing population. To complain of it, is to lament over the necessary effect and cause of the greatest public prosperity.[31]

The course of economic progress was still not clear, despite Smith's generally optimistic expectations. The behaviour of the second income share – profits – might lead to problems. As Smith saw it, the returns to capitalists and those of wage earners moved inversely: as wages increased, profits would be reduced. Smith's first attempt to explain this relationship amounted to asserting that the more employers paid their workers, the less they could retain for themselves. But this account was too static to be fully satisfactory; after all, Smith had suggested elsewhere that a régime of high wages might well lead to at least compensating increases in output per worker.[32] More basic to his explanation was the increasing competition among capitalists that he expected to accompany economic expansion. With reasoning more convincing in his day than in ours, he held that in a climate of general economic expansion businessmen would be more vigorous in pursuing their own advantage, suppressing their tendencies toward collusion, and competing down the average rate of return on capital. This tendency toward falling profits was reinforced by another consideration that Smith hinted at but did not develop systematically:

As capitals increase in any country, the profits which can be made by employing them necessarily diminish. It becomes gradually more and more difficult to find within the country a profitable method of employing any new capital.[33]

A fuller explanation of the expected effects of the 'progress of improvement' required an analysis of the relationship between profits and rents. Land-ownership and the income share attached to it clearly possessed some special attributes. The consequences of this uniqueness emerged forcefully in Smith's assertion that:

High or low wages and profit, are the causes of high or low price; high or low rent is the effect of it. It is because high or low wages and profit must be paid, in order to bring a particular commodity to market, that its price is high or low. But it is because its price is high or low; a great deal more, or very little more, or no more, than what is sufficient to pay those wages and profit, that it affords a high rent, or a low rent, or no rent at all.[34]

How was this puzzling proposition to be explained? At base, Smith's account rested on the presupposition that nature was generous. Like the Physiocrats before him he viewed agriculture as capable of yielding outputs far in excess of inputs. But unlike the Physiocrats he wished to emphasize that the extent to which this natural bounty would actually be tapped depended largely on society's requirements for the output of land. It was his expectation (and a not unreasonable one) that an expanding economy would generate rising demand for the products of land. This would occur in two ways. In the first place, population growth would swell the demand for foodstuffs. In addition an expanding non-agricultural sector would increase requirements for raw materials derived from the land. Smith, in his day, had in mind raw materials required for industrial processing (such as wool and flax) as well as land-derived materials needed for construction (e.g. timber and stone) and as sources of power (e.g. coal). In combination, these effects would draw idle lands into productive use. But he was also at pains to emphasize – as had Quesnay and his followers – that the initial expansion of non-agricultural output depended, in the first instance, on the availability of foodstuffs and raw materials needed to support industrial expansion.

Substantial growth in demand for agricultural products would have an important effect on the distribution of income between the various orders of society. Most particularly, it would benefit owners of land. Smith anticipated that the demand for the various outputs of land was likely to rise more rapidly than production could be expanded – especially when various claims on land competed with one another; the same plot could not grow corn and graze sheep simultaneously nor could timber supplies be maintained if extensions in the cultivated acreage encroached on the forested area. Prices of agricultural products were thus expected to increase. But in a system of private property land tenure the bulk of this windfall would accrue to land-owners. The rents they collected, which he described as 'naturally the highest which the tenant can afford to pay in the actual circumstances of the land',[35] would swell because tenants could be forced to part with that portion of their product in excess of the natural wage for their labour.

These arguments about the behaviour of various components of the natural price in the course of the 'progress of improvement' might be construed as indicating that economic expansion would ultimately undercut its own foundations. If a rising share of the national product was distributed to high-living landlords at the expense of frugal profit recipients, further accumulation and expansion might be dried up at its source. Smith was aware of this possibility; yet he did not push this argument to its logical conclusion. On the whole he regarded economic expansion as bringing benefits to all. It might be checked at a future point in time, but that day was distant. The emergence of a stationary state, when further expansion would be halted and capital accumulation restricted to replacement requirements, was too remote to call for serious analysis.

5. THE ANALYSIS OF CAPITAL ACCUMULATION

Smith's discussion of the problem of value and distribution set out the conceptual core of his analysis. To be completed, his model required an account of the mechanisms of economic change and of the factors governing the allocation of the labour force between productive and unproductive employments. His expectation that labour productivity would rise as the market widened could carry him only part of the way towards an explanation of economic expansion. The more fundamental analysis of dynamic change rested on the theory of capital accumulation.

Smith's treatment of the process of capital accumulation turned on a distinction between the gross and net (or in his terminology 'neat') revenue of society. This notion, which was to occupy an important place in classical thought, involves concepts rather different from those now in common use. As Smith described the point:

> The gross revenue of all the inhabitants of a great country comprehends the whole annual produce of their land and labour; the neat revenue, what remains free to them after deducting the expense of maintaining; first, their fixed; and, secondly, their circulating capital. . . .[36]

Though his development of these concepts was not altogether clear, he appears to have had in mind a

Classical Economics

subdivision of annual output into two components. The first referred to the portion of current output that would be claimed if production was to be maintained at the same level in the following year. The second component – the net revenue – was intended to isolate that portion of current output which could be made available to augment production in the future.

One attribute of Smith's definitions is especially noteworthy: unlike the net-gross distinctions used nowadays, deductions for maintenance were not restricted to capital consumption or depreciation allowances. Instead, maintenance requirements for the whole society were to be deducted from the gross revenue; i.e. in addition to the wear and tear on fixed capital and the replenishment of raw materials, provision was also made for the 'maintenance' requirements of the various classes of society. The residual represented resources which, at least potentially, could be used to enlarge production in the future.[37]

How then was the size of the net revenue established? In Smith's analysis, the greater part of the answer was to be found in the distribution of income between the various orders and, most particularly, in the shares accruing to capitalists and landowners. Wage earners, after all, were unlikely to be paid enough to permit much, if any, 'surplus' in excess of their 'maintenance' requirements. Landlords and capitalists, on the other hand, might well have larger funds at their disposal than would be necessary to finance replacements and to sustain their conventional levels of living. The 'surplus' might, of course, be allocated to the enlargement of their consumption. But the outcome for society would be happier if these 'surplus' funds were saved. In this manner, the net revenue could be converted into forms that would later enlarge production, a point Smith emphasized when asserting that 'capitals are increased by parsimony, and diminished by prodigality and misconduct'.[38]

Strictly speaking, members of both the classes receiving 'net revenue' might use their resources in ways that sup-

46

ported economic expansion. In Smith's view, however, landlords displayed a distressing tendency to indulge in high living and to engage unproductive hands. For practical purposes, capitalists were the principal agents through which the net revenue could be converted into accumulation. The size of the profit share could thus be regarded as the basic determinant of the pace of accumulation and, in turn, of the rate of economic expansion.

While saving was a vital prerequisite for economic growth, Smith was at pains to point out that saving, as he viewed it, would not lead to withdrawals of funds from the expenditure stream. 'What is annually saved', he wrote, 'is as regularly consumed as what is annually spent, and nearly in the same time too; but it is consumed by a different set of people.'[39] Hoarding, in other words, was ruled out; saving was matched almost instantaneously by expenditure for investment purposes. Smith apparently regarded this point as too self-evident to require elaboration. It was later developed more formally by J. B. Say and was to occupy a prominent position in the development of economic ideas.

The analysis of capital accumulation rounded out Smith's account of the main structural conditions important to an understanding of an economy's capability for growth. Capital accumulation, crucial though it was as a regulator of the pace of economic expansion, could not be analysed in isolation from the distribution of income between the main orders of society. Similarly, his theory of value was now integrated into the scheme as a whole. The main issue in the analysis of growth could thus be viewed in terms of the manner in which the recipients of profits and rents exercised their 'command over labour'.

6. ADAM SMITH AND ECONOMIC POLICY

Smith's theoretical model and his attitudes towards policy questions were part of a single package. He regarded economic growth as the basic goal, the desirability of which was beyond dispute. From this perspective the adequacy (or otherwise) of any particular policy should be measured by its effects on the 'progress of improvement' and, more specifically, by its consequences for the accumulation of capital and the specialization of labour.

When judged by these criteria, the mercantilist pattern of state regulation and control – which Smith saw as an expression of privilege and favouritism – was clearly objectionable. Its net effect, in his view, was to thwart the widening of the market and to divert economic activity from its natural course. For that matter virtually all government intervention – apart from the discharge of such essential functions as the maintenance of law and order, the administration of justice, and provision for national defence – was suspect. Governments were as misguided when they legislated to protect the poor as when they favoured the rich with royal charters and monopolistic privileges. Smith's attack on poor relief did not spring, however, from lack of sympathy with the plight of the less fortunate. Instead he argued that the administration of the existing Poor Laws, which called for residence within a particular parish as a condition of eligibility for benefits, restricted the mobility of labour and thereby suppressed the rate of economic growth.

Though Smith aimed much of his fire at the 'mercantile system', his argument fell short of the level of analytical sophistication reached earlier by his friend, David Hume. In the 1760s Hume had attacked mercantilism by invoking a theory linking the general level of prices to the quantity of money. The larger the supply of money, he had argued, the higher the price level was likely to rise; higher prices, in turn, would tend to make exports less competitive in foreign markets and imports more competitive in home markets. The mercantilist drive to enlarge the stock of money would thus be self-defeating; the accumulation of precious metals would produce effects that would later erode the favourable balance of trade. Hume, of course, needed another prop to this argument before it could stick; after all, a convinced mercantilist could reply that appropriate regulations could check a deterioration in the balance of trade. Hume supplied the needed reinforcement by insisting that restrictions on trade would be damaging to the national interest. A country invoking direct controls would be punishing itself by foregoing the benefits of an international specialization and division of labour. This line of critique carried more weight than did much of Smith's attack. His position, in fact, can largely be summarized in the proposition that government meant restrictions and that restrictions necessarily frustrated the natural division of labour, the operation of the invisible hand, and the progress of improvement.

Within the framework of his analytical system, Smith could quite consistently oppose many of the practices of European governments. But it did not follow directly from this part of his analysis that a régime of *laissez-faire* led to the best of all possible worlds. As he himself had recognized, unregulated private interests – fully as much as governments – might behave in ways that would suppress the progress of improvement.

How was this difficulty to be resolved? Smith's solution, though largely left implicit in his writing, amounted to the view that economic growth and a competitive order were mutually reinforcing. His case against mercantilism rested on the assumption that competition maximized growth. But effective competition could only be taken for granted in an atmosphere of economic expansion. The progress of improvement thus took on an instrumental as well as an intrinsic value; it was the essential catalytic agent for the conversion of potential discord into harmony and the solvent to the barriers to effective competition. Only then could the natural tendencies of businessmen to collude against the public interest be held in check. Similarly, a climate of expanding demand for labour was needed to neutralize the power of capitalists to take advantage of unorganized workers. If competition was

desirable as a spur to growth, economic expansion was no
less important to the promotion of effective competition.

The happy results that Smith saw from an expanding
competitive society involved yet another assumption: that
the benefits of growth would be shared by all orders of
society. Smith himself, as we have seen, was generally
confident that this would be the case. But at least some
parts of his argument could later be interpreted as suggesting that difficulties might lie ahead. Improvements in
real wages for members of the working class might, of
course, be offset by subsequent population growth;
further, the redistribution of incomes between the various
income shares to the net advantage of landowners might
also give rise to complications. These themes can be heard
in *The Wealth of Nations* but only in muted tones.

7. THE ACHIEVEMENTS OF ADAM SMITH

The Wealth of Nations was a remarkable intellectual
achievement. It provided not a piecemeal account, but a
comprehensive and integrated view of the economic process. Moreover, Smith's impressive performance at the
theoretical level was matched by a notable absence of
special-interest pleading of the type that had dominated
so much earlier economic writing.

Perhaps the clearest testimony to Smith's impact and
influence can be found in the theoretical literature produced over the three quarters of a century following the
publication of *The Wealth of Nations*. Subsequent classical writers found much to criticize in Smith's work. But
they paid him the highest compliment a theorist can
receive: both the questions they asked and their mode of
procedure in the search for answers were very largely
moulded by his writing. Moreover, mid-twentieth century
students of economic growth have profited from his exploration into these grand themes. At the popular level
Smith's influence was also considerable. His picture of the
economic universe made its complexity intelligible to

men of affairs and his central message could easily be appropriated by participants in public debates.

Little of the content of *The Wealth of Nations* can be regarded as original to Smith himself. Most of the book's arguments had in one form or another been in circulation for some time. But this fact in no way diminishes Smith's achievement. He was the first to draw the threads together, to fit them into a coherent system, and to communicate the findings to a wider audience. Measured against these standards *The Wealth of Nations* is indeed a formidable document.

Smith's talents as a synthesizer, however, were the source of some analytical imperfections in his writing. At a number of points he offered explanations that were ambiguous or inconsistent. Much of the energy of the next generation of contributors to the classical tradition was devoted to the task of tidying and tightening the basic framework he had developed. Prominent among the issues to which his successors addressed themselves were such questions as the following: how and in what circumstances might the progress of improvement be checked? did it necessarily follow that economic expansion brought gains to all orders of society? was sustained economic progress necessarily a paramount social goal? Malthus, Ricardo, and John Stuart Mill were to address themselves to these topics and to offer answers somewhat different from those Smith had supplied.

Notes

1. Adam Smith, *The Wealth of Nations*, Edwin Cannan, ed. (Methuen, London, 1961), vol 1, p. 144.

2. ibid., vol. 1, p. 278.

3. ibid., vol. 2, p. 284.

4. It is worth noting in passing that Smith's Oxford College bears him no grudge. Balliol's official historian generally seconds Smith's findings on the state of affairs in the mid-eighteenth century, a period not to be numbered among the

College's proudest; see H. W. Carless Davis, *A History of Balliol College*, revised by R. H. C. Davis and Richard Hunt (Blackwell, Oxford, 1963), pp. 154–5. Smith's bust now occupies a place of honour in the Fellows' Common Room.

5. *Lectures on Justice, Police, Revenue and Arms, delivered in the University of Glasgow by Adam Smith*. Reported by a student in 1763, Edwin Cannan, ed. (Oxford University Press, 1896), pp. 172–3.

6. As quoted by C. R. Fay, *Adam Smith and the Scotland of His Day* (Cambridge University Press, 1956), p. 150.

7. As quoted by John Rae, *Life of Adam Smith* (Macmillan and Co., London, 1895), p. 258.

8. Smith, op. cit., vol. 1, p. 7.

9 ibid., vol. 1, p. 21.

10. ibid., vol. 1, p. 2.

11. Smith, it may be noted, was not always consistent in his handling of this matter. In Book I, he spoke of wealth as the sum of 'necessaries and conveniencies' available to the nation, a usage implying the inclusion of services. When dealing in greater detail with the components of the social product in Book II, the restriction to material outputs was emphasized.

12. ibid., vol. 1, p. 352.

13. ibid., vol. 1, p. 33.

14. ibid., vol. 1, p. 53.

15. The procedure by means of which the labour 'unit' is established will be examined below.

16. ibid., vol. 1, p. 62.

17. In Smith's words: 'The natural price . . . is the central price: to which the prices of all commodities are continually gravitating. '(ibid., vol. 1, p. 65.)

18. ibid., vol. 1, p. 65.

19. Ricardo's judgement that the necessary restrictive conditions were unlikely to hold was later to be the basis for his rejection of this type of labour approach to value.

20. ibid., vol. 1, p. 37.

21. Some of the criticism has been outspoken. One writer has accused Smith of making 'waste and rubbish out of the thinking of 2,000 years. The chance to start in 1776 instead of 1870 with a more correct knowledge of value principles had been missed.' (Emil Kauder, 'The Genesis of Marginal Utility Theory', *Economic Journal*, September 1953, p. 650.)

22. As he presented this point: 'There may be more labour in an hour's hard work than in two hours' easy business; or in an hour's application to a trade which it cost ten years' labour to learn, than in a month's industry at an ordinary and obvious employment.' (ibid., vol. 1, p. 35.)

23. ibid., vol. 1, pp. 35–6.

24. ibid., vol. 1, p. 56.

25. ibid., vol. 1, p. 277.

26. ibid., vol. 1, pp. 19–20.

27. In Smith's words, 'Masters are always and every where in a sort of tacit, but constant and uniform combination, not to raise the wages of labour above their actual rate. To violate this combination is every where a most unpopular action, and a sort of reproach to a master among his neighbours and equals. We seldom, indeed, hear of this combination, because it is the usual, and one may say, the natural state of things which nobody ever hears of. Masters too sometimes enter into particular combinations to sink the wages of labour even below this rate. These are always conducted with the utmost silence and secrecy, till the moment of execution, and when the workmen yield, as they sometimes do, without resistance, though severely felt by them, they are never heard of by other people.' (ibid., vol. 1, p. 75.) In a similar vein, Smith noted that workmen also combined for the purpose of raising their wages. He further observed that existing legislation was highly inequitable: combinations of workmen were illegal, while the law was silent on collusive action by employers.

28. ibid., vol. 1, p. 89.

29. ibid., vol. 1, p. 77.

30. ibid., vol. 1, p. 88.

31. ibid., vol. 1, p. 90.

32. On this point, Smith maintained: 'The liberal reward of labour, as it encourages the propagation, so it increases the industry of the common people . . . A plentiful subsistence increases the bodily strength of the labourer, and the comfortable hope of bettering his condition, and of ending his days perhaps in ease and plenty, animates him to exert that strength to the utmost. Where wages are high, accordingly, we shall always find the workmen more active, diligent, and expeditious, than where they are low . . . .' (ibid., vol. 1, p. 91.)

33. ibid., vol. 1, p. 375.

34. ibid., vol. 1, p. 163.

35. ibid., vol. 1, p. 161.
36. ibid., vol. 1, p. 303.
37. Though Smith set out the essential notion, his treatment of the details was deficient. In his presentation of the argument, the net revenue could be used to enlarge production when allocated to the acquisition of fixed and circulating capital. He did not, however, specify wage advances as among the components of circulating capital. In order to maintain consistency with his analysis of the manner in which the progressing society increased the demand for labour (i.e., by enlarging the 'funds' destined for the maintenance of labour), he should have held that 'circulating' capital included the wage bill.
38. ibid., vol. 1, p. 358.
39. ibid., vol. 1, p. 359.

CHAPTER 2

Elaborations and Cleavages within the Classical System: Thomas Robert Malthus

THOUGH Adam Smith posed the main questions with which subsequent classical writers dealt, he left a number of loose ends in his argument. To his successors fell the jobs of refining and revising the classical theoretical structure and of probing deeper into its implications.

Thomas Robert Malthus was to play a prominent part in the next round of classical debate. High among his interests was the codification of technical terminology and late in life he devoted a book, entitled *Definitions in Political Economy*, to this subject. The development of the science, he argued, had been retarded by the absence of standardized definitions with the result that writers on economic subjects often confused the public.

But analytical tidiness was by no means his dominant interest. He also sought to place the discipline on solid empirical foundations, recognizing both the woeful deficiency of statistical data then available and the shaky empirical basis of many widely accepted theoretical propositions. In the introduction to his main work on economics, he maintained:

The principal cause of error, and of differences which prevail at present among the scientific writers on political economy, appears to me to be, a precipitate attempt to simplify and generalize; and while their more practical opponents draw too hasty inferences from a frequent appeal to partial facts, these writers run to a contrary extreme, and do not sufficiently try their theories by a reference to that enlarged and comprehensive experience which, on so complicated a subject, can alone establish their truth and utility.[1]

55

Though not himself altogether innocent of the sins he saw in others, the empirical turn of his mind was often decisive in shaping his position on controversies of the day.

By the time Malthus wrote, re-examination and re-consideration of Smith's findings were clearly in order. The economic climate had undergone a significant change. Smith's successors, though still concerned with the economy's long period prospects, were quite naturally involved in debates over immediate economic problems as well. The Napoleonic wars had stimulated sharp price increases and most particularly in the prices of food grains. Meanwhile real wages had deteriorated, bringing considerable distress to the working class. In addition, the United Kingdom became for the first time a net importer of foodstuffs. These war-induced disturbances were compounded when the end of hostilities brought with it a period of severe deflation. The post-1815 problems of re-adjustment were to stimulate important embellishments in classical theory and to spark a lively public interest in the reflections of political economists.

1. THOMAS ROBERT MALTHUS (1766-1834)

Malthus has been described by his principal biographer as 'the best-abused man of the age.'[2] Certainly he was in the thick of controversy for the better part of his days.

Born to an upper-middle class English family with aristocratic pretensions, Malthus entered Jesus College, Cambridge, in 1784 where he studied mathematics and compiled a distinguished academic record. As he himself reported, he was more noted as an undergraduate 'for talking of what actually exists in nature or may be put to real practical use'[3] than for an interest in abstract reasoning for its own sake. After a period of hesitation — apparently because of concern about a speech defect — he took Holy Orders. Though the label 'parson' was permanently attached to him, he was a practising clergyman for only a brief period. For most of his life he pursued an academic career, first in Cambridge and later as Professor of Modern History and Political Economy at a college newly established to train officials of the East India Company. This appointment, for which there was no precedent, entitles him to be regarded as the world's first professional economist.

Malthus first gained fame with the *Essay on the Principle of Population*. The first edition, published in 1798, appeared anonymously, presumably because its author feared that some readers might be disturbed to discover an ordained churchman discoursing on such delicate matters. The author's identity, however, was only thinly veiled. William Godwin, whose views were a major target of criticism in the essay, is known to have corresponded with Malthus about its contents in the year of publication.[4]

The lively reception of the essay led Malthus to prepare six further editions, the final one in 1826. The theme he dealt with was directly pertinent to current debates. Shortly before the publication of the first edition, the younger Pitt proposed legislation designed to reorganize relief for the poor by the award of special compensation and encouragement to large families on the grounds that 'those who, after having enriched their country with a number of children, have a claim upon its assistance for their support'.[5] Interest in the subject was intensified by the census of 1801 (the first comprehensive enumeration of the population of Great Britain). These tabulations appeared to indicate that population had grown substantially in the latter part of the eighteenth century. Previously, an important body of opinion had believed – along with Gregory King, the pioneer national income statistician, who had predicted in 1696 that the population of England would be unlikely to double in less than six hundred years – that the pace of population growth was slow.

Malthus's interest in population questions served as a

point of departure into more general analyses of economic and social problems. He addressed himself to broader themes in a series of pamphlets and articles on topics of the day and in his major theoretical work, *The Principles of Political Economy Considered with a View to Their Practical Application.* He found his teaching duties satisfying and regarded his subject a suitable study for young men who 'could not only understand it, but they did not even think it dull'.[6]

Contrary to many popular impressions – both in his day and since – he was by temperament a warm, generous, and gentle man. Of his many friendships the one of most significance to the history of ideas was his association with David Ricardo, an intellectual adversary on many occasions but an ally in the pursuit of truth. On his feelings toward Ricardo he once observed: 'I never loved anybody out of my own family so much.'[7]

2. THE LAW OF POPULATION

Malthus's law of population developed a point that Smith had left in disarray and was readily assimilated into the main stream of classical thought. Malthus's inquiry into the subject, however, was originally stimulated by a debate with his father over the doctrines of Godwin, an advocate of a crude form of utilitarianism who had called for the abolition of private property. In Godwin's view population growth was an unqualified social blessing: with more numbers to be happy total happiness could be increased. Feeding an enlarged population, moreover, was held to present no problem; social ownership of land was expected to unleash fresh incentives for the enlargement of production. In short, Godwin maintained that with appropriate institutional reforms a social Utopia was within reach. The sympathies of the elder Malthus with this position spurred his son to refute it and the document he wrote for this purpose became the first version of his famous essay.[8]

The basic argument was stated succinctly in the following propositions:

I think I may fairly make two postulata. First, That food is necessary to the existence of man. Secondly, That the passion between the sexes is necessary, and will remain nearly in its present state. . . . Assuming, then, my postulata as granted, I say, that the power of population is indefinitely greater than the power in the earth to produce subsistence for man. Population, when unchecked, increases in a geometrical ratio. Subsistence only increases in an arithmetical ratio. A slight acquaintance with numbers will show the immensity of the first power in comparison with the second.[9]

From these propositions Malthus deduced that a war between the powers of human reproduction and the production of food would be perpetual. In the nature of things, population could not exceed the limits set by the availability of food-stuffs. How then were the immense powers of human reproduction to be contained? The first edition described one of the mechanisms touched off by population growth as follows:

The number of labourers also being above the proportion of the work in the market, the price of labour must tend toward a decrease; while the price of provisions would at the same time tend to rise. The labourer therefore must work harder to earn the same as he did before. During this season of distress, the discouragements to marriage and the difficulty of rearing a family are so great, the population is at a stand In the meantime the cheapness of labour, the plenty of labourers, and the necessity of an increased industry amongst them, encourage cultivators to employ more labour upon their land; to turn up fresh soil and to manure and improve more completely what is already in tillage; till ultimately the means of subsistence become in the same proportion of the population as at the period from which we set out.[10]

Over a longer period, more forceful checks to the tendency of population to outstrip the means of its subsistence were also likely to be brought into play. In the first edition two checks — the positive and the preventive —

were distinguished, though both were reducible to misery and vice. Through the positive check, population might be thinned by war, famine, pestilence, plague or disease. The outcome would be less bleak if the populace could be persuaded to exercise appropriate prudence in restraining the growth of numbers. Malthus held out little hope that this outcome could be brought to pass. In any event, he maintained that lengthy postponement of marriage would probably be associated with a rise in moral depravity and unnatural attachments.

This analysis offered only a dismal future for the human race. Mankind was left on a treadmill. Any improvement in average levels of income, the message seemed to say, would soon be neutralized by expanding numbers; wages would then be pushed back to subsistence. (Modern readers should bear in mind that the age of entrance into the labour force was much lower in Malthus's day than is now the case in industrial societies; many of the textile mills in the early stages of the industrial revolution were manned by children under ten and it was by no means uncommon in the first decades of the nineteenth century in Britain to find six-year-olds in the coal pits.) The Malthus of the first edition saw the links between population and real wage levels as so unbreakable that 'to prevent the recurrence of misery, is, alas! beyond the power of man'.[11] It is small wonder that Malthus has been interpreted as converting Smith's inquiry in the 'wealth of nations' into an inquiry into 'the poverty of nations'.

In the second and subsequent editions, the argument was restated with a number of modifications. These qualifications made little difference to the public understanding of his message and indeed Malthus sometimes neglected them in his own writing. The preventive check – i.e. the restraint on population growth brought about by prudence and foresight – was upgraded with the effect of opening up some prospect for improvement in the condition of the working class. This shift in emphasis, however, involved a more substantial redefinition of one of his crucial concepts than Malthus directly acknowledged. In the first edition subsistence could generally be interpreted as referring to physiological requirements for survival. But the status accorded to the preventive checks in subsequent editions introduced a complication. Subsistence could no longer be understood in terms of survival needs. A psychological version of subsistence – i.e. the minimally acceptable level of income that a potential parent would insist upon before raising a family – was now brought to the foreground. These two interpretations of subsistence yield divergent results. Should popular tastes be elevated, the likelihood that an improvement in real income would soon be eaten up by more mouths would be considerably diminished.

In his essays on population Malthus attached little weight to the possibility of this outcome. He appeared to believe that significant changes in the habits and attitudes of the population (and, most particularly, of the working class) could take effect only over long periods. In his major piece of economic writing, the alternatives were given fuller recognition:

From high wages, or the power of commanding a large portion of the necessaries of life, two very different results may follow; one, that of a rapid increase of population, in which case the high wages are chiefly spent in the maintenance of large and frequent families: and the other, that of a decided improvement in the modes of subsistence and the conveniences and comforts enjoyed, without a proportionate acceleration in the rate of increase.[12]

This concession, however appealing as a withdrawal from the harshness of the first edition, stripped his population theory of much of its bite. No longer could it be maintained that Malthus had uncovered a scientific law with direct and immediate bearing on social reality. Instead, his principle was reduced to a tautology, empty of empirical content. Despite its appearance, the proposition that pressure of population will naturally perpetuate a subsistence wage level says nothing specific about the future condition of the working class. With growth in national output, real wages might be constant or they might rise, depending on which notion of subsistence was operative. No evidence can falsify a statement of this form. The cost of this immunity, however, is loss of contact with the world of events.

In his recommendations on economic policy Malthus largely ignored these qualifications. Moreover, most classical economists interpreted his 'principle of population' as providing a convincing demonstration that real wages would naturally gravitate to an equilibrium at a fixed level of subsistence. Nor in the popular under-standing was the gloom of the original version noticeably relieved. As one of the characters in Thomas Love Peacock's novel, *Melincourt*, observed:

Bachelors and spinsters I decidedly venerate. The world is overstocked with featherless bipeds. More men than corn is a fearful pre-eminence, the sole and fruitful cause of penury, disease and war, plague, pestilence and famine.[13]

If Malthus's logic was not impeccable, his inter-pretation of the causal mechanics of population change was also open to challenge. Malthus had argued that adjustment of population size to econo-mic change occurred largely through effects on natality. If real incomes improved, marriages would be contracted earlier and births would increase. He assigned little importance to the possible relationships between economic improvement and reductions in mor-tality. There is considerable evidence to suggest, however, that the 'population explosion' of his day was heavily influenced by reductions in death rates. These demo-graphic changes, moreover, were linked more closely to improvements in public health and sanitation than to improvements in real wages. The facts of the case, how-ever, are not yet conclusively established. The inade-quacies of the national statistics on the British population in the late eighteenth and early nineteenth centuries are such that, as one close student of these problems has commented, a thorough understanding of the mechanisms of population growth in that era would require 'a generation of collaborative work on parish registers and other local sources'.[14]

With the benefit of hindsight, it is now clear that Malthus considerably underestimated the pace of technological progress and its impact. He could not reasonably have been expected to anticipate the revolution in agricultural science that was later to alter radically the capacity of the limited supply of land to feed much enlarged populations. Nor did he foresee improvements in the techniques of fertility limitation. Similarly, Malthus did not appreciate the opportunities offered by international trade for expanding a small island's capacity to provide subsistence to larger numbers. It was, in fact, through international specialization and trade that Britain first managed to evade the Malthusian danger in the nineteenth century.

These shortcomings are easy to identify a century and a half after Malthus wrote. But in his time there was no basis for a confident expectation that technology and trade could produce such a transformation. Indeed, it was then not inappropriate to sound warnings that mankind might be poised on the brink of disaster. After all, Britain, though it managed to escape the distresses of the positive checks, did not do so by a very comfortable margin. In Ireland they came into play with a vengeance; the potato famine of the 1840s reduced the population – through the combined effects of mortality and emigration – from nearly nine million to six and a half million in only six years.[15]

In Western countries, the tone of fatalism that ran through Malthus's discussion of the relationship between population growth and real wage changes now has no justification. The experience of the past century in industrial societies provides abundant evidence that the coefficients of human reproduction and food production are more variable than Malthus and many of his contemporaries believed them to be. In many of the poorer parts of the modern world, however, Malthusian presuppositions are dangerously approximated. Agrarian technology is backward and not readily responsive to stimuli for change, fertility is largely unchecked by modern contraceptive techniques, while mortality rates have been sharply reduced by public health and sanitation measures. In these areas Malthusian warnings have not lost their relevance. This issue is one of the central problems of our times.

3. THE MALTHUSIAN ANALYSIS OF THE LAWS OF PRODUCTION IN AGRICULTURE

The population question provided Malthus's point of departure into political economy. But the postulates on which the principle of population rested – especially his views on the productive possibilities of agriculture – required further analytical support before they could carry conviction. In particular it was incumbent upon him to demonstrate why food supplies could not be expected to expand more rapidly than mouths.

His work in economic theory provided an underpinning of the type required. The basic insight he developed is now often referred to as the 'law of diminishing returns' and a notion of much the same sort was hit upon almost simultaneously by three other writers: Ricardo, West and Torrens. The discussion of the point at issue thus marked one of those occasions – of which there have been several in the history of economic ideas – of a co-incidence in formulation of a fundamental theoretical proposition by several active minds.

Tempting as it is to describe the message of these contributors to classicism in modern terminology, it would distort part of their argument to do so. In current practice the concept of 'diminishing returns' is commonly stated in the following form: if all factors of production save one are held constant, the increments to output obtainable from the addition of successive units of a variable factor will, beyond a certain point, diminish. Thus, for example, if more and more labour is engaged to work a fixed acreage with an unchanged amount of capital equipment, total output may thereby be expanded but when the number of workers is substantially enlarged the rate of increase in product will decline. This principle is usually interpreted as applying quite generally to all lines of production in any sector of the economy.

The divergence between the modern concept and the one worked out by writers in the classical tradition can be observed in the manner in which Malthus developed the analysis. His opening move was to offer a three-fold account of the origins of rent:

First, and mainly, That quality of the earth, by which it can be made to yield a greater portion of the necessaries of life than is required for the maintenance of the persons employed on the land.

Secondly, That quality peculiar to the necessaries of life of being able, when properly distributed, to create their own demand, or to raise up a number of demanders in proportion to the quantity of necessaries produced.

And, Thirdly, The comparative scarcity of fertile land, either natural or artificial.[16]

The first of these observations is reminiscent of the 'bounty of nature' view advanced by the Physiocrats and appropriated by Smith. The second links his population principle to an account of a perpetually assured demand for the products of the land. But it is the third that turns the analysis in a new direction. Land is not only limited in supply, but its quality is uneven. As population growth swells the demand for food and raises its price, cultivation will be extended to less fertile acreages and/or will be intensified on lands already under the plough. In either case, the average costs of production will rise because the effort required per unit of additional output increases. By the same token, the rise in prices necessary to induce landowners to extend cultivation to new lands or to improve cultivation on older ones will benefit the owners of the more fertile acreages. They can enjoy higher receipts without an increase in their costs; thus their rents will swell.

In appearance this argument bears a striking similarity to the latter-day version of 'diminishing returns'. Yet there are two important points of contrast. In the hands of Malthus and his contemporaries the analysis of the tendency for returns per successive unit of input in agriculture to diminish was not developed around static conditions in which all factors, save one, are held constant. Instead the argument was constructed in a context of change – particularly of population and of the size of the capital stock. In the form presented, it provided an answer to those who had maintained that the Malthusian population prognosis should be rejected on the grounds that for each mouth God sends a pair of hands. Now it appeared that food output, though it could still grow, was likely to do so at a declining rate and that in consequence the problem of maintaining food availability per head could be expected to become more serious as the population mounted. Malthus did recognize, however, that considerable relief could be afforded if capital were poured into agricultural improvement even though it could not be 'laid out without diminished return'.[17] Unlike Smith, he held that the landlord could be an important improver and investor. The intensification of agricultural production, however, was not likely to occur until rents had already risen.

In another respect the classical notion of diminishing returns diverged from the interpretation that later acquired currency. For Malthus (and for most classical economists) this analysis was intended to refer only to agricultural production. The tendency to 'diminishing return' was not extended to all lines of production. On the contrary, they anticipated that in manufacturing –

66

where the basic instruments of production could be multiplied without natural limit – the same problem would not arise. The returns reaped by capitalists (i.e. profits) were likely, over the long term, to diminish. But this phenomenon was related more to the effect of rising rents and food prices than to the conditions attached to the production of manufactured goods.

This analysis of production problems in agriculture buttressed Malthusian population arguments, but it also had a number of further consequences. In effect it challenged one of the presuppositions on which *The Wealth of Nations* had been built. Smith had viewed rent as an unearned income arising primarily from the bounty of nature. Malthus brought another side of nature to the foreground – its stinginess in limiting the cultivable acreage and in restricting the supply of lands with high fertility. Natural conditions thus imposed severe limitations on the rate at which agricultural output could grow.

This finding, in turn, was symptomatic of a broader re-orientation in the classical outlook. Given the nature of agricultural production as it was seen by Malthus and by Ricardo, a re-distribution of income in favour of rents and at the expense of profits was likely to occur at a faster pace than Smith had been prepared to allow. Malthus added the qualification that rents, while rising in absolute magnitude in the course of economic expansion, would not necessarily increase as a proportionate share of total revenue. But his view – which Ricardo, among others, did not share – rested on the assumption that rising rents would spur capital improvements in agriculture with the result that a growing share of the income of landowners could be treated as profit. In any event, the combined effects of capital accumulation and population growth were likely to be associated with rising food prices, higher money wages (even though the real wage was unchanged), and a squeeze on the profits of capitalists. The prospect of the stationary state – when growth would cease and capital accumulation would be restricted to replacement requirements – thus became a less distant possibility.

Malthus's analysis of population and of agricultural production did much to cast a shadow over the optimism of early classicism. In some degree this part of his message was absorbed into the mainstream of later classical thought. The inferences flowing from these findings were largely responsible for provoking Carlyle to label political economy as 'the dismal science'.

4. MALTHUS AND THE LAW OF MARKETS

Malthus's place in the history of economic ideas rests on more than his contribution to the classical analysis of population and of productivity in agriculture. He is also renowned for an important dissent from one aspect of orthodox classical doctrine. The crucial point on which he parted company with most of his contemporaries concerned the allegedly 'self-adjusting' properties of markets. This weapon in the arsenal of classical economic laws has usually been associated with the name of a Frenchman, J. B. Say (1767–1832), though its central idea had been spelled out earlier by James Mill. For that matter, Smith – without arguing the point – had anticipated its conclusions in *The Wealth of Nations*.

Say's Law has figured so prominently in economic controversies over the past century and a half that the form in which it was originally stated deserves to be set out. It proceeded deductively from two propositions: (1) that products are given in exchange for products; and (2) that goods constitute the demand for other goods.

The significance of the first of these statements lay as much in what was not said as in what was said. By asserting that 'products are given in exchange for products', Say restricted money to the role of a medium of exchange as a catalyst to commerce. Its use, however, did not alter the basic fact about transactions: that they represented exchanges of goods. This was not an original view; Smith and Hume before him had reached essentially the same conclusion. Say regarded this finding as revolutionary, and as demonstrating conclusively the fallacies of a mercantilist view that money was worth acquiring as an asset.

Say's second proposition was to have a marked influence on the development of economic thinking. The statement that 'goods constitute the demand for other goods' was interpreted to mean that the act of producing generates incomes sufficient to buy back the product or, more simply, that 'supply creates its own demand'. This proposition, of course, was understood to refer to the economy as a whole and not to the situation of individual firms or industries. Because a deficiency in aggregate demand allegedly could never exist, Say's Law ruled out the possibility of 'general over-production'.

This conclusion rested on an important, though implicit, assumption: that all income was spent and none hoarded. For Say and most writers in the classical tradition, the basic premise was too self-evident to call for detailed argument. As they viewed the world, there was no reason why anyone should ever wish to hoard. After all, no intelligent man (as opposed to the exceptional case of the misguided miser) would accumulate idle balances when he could increase his income by lending the same funds at interest. This attitude was held with the force of dogma by the orthodox classical mind, a phenomenon not unrelated to its antipathy toward the mercantilist attitude that hoarding on a national basis was socially beneficial.

While 'general over-production' was thus ruled out, 'partial over-production' – a situation in which individual firms or industries were unable to dispose of all their output – could clearly occur. Even though an individual producer added as much to total demand as to total supply, he was not thereby assured that all his output would find a buyer. Disturbances might arise – stemming, for example, from entrepreneurial miscalculation or changes in the public taste – that would confront the seller with a partial glut of unsold commodities.

But that was not the end of the matter. It was essential to this argument to insist that if and when partial over-production occurred, the disturbance would not escalate into a general glut. The doctrine maintained that if one seller was unable to dispose of all his product, then others could be expected to enjoy an abnormally strong demand for theirs. This conclusion followed from the condition that all income was spent on either consumption goods or investment goods.

With one further step it could also be maintained that a situation of partial over-production would tend, in the normal course of events, to correct itself. If it could be assumed that there were no significant obstacles to the mobility of capital and labour, then partial over-production could be expected to induce a re-allocation of productive resources. Capital and labour would be withdrawn from the glut sectors and put to work in those enjoying buoyant demand. The required adjustment could not be made instantaneously. Nevertheless the natural forces of the market, if left alone, would supply the impetus required to eliminate a temporary partial glut.

The tidiness and elegance of this argument gave to it an obvious appeal. But to Malthus, who observed the distresses following the Napoleonic Wars, the impossibility of a general glut was not self-evident. Nor was he confident that the problem was only temporary and remediable through the untampered processes of the market. Producers of many kinds of goods experienced difficulty in disposing of their product and 'unemployment' – at least as measured by registrants for parish relief who numbered nearly one and a half million in 1818 [18] – was at an unprecedented level. The glut, he feared, might be both general and chronic.

By modern standards, Malthus's counter-argument was not systematically worked out. His views were developed around a distinction between two categories of outputs – essentials (primarily food) and non-essentials. In the case of the former there was never a problem of glut. As his argument on population had demonstrated, increased supply (in the form of an enlarged availability of food-stuffs) automatically created its own demand (in the form of a larger number of mouths). In the case of the non-essentials, however, the problem was different. Whether or not the market was cleared of these goods depended on the tastes of those – primarily landlords and capitalists – with incomes high enough to acquire them. Malthus might well have added another sub-group (though he did not): the *nouveaux rentiers* who held the enormously enlarged government debt created by the Napoleonic wars. At the time their economic position was not unimportant, as service charges on the national debt amounted to about ten per cent of the national income.[19]

Malthus's diagnosis of the 'glut' problem had much in common with the attitude that led him to put little faith in the efficacy of the preventive check to population growth. The tastes and habits of the working class could not be altered except over a prolonged time period, he maintained, nor were those of potential buyers of luxuries likely to be much more pliable. As he elaborated the signi-ficance of this point in a letter to Ricardo in 1817:

You seem to think that the wants and tastes of mankind are always ready for the supply; while I am most decidedly of opinion that few things are more difficult, than to inspire new tastes and wants, particularly out of old materials; that one of the great elements of demand is the value that people set upon commodities, and that the more completely the supply is suited to the demand the higher will this value be, and the more days' labour will it exchange for, or give the power of commanding. . . . I am quite of opinion that *practically* the actual check to produce and population arises more from want of stimulus than want of power to produce.[20]

To deal with these distresses Malthus proposed several heretical remedies. Fearing that – in the absence of extra-ordinary measures – demand might be insufficient to absorb the product of the economy, he maintained that encouragement of unproductive expenditures was the course of wisdom. In his view it was to society's advantage when the rich (particularly large landowners) augmented their complement of retainers. The results would be even happier if landlords engaged workers who would otherwise be unemployed to improve their estates. In addition, the state – the unproductive spender *par excellence* – might well undertake public works in order to create jobs. As he summed up his proposals:

And altogether I should say, that the employment of the poor in roads and public works, and a tendency among landlords and persons of property to build, to improve and beautify their grounds, and to employ workmen and menial servants, are the means most within our power and most directly calculated to remedy the evils arising from that disturbance in the balance of produce and consumption, which has been occasioned by the sudden conversion of soldiers, sailors, and various other classes which the war employed, into productive labourers.[21]

Malthus's views on the problem of gluts in the post-Napoleonic war period have been described as an anticipation of later Keynesian arguments on the importance of aggregate demand to the determination of total income and employment. Despite the surface resemblance between these lines of argument such claims place an undue strain on the facts. Malthus's thought was still very much in the classical mould. Though he sensed something amiss, he was unable to rise above the limitations of this tradition. In fact, the main manoeuvre that would have permitted him to make a counter-argument stick – an analysis of the likelihood of hoarding in periods of 'glut' – he did not seriously entertain.

5. MALTHUS AND ECONOMIC POLICY

If Malthus was at odds with the mainstream of the classical tradition in his analysis of 'gluts', he also parted company with many of his contemporaries on other matters. While most classicists favoured free trade (particularly in agricultural commodities), Malthus defended the agricultural protection provided by the Corn Laws. While most of his contemporaries opposed unproductive expenditures (particularly government spending), Malthus – at least in certain circumstances – made a positive case for them. Perhaps even more puzzling was his attitude towards population control. In view of his fears of a population explosion and its consequences for human misery, one might have expected him to be a strong advocate of birth control. In fact, however, he opposed contraceptive practices, technically deficient (by modern standards) as they were in his day.

Underlying these positions was a consistent, if dubious, rationale. Malthus attached prime importance to an expanded production of foodstuffs and he regarded a sharpening of incentives as essential to its achievement. Agricultural protection was thus justified on the grounds that high food prices would encourage productivity-raising investment in agriculture. This attitude was bolstered by a subsidiary non-economic argument: it would be unwise, he maintained, for a small island to rely on imports for a substantial part of its nourishment. In times of war or national emergency, its position would be uncomfortably vulnerable.

Similarly, his opposition to birth control rested on the view that family responsibilities helped men to overcome their natural tendency to indolence and sloth. The pressure of necessity was an unrivalled spur to diligent and intensive work. His heretical recommendations on unproductive expenditures were addressed to a specific situation and were not defended as general propositions. The remedies proposed, however, gave an important place to the employment of idle labour in tasks that would raise the productivity of the land.

Though Malthus made some conspicuous departures from the standard classical position, his views on a wide range of policy issues were in full accord with those of the orthodox tradition. Apart from the exceptions already noted he was generally an advocate of the free market and an opponent of governmental restrictions. Like most of his classical contemporaries he attacked the Poor Laws. While he followed the path cleared by Smith, he provided – with the aid of his population analysis – some additional arguments for repeal or amendment. No longer were the Poor Laws objectionable primarily on the grounds that they interfered with labour mobility; Malthus also argued that they had the unfortunate effect of swelling claims on the nation's food supplies while making no contribution to their enlargement. Moreover, the existing system compounded the difficulties in at least two respects: not only did parish relief deaden incentives to work but it also enabled its recipients to reproduce at rates higher than would otherwise have been possible, thus intensifying the competition for a limited food supply.

Harsh though some of Malthus's views on policy appeared to be, it must be noted that, by his lights, they were inspired by a genuine concern for humanity. Malthus was almost alone among his contemporaries in urging public measures to alleviate post-war unemployment. His recommendations on the Poor Laws – to which he was militantly opposed – called for a gradual phasing out of parish relief. He advised withdrawal of public assistance only from the able-bodied; persons unequipped to earn their own living would retain a claim on state charity. But, most important, all of his views on economic policy stemmed from a conviction that constraints on food production imposed severe limits – limits that men could ignore but only at their peril – on the prospects for improvement in material circumstances.

Notes

1. Malthus, *Principles of Political Economy Considered with a View to Their Practical Application* (Wells and Lilly, Boston, 1821), pp. 4–5.
2. James Bonar, *Malthus and His Work* (George Allen and Unwin, London, second edition, 1942), p. 1.

3. As quoted by Bonar, op. cit., p. 409.

4. Bonar, op. cit., p. 43.

5. Parliamentary Debates, 12 February 1796, as quoted by G. F. McCleary, *The Malthusian Population Theory* (Faber and Faber, London, 1953), p. 35.

6. As quoted by John Maynard Keynes, 'Robert Malthus' in *Essays and Sketches in Biography* (Meridian Books, New York, 1956), p. 27.

7. As quoted by Keynes, op. cit., p. 29.

8. The full title of the first edition is worth noting: *An Essay on the Principle of Population as It Affects the Future Improvement of Society with Remarks on the Speculations of Mr Godwin, M. Condorcet, and Other Writers*. The second edition was retitled as *An Essay on the Principle of Population or a View of its Past and Present Effects on Human Happiness with an Inquiry into the Prospects Respecting the Future Removal or Mitigation of the Evils which it Occasions.*

9. Malthus, *An Essay on the Principle of Population*, first edition (Macmillan Company reprint, 1909), pp. 6, 7.

10. ibid., pp. 14–15.

11. ibid., p. 37.

12. Malthus, *Principles of Political Economy*, p. 195.

13. As quoted by Alan T. Peacock, 'Malthus in the Twentieth Century' in *Introduction to Malthus*, edited by D. V. Glass (John Wiley and Sons, New York, 1953), p. 57.

14. H. J. Habakkuk, 'English Population in the Eighteenth Century', *Economic History Review*, second series, vol. 6 (1953), p. 130.

15. For a fascinating account of these events, see Cecil Woodham-Smith, *The Great Hunger: Ireland 1845 to 1849* (Signet Books, New York, 1964).

16. Malthus, *Principles of Political Economy*, p. 110.

17. ibid., p. 137n.

18. Mark Blaug, *Ricardian Economics* (Yale University Press, 1958), p. 197.

19. B. R. Mitchell and Phyllis Deane, *Abstract of British Historical Statistics* (Cambridge University Press, 1962), pp. 366, 396.

20. Malthus to Ricardo, 26 February 1817, *The Works and Correspondence of David Ricardo*, Piero Sraffa, ed. (Cambridge University Press, 1952), vol. 7, pp. 122–3.

21. Malthus, *Principles of Political Economy*, p. 395.

CHAPTER 3

David Ricardo and the Formalization of Classical Analysis

RICARDO and Malthus worked much the same theoretical territory. Both were concerned with extending the tradition launched by Smith and with sharpening its insights. Moreover the writings of both responded to the unusual circumstances of the Napoleonic wars and their aftermath. On a number of specific points they arrived at quite different conclusions. Nevertheless, both aimed their analytical sights on the classical problem. For his part, Ricardo identified himself with its central issues when he declared that the 'principal problem in Political Economy' was to 'determine the laws' regulating distribution between the various classes and their relation to the general circumstances of society.

The aspect of this theme on which Ricardo initially focused attention was more restricted in scope: the effects on the economy as a whole of the protection afforded to agriculture by the Corn Laws. In the circumstances of the time, it was by no means accidental that this issue should have occupied a dominant place in Ricardo's thought. The Napoleonic wars – combined with a run of poor harvests – had, as noted earlier, converted the British economy into a net importer of food grains. Corn prices had skyrocketed and meanwhile the income of landlords had been swollen. On one estate for which systematic records have been kept, for example, the landlord's return increased by nearly tenfold between 1776 and 1816. Not all of this return can be interpreted as an 'economic rent' in the sense in which Ricardo and Malthus wrote about it in their theories; part represented a return on investments to raise the productivity of the soil. Nevertheless it was abundantly apparent that a fundamental change in the balance of agriculture (relative to the rest of the economy) had occurred.

These problems were aggravated by amendments to the Corn Laws passed shortly after the end of the war. Their effect was to make the protection of domestic agriculture virtually absolute by prohibiting the importation of foreign grain until the domestic price of wheat exceeded sixty shillings per quarter. The problem to which Ricardo addressed himself was clearly real and important. His preoccupation with the significance of agriculture was apparent in the phrasing he chose to preface his major work:

The produce of the earth – all that is derived from its surface by the united application of labour, machinery, and capital, is divided among the three classes of the community; namely, the proprietor of the land, the owner of the stock or capital necessary for its cultivation, and the labourers by whose industry it is cultivated.

But in different stages of society, the proportions of the whole produce of the earth which will be allotted to each of these classes, under the names of rent, profit, and wages, will be essentially different; depending mainly on the actual fertility of the soil, on the accumulation of capital and population, and on the skill, ingenuity, and instruments employed in agriculture.[1]

In much of his writing Ricardo viewed the whole economy as if it were one giant farm.

The method Ricardo employed in dealing with this problem gave to his analysis a tone of generality. His prose style – by contrast with that of Smith and Malthus (which had been embellished with homely illustrations and the occasional parenthetical homily) – was spare and formal. Moreover, his acute analytical perception led him well beyond the practical issue that had originally turned his mind to theoretical investigations. It was the more general version of his model that was to leave a lasting mark on the techniques of economic theorizing.

1. DAVID RICARDO (1772–1823)

Ricardo began to make his way in the world when, at the age of fourteen, he entered the London Stock Exchange in the employ of his father. Upon the son's marriage outside the Jewish faith seven years later, family relationships were strained and the younger Ricardo struck out on his own. Specializing in dealings in government securities, he soon flourished and, by 1815, had amassed a sizeable fortune.

His interest in the abstract problems of economics was developed in the middle years of his life. His acquaintance with the subject appears to have dated from 1799 when, on a visit with his wife to the spa town of Bath, he read Adam Smith. A decade later his first published views – dealing with the depreciation of the currency – appeared in the form of letters to the press signed 'R'. Shortly thereafter, he expanded his thoughts on currency questions into a pamphlet which was to bring him public notice and the attention of several prominent literary figures – among them, James Mill. Without the goading of Mill (who insisted that 'as you are already the best *thinker* on political economy, I am resolved that you shall also be the best writer')[2] it is unlikely that Ricardo's *Principles* would ever have been produced. Ricardo feared that 'the undertaking exceeds my powers',[3] and lamented after he had begun the work: 'I make no progress in the very difficult art of composition. I believe that ought to be my study before I introduce any more of my crude notions on the public.' [4] Despite delays and the author's recurrent periods of despondency, *Principles of Political Economy and Taxation* appeared in 1817.

This work solidly established his reputation as the leading economic analyst of his day. When he entered Parliament in 1819, it gave to his opinions (expressed though they were in a quiet high-pitched voice) a tone of authority. Indeed he has been described as the first to educate the House of Commons in economic analysis. But his

opinions were not unchallenged; the most articulate dis-
senter was his warm friend Malthus. His last letter to
Malthus conveys the manner of the man:

Like other disputants after much discussion we each retain
our own opinions. These discussions however never influence
our friendship; I should not like you more than I do if you
agreed in opinion with me.[5]

Late in life, despite his protestations on the malevolence
of landlords, Ricardo placed the larger part of his substantial fortune in land. On this aspect of his friend's
behaviour, Malthus once observed:

He [Ricardo] is now become, by his talents and industry, a
considerable landholder; and a more honourable and excellent
man, a man who for the qualities of his head and heart more
entirely deserves what he has earned, or employs it better, I
could not point out in the whole circle of landholders.

It is somewhat singular that Mr Ricardo, a considerable
receiver of rents, should have so much underrated their
national importance; while I, who never received, nor expect
to receive any, shall probably be accused of overrating their
importance. Our different situations and opinions may serve
at least to shew our mutual sincerity, and afford a strong pre-
sumption, that to whatever bias our minds may have been
subjected in the doctrines we have laid down, it has not been
that, against which perhaps it is most difficult to guard, the
insensible bias of situation and interest.[6]

2. RICARDO'S ANALYTICAL PROGRAMME

The central core of Ricardian theoretical argument was
contained in one fundamental proposition: 'that in all
countries, and all times, profits depend on the quantity of
labour requisite to provide necessaries for the labourers,
on that land or with that capital which yields no rent'.[7]
Indeed the bulk of his analysis was dedicated to supplying
arguments to support this conclusion.

The importance of this proposition within the larger
context of classical thought can be readily appreciated.
The rate of profit for Ricardo, as for the earlier classicists,
was a primary regulator of the rate of economic growth.

An understanding of the mainsprings of economic expansion and of forces that might check it clearly required a firm grasp on the determinants of this income share.

But what justification had Ricardo for maintaining that the conditions of production in agriculture had a decisive bearing on profit rates throughout the economy? Could it not be held with equal plausibility (as Malthus observed when criticizing Ricardo's position) that the circumstances of other branches of the economy determined rates of return within agriculture? A fully satisfactory answer to this question cannot be found within the pages of Ricardo's *Principles*. The evidence compiled by Piero Sraffa, the tireless collector and editor of Ricardo's papers, now permits a reconstruction of the argument Ricardo must have had in mind.

Agriculture, it would appear, was to be regarded as unique because of two special attributes. It was the only sector in which the same commodity (Ricardo used 'corn' as a composite term to embrace all agricultural output) figured as both input and output. Corn was obviously an input when used as seed. Moreover, because corn was the basic component of subsistence, it was also crucial to the other indispensable input – labour. Following the classical view of 'advances' to labour, wages could be reduced to advances of corn and, in turn, all inputs could be expressed in terms of corn. But, as corn was also the output of agriculture, the net return to producers could be measured in corn terms by subtracting inputs from outputs.

The net return in agriculture, calculated in this fashion, would not, in all cases, provide a measure of profits. Much of the land under cultivation would also yield rent. In their handling of this matter, Malthus and Ricardo adopted much the same approach. The 'niggardliness of nature' had made land scarce and uneven in quality. Acreages of high fertility (which, it could be reasonably assumed, would be the first to be drawn into cultivation) would provide a windfall to their owners. Moreover, the size of this windfall would swell as population growth enlarged the demand for food. As food prices rose, less fertile areas would be brought under the plough, so long as their cultivators could obtain going rates of return for their efforts. Meanwhile, the owners of fertile acreages would reap higher and higher rents. The outputs of the last units, on the other hand, would be sufficient only to cover the costs of cultivation and would fail to yield a rent.

With the aid of this argument, it could thus be maintained that rent and profit could be isolated by observing zero-rent land where the net return would consist entirely of the return on capital – profits. The rate of profit could then be calculated as a percentage by dividing the net return (corn outputs less corn inputs) by total inputs (measured in terms of corn).

With this exercise part of the claim to a unique status for agriculture could be established. In this sector of the economy, profit rates could be determined without reference to prices. In no other sector could a similar calculation be undertaken in real terms (i.e. with physical rather than monetary units of measurement). But agriculture had a further claim to a special position. Its outputs were indispensable as inputs in all other lines of production. The availability of food supplies was required if non-agricultural employers were to make wage advances to their work force.

While Ricardo's argument assigned a special role to agriculture, he rejected the Physiocratic view that agriculture was the economy's only productive sector. For Ricardo, agricultural production had only an analytical primacy in that it supplied useful leverage on the economy as a whole. Once conditions in agriculture had been established, other pieces in the analytical puzzle fell into place. So long as it could be assumed that the market tended to produce uniform rates of return in all sectors of the economy, then profits in agriculture could be interpreted as typical of profit rates prevailing throughout the economic system. By looking first at agriculture, the general behaviour of profits could thus be derived in a manner independent of monetary valuation.

The argument on uniform rates of return throughout the economy applied with equal force to wages. But wages were likely to be tied to an even more basic regulator – the requirements for subsistence. In his handling of this point Ricardo largely absorbed Malthusian teaching on population. He was aware of the differing results yielded by psychological and physiological interpretations of sub-sistence and his personal hope was that the habits of the working class could be elevated.[8] But he saw little prospect that these tastes could be altered except over a prolonged time period. For the immediate future it thus appeared that a natural wage gravitating around the conventional level of subsistence should be regarded as normal.

With population growth, rates of profit were likely to deteriorate even though real wages were unaltered. The margin of cultivation would then be extended to poorer lands where more labour input per unit of output would be required than had previously been the case. More corn would thus have to be advanced to labour in order to obtain the increments to corn output needed to feed a larger population. As Ricardo phrased the outcome, 'the quantity of labour required to produce necessaries on zero-rent land' would rise. Hence, rates of profits in agri-culture and throughout the economy would be squeezed.

Ricardo's simple model, though built around an analy-sis of productive conditions in agriculture, thus had con-tained within it a broad vision of the forces regulating the distribution of the social product and, in turn, of the forces likely to frustrate its continued expansion.

3. THE RICARDIAN REFORMULATION OF THE THEORY OF VALUE

Ricardo's simplified model of the corn-based economy permitted the mechanisms of distribution to be analysed in real terms without reference to valuation. If, in fact, society had been organized exclusively along the lines of a giant farm in which corn was both the basic input and the only output, this formulation would have required no elaboration. But Ricardo appreciated that the world of reality was more complex. Some headway towards a formulation of rules governing the behaviour of the economic system could be made by isolating a 'basic' sector possessing convenient analytical properties and by arguing that all other sectors would conform to its results. Nevertheless a closer inspection of the linkages was clearly in order.

At a more general level of analysis the problem became less tidy. Outside agriculture, outputs were considerably more heterogeneous and their variety called for the aid of a device capable of reducing them to a common denominator. In short, statements about the division of the national revenue between the various income shares – when pursued in any depth – required a procedure for valuation.

In his search for a common factor linking all lines of production, it was not surprising that Ricardo should have hit upon labour as the crucial common denominator. In one form or another, a labour approach to value had already been built into the classical tradition. But that was not all. Labour, it could be plausibly maintained, did indeed provide a realistic link: it entered into all lines of production.

Ricardo approached the problem of value along a path somewhat different from the one his predecessors had taken and he emerged from his inquiries with a different solution. Smith, for example, had addressed himself to the issue for the primary purpose of measuring changes in total output between time intervals of considerable length. Ricardo, though not insensitive to the importance of this problem, was doubtful that labour could serve as a 'stable' and 'invariant' measure. In any event, it was more pertinent to his concerns to analyse the consequences of changes in the relative prices of output for the distribution of income.

The tack Ricardo took was thus to come closer to the questions that were to dominate economic theorizing in a later stage – in particular, the analysis of price determination – than had Smith's. Even had he chosen to do so, Smith, with the tools he worked with, would have been precluded from offering a systematic account of relative price in labour terms. His procedure, it will be recalled, used labour as a 'measure of value' by reducing income to labour units that could be 'commanded'. On the input side, however, he lacked a basis for dissolving the non-labour factors of production into labour units.

The Ricardian analysis of rent re-opened the labour input route to the analysis of value. Because he maintained that the price of corn was regulated by labour inputs on zero-rent land, the land factor of production could effectively be eliminated from the explanation of value. Capital, of course, was a different matter. But it appeared to be readily reducible to labour inputs. A machine, for example, could be viewed as embodied or accumulated labour, the productive powers of which would be transferred to current output over the course of its life. The value of a commodity could then be expressed in terms of labour inputs (both those applied directly and indirectly through embodiment in machines) required in its production.

At first glance it might appear that a satisfactory common denominator had been found. But, as Ricardo came increasingly to realize as he grappled with this issue, a labour-content interpretation of value became awkward precisely at the point where it was most needed – in the analysis of long-period economic change. A crude labour-content explanation of relative price ran into heavy weather when important dynamic considerations were introduced into the analysis: e.g. changes in money wage rates and the accumulation of fixed capital.

With the accumulation of capital, Ricardo saw that a

number of complications were introduced. After all, it could not be assumed that the fixed capital stock employed in an economy would have uniform durability; nor could it be assumed that fixed and circulating capital were allocated in identical proportions in all lines of production. Once these elements of diversity in the productive structure were allowed, there was no longer any basis for holding that prices would correspond to labour inputs in a growing economy. Divergent price results could be obtained, for example, if wage rates were altered, even though production processes themselves were unchanged. The basic point to which Ricardo wished to draw attention was that a production process dominated by direct labour inputs would be more vulnerable to an increase in money wage rates than would one in which indirect labour inputs (i.e. labour embodied in fixed capital) were used. If a uniform rate of profit were to be maintained in all branches of production, then relative prices would diverge from ratios of labour inputs in production. Moreover, a divergence might arise from inequalities in the time periods of production. Two commodities produced with identical quantities of labour input would differ in price if one required longer commitments of capital before revenues were realized through sales than the other.

In short, the strict labour interpretation of value broke down. Ricardo still maintained that the discrepancies would be constrained within narrow limits. At one point in his treatment of the divergence of price ratios from labour input ratios of two commodities produced with differing proportions of direct and indirect labour, he asserted: 'The greatest effects which could be produced on the relative prices of these goods from a rise of wages, could not exceed six or seven per cent. . . .' [9] Labour content was only a crude approximation or, as he later put it, 'the foundation of value'.[10]

This unsuccessful detour into value theory in a dynamic setting was not, however, devoid of significance. It produced a fresh insight into the relationships between increases in money wage rates and the accumulation of fixed capital, the phenomena responsible for undercutting his labour input approach. Both of these changes were expected to accompany economic expansion. But there was another important connexion between them. Rising wage rates would induce employers to substitute fixed capital for labour in order to reduce costs of production. Ricardo expected that the resulting economies would, at least in part, be passed on to consumers through price reductions, a result that competition was expected to assure. But what would be the consequence for the volume of employment? The Ricardo of the first two editions of *Principles* was confident that technological unemployment was an impossibility and that productivity gains brought by the introduction of machinery were an unmixed blessing. All classes of society would benefit from the ensuing reductions in prices of output, and profits would be higher than would otherwise have been the case. The rate of growth could thus be sustained and the total demand for labour enlarged to the benefit of the entire community.

In the third edition of *Principles*, Ricardo shifted his ground. After recounting his earlier opinions, he observed:

> . . . I am convinced, that the substitution of machinery for human labour, is often very injurious to the interests of the class of labourers. My mistake arose from the supposition, that whenever the net income of a society increased, its gross income would also increase; I now, however, see reason to be satisfied that the one fund, from which landlords and capitalists derive their revenue, may increase, while the other, that upon which the labouring class mainly depend, may diminish, and therefore it follows, if I am right, that the same cause which may increase the net revenue of the country, may at the same time render the population redundant, and deteriorate the condition of the labourer.[11]

At base, Ricardo's worry about the possibly detrimental effects of machinery on employment stemmed from the view that the volume of circulating capital available to hire labour would be reduced by the purchase of fixed capital. This finding, of course, touched a sensitive nerve in contemporary controversy. The Luddites, dispensing with the qualifications Ricardo added to his conclusion, were convinced that the machine was inimical to the interests of working men and, acting on this premise, had sparked the machine-smashing riots in textile districts in 1811 and 1812.

Ricardo was still hopeful that unemployment in this form could be averted, arguing that technological discoveries were necessarily gradual and could thus be assimilated without sudden shock. Ricardo saw the danger, but played down its practical significance. Nevertheless, his argument conflicted sharply with Smith's faith in the 'harmony of interests' between the various classes of society. Marx was later to pick up this theme and to give it a central position in his theoretical system.

4. RICARDO AND THE LONG-PERIOD PROSPECTS OF THE ECONOMY

Classical analysis of the problem of value underwent a subtle but profound change from Smith to Ricardo. Ricardo's approach, imperfect and approximate though it was, not only yielded fresh findings but buttressed a number of familiar ones. In his hands, the analysis of value provided an underpinning to the long-term prognosis of economic expansion. With its support, he could write: 'The reason then, why raw produce rises in comparative value, is because more labour is employed in the production of the last portion obtained, and not because rent is paid to the landlord. The value of corn is regulated by the quantity of labour bestowed on its production on that quality of land, or with that portion of capital, which pays no rent.' [12]

The implications of this conclusion extended far beyond their direct bearing on differential rates of change in the prices of agricultural and manufactured goods.

Among other things this analysis pinned down the connexions between economic expansion and income distribution. As population growth was thought likely to accompany economic expansion, food requirements – which could only be satisfied at substantially higher cost – would grow. Higher money wages would be called for in order to maintain real wages at their conventional level. The profit share of income would thus be squeezed. Meanwhile, the distribution of income would shift in favour of rents. This outcome, however, was directly linked to 'the increasing difficulty of making constant additions to the food of the country'. Conversely, Ricardo maintained, 'if the necessaries of the workman could be constantly increased with the same facility, there could be no permanent alteration in the rate of profits or wages, to whatever amount capital might be accumulated'.[13]

The upshot of this argument was that the process of economic expansion might erode its own foundation – i.e. accumulation out of the profit share of income. Ultimately, as the rate of profit fell, the stationary state would emerge when further net accumulation would be halted. Nor was it necessary for profits to be eliminated altogether before growth was checked. Ricardo anticipated that a critical point might be reached earlier. As he put it:

The farmer and manufacturer can no more live without profit, than the labourer without wages. Their motive for accumulation will diminish with every diminution of profit, and will cease altogether when their profits are so low as not to afford them an adequate compensation for their trouble, and the risk which they must necessarily encounter in employing their capital productively.[14]

The day when growth was halted could, however, be postponed by measures that reduced the labour costs involved in enlarging food supplies. The tendency of profits to fall, Ricardo noted, 'is happily checked at repeated intervals by the improvements in machinery, connected with the production of necessaries, as well as by discoveries in the science of agriculture which enable us to relinquish a portion of labour before required, and therefore to lower the price of the prime necessary of the labourer'.[15] But relief via technological innovations could not be predicted with confidence. The upward pressure on the prices of subsistence goods and, in turn, on money wage rates, might be more reliably restrained through the importation of foodstuffs from lower-cost producers abroad. This consideration figured prominently in Ricardo's hostile attitude toward the protection to home agriculture afforded by the Corn Laws.

5. RICARDO ON ECONOMIC POLICY

On most points of public controversy in his day Ricardo accepted and extended the mainstream of classical thinking. With respect to the Poor Laws he maintained that 'every friend to the poor must ardently wish for their abolition',[16] though, with Malthus, he recommended that relief payments should be withdrawn gradually. In general, he opposed government intervention in economic activity and endorsed the beneficence of a self-regulating market system, the virtues of which he defended against Malthus's doubts about the efficacy of Say's Law.[17]

His most important contribution to debates on policy focused on the issue that had originally inspired his investigations – the Corn Laws. Ricardo advocated repeal, but with a more powerful battery of arguments than had earlier been mustered. With the aid of his analytical model it could now be demonstrated that the Corn Laws were objectionable – not simply because they obstructed the free movement of resources – but, more importantly, because they tightened the squeeze on profits, the mainspring of sustained economic expansion.

In support of his arguments for free trade in agricultural products, Ricardo worked out the basic format of the doctrine that now enters introductory textbooks as the theory of comparative advantage. He formulated the problem in terms consistent with his general approach: by way of a comparison between the labour inputs required to obtain commodities from home production in different countries. If cost ratios of internationally tradeable commodities (measured in terms of labour inputs) differed in the home economies of two countries, each could benefit by specializing in the production of the good in which it held a comparative advantage (and offering part of the output for export) and by importing its requirements of the other. In this fashion, gains from trade would accrue to all parties. A greater quantum of output could be acquired than would have been possible through exclusive reliance on domestic resources.

But it was not simply the general gains from specialization and trade that Ricardo wished to emphasize. It was important that British trade should flow in channels that would arrest the erosion of profits. Thus it was not a matter of indifference which goods predominated in the trading pattern. On the contrary, the national interest was best served when imports were concentrated on foodstuffs, with British manufacturers supplying the exports to pay for them. Specialization along these lines would reduce pressures on money wage rates by making subsistence goods available at lower cost than would otherwise have been possible. As Ricardo argued the point:

If, therefore, by the extension of foreign trade, or by improvements in machinery, the food and necessaries of the labourer can be brought to market at a reduced price, profits will rise. If, instead of growing our own corn, or manufacturing the clothing and other necessaries of the labourer, we discover a new market from which we can supply ourselves with these commodities at a cheaper price, wages will fall and profits rise; but if the commodities obtained at a cheaper rate, by the extension of foreign commerce, or by the improvement of machinery, be exclusively the commodities consumed by the rich, no alteration will take place in the rate of profits.[18]

The realization of the full benefits of international trade required, however, a sound international financial system. Ricardo's views on monetary and financial questions – which left a formidable imprint on the thought of his time – were dominated by this concern. The domestic monetary system, he maintained, should be regulated to insure against disruption in the international division of labour. Conceivably, increases in the note issue at home might threaten a country's trading position should they lead to price increases that made its exports less competitive in foreign markets and imports more attractive in home markets. These considerations led Ricardo to adopt what was described as a 'bullionist' position in the debates of the time. He maintained that the domestic money supply should be directly tied to the country's gold supply. Under such an arrangement, the note issue of a country suffering a loss of gold through an unfavourable balance of trade would automatically be contracted. A reduced money supply would tend to depress the price level which, in turn, would encourage the desired adjustments in the international accounts. The deficit country's exports would become more attractive to foreigners while imports could compete less successfully in home markets as the prices of domestically-produced items declined. In embryonic form, Ricardo had sketched the theory of the nineteenth century gold standard.

Considerations of the problems of growth also informed Ricardo's basic strategy with respect to matters of taxation. Though he was at one with the mainstream of the classical tradition in his suspicion of government intervention in the economy, he recognized that some necessary functions could only be discharged on the public account. In the choice between various types of tax levies that might be used to finance these services, one consideration was paramount: that taxes falling on profits should be minimized, if not avoided altogether. He was aware, of course, that the impact of taxation could not always be easily ascertained. If wages were at the 'subsistence' level, for example, a tax on labourers would be shifted to capitalists; the latter would be obliged to increase money wage rates by an amount sufficient to maintain subsistence standards. From the point of view of the future expansion of the economy, taxes that threatened to choke accumulation from profits were undesirable. Far preferable were levies that fell on unproductive spenders and expenditures, particularly on the rent share of income and on luxury consumption.

Notes

1. Ricardo, *Principles of Political Economy and Taxation*, Piero Sraffa, ed. (Cambridge University Press, 1953), p. 5.

2. James Mill to Ricardo, 22 December 1815, *The Works and Correspondence of David Ricardo*, Piero Sraffa, ed. (Cambridge University Press, 1952), vol. 6, p. 340.

3. Ricardo to J. B. Say, letter of 18 August, 1815, loc. cit., vol. 6, p. 249.

4. Ricardo to Malthus, 7 February 1816, loc. cit., vol. 7, p. 19.

5. Ricardo to Malthus, 31 August 1823, loc. cit., vol. 9, p. 382.

6. Malthus, *Principles of Political Economy* (Wells and Lilly, Boston, 1821), p. 186n.

7. Ricardo, op. cit., p. 126.

8. In Ricardo's words, 'The friends of humanity cannot but wish that in all countries the labouring classes should have a taste for comforts and enjoyments, and that they should be stimulated by all legal means in their exertions to procure them. There cannot be a better security against a superabundant population.' (Ricardo, op. cit., p. 100.)

9. ibid., p. 36. It is on the basis of this passage that one commentator has described Ricardo as holding a '93 per cent labour theory of value'.

10. ibid., p. 88.

11. ibid., p. 388.

12. ibid., p. 74.

13. ibid., p. 289.

14. ibid., p. 122.

15. ibid., p. 120.

16. ibid., p. 106.

17. In the third edition (1821) of his *Principles*, Ricardo inserted one comment on this controversy indicating that the distresses of the time should be regarded as transitional:

David Ricardo

'The termination of the war has so deranged the division
which before existed of employments in Europe, that every
capitalist has not yet found his place in the new division
which has now become necessary.' (p. 90.)

But he also asserted. 'M. Say has . . . most satisfactorily
shewn, that there is no amount of capital which may not be
employed in a country, because demand is only limited by
production. . . . Productions are always bought by productions, or by services; money is only the medium by which the
exchange is effected.' (pp. 290, 291-2.)

18. ibid., p. 132.

CHAPTER 4

The Revisionism of John Stuart Mill

JOHN STUART MILL regarded his writing in economics – which formed only a part of his larger intellectual enterprise – as primarily an exercise in synthesizing the findings of the classical tradition. His professed objective was not to originate, but to consolidate classical analysis as it had evolved since Smith. In fact, however, his contribution to economics went well beyond this stated aim. In the course of his work, he managed – while always protesting his loyalty to the classical tradition – to amend some of its premises and with consequences more far-reaching than he himself realized.

Mill's revision of the premises of classical political economy was parallelled by his revisionist attitude towards the philosophical tradition in which he had been brought up. Schooled originally in the Benthamite tradition of the pleasure-pain calculus, he turned away from the cruder formulations of this doctrine. As he came to view matters, pleasures could not be as readily measured and aggregated as Bentham's version of utilitarianism required. Instead, Mill insisted, qualitative considerations should count fully as much as quantitative ones. He wished to draw attention to the different orders of pleasure, which he did emphatically when he asserted that it is 'better to be Socrates dissatisfied than a fool satisfied'. With this amendment, the props to Benthamite confidence in the felicific calculus as a guide to social policy were shaken.

The economic world Mill observed had also undergone considerable change from the state of affairs with which Ricardo and Malthus had been concerned. Many of the specific policy battles in which the earlier classicists had

been engaged had been won, though not always in quite
the form they had intended. By 1846 the Corn Laws had
been repealed, banking and currency arrangements had
been reorganized and effectively tied to gold as the international means of payment, and the Poor Laws had been
amended to attack the restraints on labour mobility imposed by the earlier system of parish residence as a
condition of eligibility for relief. England was close to
becoming a nation dedicated to free trade, both in theory
and in fact. Meanwhile the worst disasters of the years
of deflation in the immediate post-Napoleonic war
decades had passed.

Even so, the quality of life – as well as the means for its
full enjoyment – left much to be desired for the bulk of
the population. *Laissez-faire*, whatever its contribution
to the growth of international trade and to the enlargement of the national product, seemed not to have meant
that a substantial share of the gains were distributed to
the benefit of the least advanced groups in the community. Sensitivity to growing inequalities was clearly
part of the political protest of the Chartist movement and
it was also reflected in the stirrings of the trade union
organizations (relieved after 1824 of many of their former
legal disabilities with the repeal of the anti-combination
laws) and of the cooperative movement.

1. JOHN STUART MILL (1806–73)

Few economists or political philosophers can ever have
had a more thorough preparation for intellectual pursuits than John Stuart Mill. From a tender age he was
tutored by his father, James Mill, a political economist
of note in his own day, but now remembered more for his
close association with Ricardo and Bentham. By the age
of eight, the younger Mill was reading Greek classics in
the original and at thirteen was set to work on Smith and
Ricardo. Later in life John Stuart Mill was to observe
that his remarkable education – which covered most

branches of knowledge – gave him twenty-five years' head start on most of his contemporaries.

In 1823, after abandoning earlier plans to take up the study of law, Mill entered the employ of the East India Company. He began as an assistant to his father in the examiner's office, the division of the company charged with the conduct of its affairs with the native states. The younger Mill spent the next thirty-five years of his life as an official of the company, ultimately rising to the highest post in the examiner's department, a position held earlier by his father. This connexion was severed only when Parliament relieved the company of its political and administrative responsibilities in 1858.

His involvement in Indian affairs, despite its duration, had little influence on the development of his thought. He did not share his father's zeal for translating Ricardian and utilitarian doctrine into a massive programme of reform in India. For that matter, he never visited India and there is no evidence that he ever expressed a desire to do so. His attitude toward his official duties appears to have had something in common with that held by a few university professors nowadays towards their teaching responsibilities: the latter, however, seldom express themselves so candidly in print. As Mill observed:

I do not know any one of the occupations by which a subsistence can now be gained, more suitable than such as this to any one who, not being in independent circumstances, desires to devote a part of the twenty-four hours to private intellectual pursuits.[1]

More potent as an influence on the development of his thought was Mill's companionship with Mrs Harriet Taylor, whom he married after the death of her husband. Mill described her as the 'inspirer of my best thoughts'.[2] Though she shaped the details of his teaching on only one issue – the 'subjugation' of women – he regarded her influence as crucial to his re-assessment of classical postulates and to his attempts to reformulate political economy along lines that offered less cramped prospects for the bulk of mankind. His appraisal of her influence was, perhaps understandably, exaggerated.

Late in life, Mill served briefly as a member of Parliament. During his term, he championed the extension of the franchise to the working classes and to women and called for land tenure reform in Ireland. His attempt to win re-election was unsuccessful.

2. THE MODIFICATION OF THE APPROACH TO VALUE

From an early stage in his work, it was apparent that Mill was prepared to re-define some familiar classical terms. One of his first essays on economic theory was addressed to the definition of 'productive' and 'unproductive' labour. In his view the argument that labour was 'productive' only when it produced material objects called for a re-examination. One intangible in particular – the transmission of skills – should be regarded as productive, at least under certain conditions. But Mill was still enough in the classical mould to insist on a qualification: labour involved in training workers was productive, 'provided that an increase of material products is its ultimate consequence'.[3]

Mill quarrelled more seriously with orthodox definitions when he protested that standard classical terminology conveyed an unfortunate impression that the functions discharged by governments were essentially unproductive. In principle, he maintained, there was little to distinguish the protective works on a farm (such as hedges and ditches) from those supplied by governments when they financed police officers and courts of justice.[4] He carried the critique a step further by arguing that some types of labour, though embodied in material objects, might still be unproductive. Indeed, productive labour might 'render a nation poorer' if the wealth it produces, that is, the increase it makes in the stock of useful or agreeable things be of a kind not immediately wanted. . . .'[5] There was more than a hint in this attitude that the conventional classical approach to problems of value did less than justice to considerations of utility and demand. But this was not the only limitation from which it suffered. Labour might also be wasted if it produced material outputs with outmoded techniques. Though Marx was also to emphasize this point (arguing that only 'socially necessary' labour should count in the calculation of value), it had been given little attention by earlier classicists, largely because they assumed that the extension of the market would be a sufficient antidote to inefficiency.

While adding qualifications to familiar classical distinctions, Mill nevertheless accepted the basic point stressed by earlier classical writers. He, as much as they, saw the importance of isolating that part of society's product likely to give rise to subsequent increases in the national output from that less likely to do so. If in practice the dividing line might involve more than a pinch of arbitrariness, the basic concept was both clear and significant.

Mill moved further away from the tradition of his orthodox classical predecessors in his formulation of the specific ingredients of value. When explaining the difference in value of two commodities, for example, he observed:

If one of two things commands, on the average, a greater value than the other, the cause must be that it requires for its production either a greater quantity of labour, or a kind of labour permanently paid at a higher rate; or that the capital, or part of the capital, which supports that labour must be advanced for a longer period; or lastly, that the production is attended with some circumstance which requires to be compensated by a permanently higher rate of profit.[6]

This view took into account the exceptions Ricardo had observed to his labour-input account of value, but it also severed the earlier classical link between labour and value. None of Smith's concern to use a labour measurement to solve the index-number problem remained; Mill, in fact, devoted a chapter in his *Principles* to demonstrating that the search for an invariant measure of value was misguided on both logical and empirical grounds.

At the same time Mill retained the classical terminology of 'natural' and 'market' prices. The former, he held, represented market prices in long-period equilibrium and – barring the case of monopoly – would normally be adjusted to the cost of production. He noted, however, that competition could not always be relied upon as an effective force in the pricing process. In some instances – particularly in the case of public utilities – 'competitors are so few that they always end by agreeing not to compete'.[7] Moreover, this problem was likely to become more serious as economies of large-scale operations increased the size and reduced the number of sellers. He did not grasp the full significance of this matter, but he at least caught the scent of an issue that was later to preoccupy a generation of economists.[8]

Mill summed up his position with a judgement that was rashly immodest. 'Happily', he wrote in 1848, 'there is nothing in the laws of value which remains for the present or any future writer to clear up; the theory of the subject is complete.'[9] Later strands of economic theory were to offer a completely different account of this problem. But within a tradition bearing any resemblance to classicism, Mill's conclusion was largely correct. The territory bounded by classical presuppositions had been fully explored. New departures required another analytical framework.

3. THE REVISIONIST VIEW OF THE LAWS OF PRODUCTION AND DISTRIBUTION

Perhaps the most significant of Mill's modifications in the orthodox classical tradition was his re-interpretation of the laws governing economic activity generally and of income distribution most particularly. At an abstract level Mill shared many of the standard conclusions about the likely redistributional effects of economic growth. He agreed with the classical mainstream that a period of expansion would generate tendencies towards rising rents, falling profits, and rising money (though not real) wages. But he also argued that there might be counteracting forces to relieve the cramp on the working class.

Mill proceeded by distinguishing between two types of economic laws. Those of the first type governed production; they were immutable, fixed by nature and technology. Men could adjust to these laws, but were powerless to amend them. The laws governing the distribution of the social product, however, fell into a different category. In this case the outcome was socially determined and subject to human control.[10] In support of this proposition Mill examined at length the different sets of distribution arrangements associated with various types of social organization. His point was not simply that a variety of distributional systems had existed. More important was his assertion that the prevailing distribution of income could be altered.

Mill perceived clearly that the Malthusian population argument – which had been interpreted to mean that the working class could never escape from poverty – provided the basic prop to orthodox classical thinking about the shape of income distribution. He accepted the conclusion that subsistence wages at a meagre level might be sustained if Malthus's gloomiest prognosis was borne out in fact. But this result was by no means the only one possible.

Malthus, of course, had recognized that other outcomes were conceivable, though he placed no confidence in the possibility that the working class would adopt prudential restraint. Mill took quite the opposite position, arguing that the behaviour of the working class was more readily changeable than earlier classicists had allowed and that population growth could indeed be constrained. Wide-

John Stuart Mill

spread and intensive education might be required, but he had no doubt that it would be effective in raising the tastes and aspirations and altering the behaviour of the working class. This confidence, he insisted, was more than a leap of blind faith: it was supported by observable developments. The masses of the population were emancipating themselves from a traditionally dependent status and 'a spontaneous education was going on in the minds of the multitude'.[11] The pace of these changes was quickened by the institutes for lectures and discussion and by the formation of trade unions. This led him to conclude:

It appears to me impossible but that the increase of intelligence, of education, and of love of independence among the working classes, must be attended with the corresponding growth of the good sense which manifests itself in provident habits of conduct, and that population, therefore, will bear a gradually diminishing ratio to capital and employment.[12]

With this elimination of the overtones of inevitability attached to earlier classical interpretations of economic laws, the Malthusian spectre was banished. Brighter prospects for the improvement and perfectability of mankind could now be seriously entertained. This outlook also implied that a re-definition of one of the basic concepts of classicism was in order. No longer could the net product of society be identified with the profit and rent shares of income; saving to facilitate capital accumulation might also arise from the wage share of income.[13]

4. THE REVISION OF IMPLICIT GOALS

Mill's re-interpretation of the nature of economic laws was to have notable consequences. Not least among them was a challenge to an implicit value premise that had run through the whole of classical writing: that uninterrupted economic expansion was a goal of such obvious importance that it required no justification. Mill attacked the orthodox position when he wrote:

I know not why it should be matter of congratulation that persons who are already richer than anyone needs to be, should have doubled their means of consuming things which give little or no pleasure except as representatives of wealth. . . . It is only in the backward countries of the world that increased production is still an important object . . .[14]

In his view the stationary state was not necessarily a grave social ill. On the contrary, Mill observed:

I cannot . . . regard the stationary state of capital and wealth with the unaffected aversion so generally manifested towards it by political economists of the old school. I am inclined to believe that it would be, on the whole, a very considerable improvement on our present condition. I confess that I am not charmed with the ideal of life held out by those who think that the normal state of human beings is that of struggling to get on; the trampling, crushing, elbowing, and treading on each other's heels, which form the existing type of social life, are the most desirable lot of human kind, or anything but the most disagreeable symptoms of one of the phases of industrial progress.[15]

These remarks, of course, were addressed to Mill's contemporaries in England. But affairs in the United States did not escape his notice; indeed his most barbed comment was reserved for the Northern and the Middle States of America. He viewed the population of this area as enjoying the highest stage of economic advance. Poverty had been eliminated, abundance was assured to all who were willing and able to work, and social injustices had been eliminated – at least all 'inequalities that affect persons of a Caucasian race and of the male sex'. But what had this opulence produced? Mill's judgement in 1848 was outspoken '. . . all that these advantages seem to have done for them is that the life of the whole of one sex is devoted to dollar hunting, and of the other to breeding dollar hunters'.[16]

From the perspective of classical orthodoxy, these assertions amounted to heresy – a point his lay readers were quick to grasp. One reviewer commended the first edition in these words: '... here is no indifference to human suffering, no inordinate estimation of wealth, no sordid and groveling morality'.[17] Another, noting with approval Mill's attitude toward the dread stationary state, observed: 'It is no little novelty to hear a political economist speak in the following manner of the mere elements of national wealth.'[18] Mill was congratulated for demolishing those arguments 'by which his scientific predecessors had attempted to mislead the man of experience or of empirical knowledge'.[19]

It was not solely a distaste for some of the social manifestations of affluence that led Mill to this conclusion. He was also concerned about tendencies towards instability likely to be associated with the approach of the stationary state and with declining rates of profit. These circumstances would impel some entrepreneurs to reject prevailing rates of profit and to seek out high-risk ventures with the expectation of reaping above-average gains. With arguments like those heard more recently from bankers who voice concern about deterioration in the quality of credit risks during a period of expansion, Mill maintained that these conditions easily generated speculative rashness which, in turn, was likely to be followed by disappointments. The behaviour of those who tried to evade the natural tendency for profit rates to fall could thus lead to oscillations between boom and bust.

Mill was too closely associated with the Say's Law tradition of the classical mentality to press the analysis of this issue very far. Nevertheless, he perceived more clearly than had earlier contributors to the classical mainstream that the approach of the stationary state at a high level of economic activity was likely to increase the sensitivity of the economy to substantial fluctuations. Indeed, tendencies toward instability were inherent within an unregulated economic system.

5. MILL AND ECONOMIC POLICY

In several important respects, Mill's attitude towards questions of economic policy departed substantially from the positions that had characterized orthodox classicism. Perhaps his sharpest break with orthodoxy concerned the economic role of the state. Mill's frame of reference contained at least the outlines of a more active programme of state intervention in economic life than his predecessors would have tolerated. In the first instance he emphasized the economic importance of the state as a 'civilizer' – i.e. as the sponsor of improved educational facilities, as well as such cultural amenities as parks and museums. Elevation in popular tastes and aspirations, especially among members of the working class, was vital to the banishment of the Malthusian devil and to the exercise of human control over the distribution of income. Nevertheless, like his classical forebears, Mill was critical of the administration of poor relief on the ground that it had unfortunate effects on the mobility of the labour force and on its allocation to socially most effective uses.

While pursuing their civilizing mission, governments could also perform a significant stabilizing function. Mill, in his revisionist analysis of the onset of the stationary state, had held that falling rates of profit were likely to be associated with speculative rashness which in turn led to unintended wastages of capital. How much better the outcome would be, he maintained, if the state taxed an increasing share of potentially investible funds and used its receipts to finance socially beneficial projects. In this fashion two worthwhile purposes would be served simultaneously: deterioration in rates of return on private capital would be slowed and the volatility of the economic system dampened. But this technique was not the only one available for slowing reductions in the rate of profit as the stationary state was approached. If part of domestic savings were channelled into overseas investment, the erosion of home rates of profit would be slower than would otherwise have been the case. The results would be doubly beneficial if capital exports were directed into the development of low-cost sources of food and raw materials required in the lending country. This interpretation of capital export has much in common with the analysis of imperialism as a prop to the capitalist order that was later devised by Hobson and Lenin.

Mill also placed himself outside the classical mainstream in his attitudes toward private property. Existing social institutions he regarded as 'merely provisional', though he reached this position only after a struggle against his early beliefs. In his personal summing up he recorded:

> We were now much less democrats than I have been, because so long as education continues to be so wretchedly imperfect, we dreaded the ignorance and especially the selfishness and brutality of the mass: but our ideal of ultimate improvement went far beyond Democracy, and would class us decidedly under the general designation of Socialists. While we repudiated with the greatest energy that tyranny of society over the individual which most Socialist systems are supposed to involve, we yet looked forward to a time when society will no longer be divided into the idle and the industrious; when the rule that they who do not work shall not eat, will be applied not to paupers only, but impartially to all; when the division of the produce of labour, instead of depending, as in so great a degree it now does, on the accident of birth, will be made by concert on an acknowledged principle of justice; and when it will no longer either be, or be thought to be, impossible for human beings to exert themselves strenuously in procuring benefits which are not to be exclusively their own, but to be shared with the society they belong to.[20]

Despite his sympathy for social change, Mill did not work out carefully the details of a future and happier order of society. But one point was at least clear: his version of socialism was not one in which the state would play a commanding role. He thought more in terms of voluntary cooperative arrangements and of co-partnerships between capital and labour.

Notes

1. *Autobiography of John Stuart Mill* (Columbia University Press, New York, 1944), p. 58.
2. ibid., p. 184.
3. Mill, *Principles of Political Economy*, W. J. Ashley, ed. (Longmans, Green, and Co., London, 1926), p. 48.
4. Mill, *Essays on Some Unsettled Questions in Political Economy* (John W. Parker, London, 1844), p. 78.
5. Mill, *Principles*, p. 51.
6. ibid., p. 480.
7. ibid., p. 143.
8. As Mill put it: 'In the countries in which there are the largest markets, the widest diffusion of commercial confidence and enterprise, the greatest annual increase of capital, and the greatest number of large capitals owned by individuals, there is a tendency to substitute more and more, in one branch of industry after another, large establishments for small ones.' (ibid., p. 142.)
9. ibid., p. 436.
10. Though arrived at by a different route and employed for quite different purposes, Mill's distinction between the laws of production and the laws of distribution has much in common with Marx's distinction between the mode of production and the productive relations. See Chapter 5.
11. ibid., p. 757.
12. ibid., p. 759.
13. ibid., p. 163.
14. ibid., p. 749. Some readers may detect an analogy with J. K. Galbraith's more recent analysis of the 'affluent society'.
15. ibid., p. 748.
16. ibid., p. 748.
17. *Frazer's Magazine*, September 1848, p. 247.
18. *Blackwood's Edinburgh Magazine*, October 1848, p. 412.
19. ibid., p. 407.
20. *Autobiography of John Stuart Mill*, p. 162.

Postscript to Classical Economics

THE classical tradition underwent considerable modification between the publication dates of *The Wealth of Nations* and John Stuart Mill's *Principles of Political Economy.* Nevertheless, an important thread of continuity – a common concern with the process of economic growth – linked the work of its main contributors.

Measured against this primary analytical objective the achievement of the classical economists was impressive. The perspective they provided on an economic system undergoing dynamic change was markedly superior to analyses available earlier. Moreover, many of their insights into the causes and consequences of economic growth have proved to be of lasting value. In the mid-twentieth century, students of growth and development have revisited classical literature for inspiration in the handling of a persistent set of problems. The classical economists were, after all, interested in the big questions: the process of economic growth over prolonged time periods and the relation of the resulting distribution of income to its prospects. The relevance of these issues has not diminished since they wrote; in fact, in much of the modern world, the questions to which they addressed themselves are the dominant economic issues. The classical approach, though susceptible to considerable updating and refinement, still has much to offer to mid-twentieth century readers.

It is thus not surprising that the analytical achievement of classical economists has left an impressive legacy. Their imprint on an important strand of modern analysis is conspicuous. Among the more interesting statements of updated classicism is the model of growth in underdeveloped economies devised by W. A. Lewis. His analysis, which is of considerable interest in its own right, provides an excellent illustration of the manner in which variations on classical themes can enrich understanding of a wide range of current issues.[1]

Lewis views the typical underdeveloped economy as divided into two compartments: a capitalist sector and a traditional subsistence sector. In his dualistic system, the capitalist sector is the source of dynamic stimuli and the rate of growth in the economy as a whole is held to be regulated primarily by re-investment from capitalist profits. Expansion of the capitalist sector, however, involves contact with the subsistence sector which, in Lewis's view, is characterized by backward techniques, low output per head, and a substantial volume of underemployment. In these circumstances, capitalists can draw off labour from the subsistence sector by offering wages sufficient to provide a slight improvement over the low real incomes that workers could otherwise have obtained in traditional agriculture. Moreover, capitalists can continue to tap the labour reserve of the subsistence sector indefinitely on low wage terms.

By substituting sectoral distinctions for the class divisions with which the original classicists worked, Lewis managed to reinstate much of the classical framework for the analysis of distribution and growth. The existence of a subsistence sector as a supplier of wage labour replaces Malthusian population postulates in the original classical model to yield the conclusion that output and employment can expand without raising real wages. Moreover, as in the classical scheme, profits are interpreted as the source of accumulation and expansion. The rate of profit, however, may be eroded for reasons similar to those underlying classical explanations of income redistribution in favour of rents. In Lewis's model, this problem is presented as a shift in the 'terms of trade' of industrial for agricultural products. Thus, for example, should the capitalist sector rely on the subsistence sector to feed the growing wage labour force, food prices would probably rise. The money wage would have to be adjusted upward in order to maintain real wages at established levels. Should this be the outcome, the rate of profit would be reduced and accumulation retarded. These tendencies, however, might be offset by improvements in agricultural productivity or through the creation of a self-contained capitalist enclave which produced its own food requirements and thus by-passed traditional agriculture. Ultimately, in Lewis's interpretation, expansion might reach a stage at which the subsistence sector's labour force would be completely absorbed in capitalistically-organized lines of production. At that point '. . . an economy enters upon the second stage of development. Classical economics ceases to apply; we are in the world of neo-classical economics. . . .' [2]

Though Lewis's analysis is open to criticism on points of detail it has supplied a highly stimulating point of departure for a substantial body of current discussion of problems of underdevelopment. In particular, it has directed attention to some of the unique aspects of economic expansion in underdeveloped economies. Moreover, it is clearly oriented towards the basic questions relevant to the study of underdeveloped economies: the inter-relationships between growth and income distribution over a prolonged period of dynamic change. With these considerable points to its credit, it is also of interest to note that an updated classical analysis also inherits some of the deficiencies of its predecessors: problems of short-run price determination are slighted and, implicitly, Say's Law is assumed to hold. For Lewis's analytical problem a sophisticated treatment of these issues is no more relevant than it was for the original classicists.

In the modern literature, Lewis's model of growth is perhaps the most explicitly classical in form. But a number of classical themes, on a less comprehensive basis, have crept back into current discussions of long-period growth problems. Several recent analyses of economic growth in advanced economies, for example, have been constructed on the assumption that the distribution of income between the profit and non-profit shares of income is the basic determinant of the rate of growth. In these lines of argument it has been assumed that for the community as a whole, wage and salary earners save little or nothing even though their incomes are well above the classical subsistence level. This conclusion, moreover, is reasonably well supported by recent empirical studies. This is not to suggest, of course, that all wage and salary earners save nothing, but rather that the saving of some members of these groups has been roughly counterbalanced by expenditures in excess of income by others (i.e. from withdrawals of past savings to cover retirement or emergency expenditures, through the financing of consumption by credit, etc.). The analysis of saving can thus be reduced to an inspection of the forces governing the behaviour of the non-labour shares of income. Those who have built theories on this basis have usually made the further assumption that income which is not spent on consumption is channelled into investment. All of this sounds very much like Say's Law refurbished in modern dress, as indeed is the case. It is part and parcel of this line of reasoning to regard full employment as a norm.

Other classical themes re-emerge in modern theories exploring the relationship between growth and distribution. In certain recent formulations, the share of profits is held to be the main regulator of the volume of accumulation and of the rate of economic growth. Though the classical belief that the rising rents associated with population growth would tend to erode the rate of profit has largely been discarded, models constructed with classical categories now usually maintain that profits are likely to be squeezed for another reason – the existence of diminishing returns to capital investment. Unless this tendency is offset by 'technological progress' – a possibility that classical writers also allowed for in their worries about the future course of rents –, the rate of profit will be depressed and a situation analogous to that of the stationary state may arise.[3]

Similar considerations have left their mark on contemporary analyses of growth problems in underdeveloped economies. For example, classical conclusions about the role of profits in stimulating capital formation and economic expansion have been invoked to support the case for the application of capital-intensive technologies in developing countries. Highly capitalistic techniques, it has been maintained, are likely to produce a distribution of income more favourable to profits than would more labour-intensive techniques. This conclusion, like its classical ancestors, implicitly assumes that maximization of the growth in output (irrespective of considerations of effective demand) is the primary economic objective and that profits, once generated, will in fact be re-invested productively.

Perhaps the most ingenious of the recent revisitations to the classical tradition has sprung from the the work of Piero Sraffa, the indefatigable editor of the ten-volume edition of Ricardo's works and correspondence. By building on the base provided by Ricardo's attempt to derive a rate of profit from the corn economy without reference to valuation (rather than on the dynamic thrust of classical analysis), Sraffa has constructed a system in which the problems of an economy are viewed in terms of the conditions it must satisfy in order to sustain itself and to grow.[4] This approach provides a highly illuminating statement of the technical requirements for economic survival and growth. Again all of the familiar classical puzzles re-emerge but in a form altered by the use of the notations of linear algebra. The substantive problems with which Ricardo wrestled – such as the derivation of natural prices and the determination of the rate of profit – remain and their solution is subject to the same constraints. The analysis of the demand side of market behaviour is truncated and the problem of aggregative instability (though not entirely ignored) is not accorded detailed attention.

While classical motifs have left an imprint on modern analysis, most classical thinkers were more concerned with promoting economic improvement than with advancing the techniques of economic analysis. Though they differed among themselves about specific issues they adopted a common procedure when approaching matters of public policy. For them all, one overriding question – the likely consequences of policy actions on the course of economic expansion – set the context of controversy. Classicists generally proclaimed the virtues of a free market, but they did so on grounds quite different from those invoked by later generations of economists. To members of the classical school, the unregulated market was more important as an engine of growth than as a process for optimizing the allocation of economic resources. Their views contrasted even more sharply with those of the Social Darwinists of the late nineteenth century who held that the struggle of unfettered competition insured that only the fittest and most deserving should flourish and that no sympathy should be wasted on the less fortunate. Theorists in this tradition cannot fairly be indicted, however, on the charge of insensitivity to human suffering. Their concern for the miseries of poverty was genuine. The message of those in the mainstream of classicism was that amelioration of distresses could best be achieved through the enlargement of production. Tampering with the distributional mechanism would simply increase claims on the social product and might even have a negative effect on the desired expansion of output. These conclusions followed from the view that the economic process was governed by laws beyond human control. Mill's re-interpretation of economic laws was required before the classical tradition could begin to erase the stigma of 'the dismal science'.

Nor, in the circumstances of their times, did classical writers lack a substantial basis for their suspicion of governmental involvement in economic affairs. The political environment they observed was not one in which governments could be regarded as champions of the general welfare. Before the franchise was widened, no government was obliged – as a condition of its survival – to respond to the concerns of a mass electorate. In these circumstances, it was not unreasonable to argue that the social consequences of diffusing economic power impersonally in unregulated markets were likely to be superior to those produced by a system in which narrowly based governments intervened forcefully in the economy. However plausibly grounded such an attitude may have been in the era classical writers observed, this political case for *laissez-faire* evaporated with the advent of broadly based social democracy.

To be sure, the classical tradition left some questions – questions that were to be elevated to importance by later schools of thought – unanswered. In particular, the classical frame of reference precluded a full exploration of two issues: the process of market price formation and the problem of economic fluctuations. Part of the neglect of these avenues of inquiry was related to the institutional setting of classicism. In the early stages of Western industrial emergence – when poverty and scarcity were the dominant facts of economic life – it was probably appropriate to concentrate attention on the expansion of output. A sophisticated analysis of demand and its significance in the economic process appeared to be unnecessary as, for most practical purposes, it could be taken for granted that additions to output could readily be absorbed. It was only in 'abnormal' circumstances (such as those immediately following the Napoleonic wars) that writers of a classical persuasion diverted their attention from the supply to the demand side of production, and then only temporarily.

Nor did classical analysis attempt to offer a full account of costs and conditions of supply. In the circumstances of the first half of the nineteenth century, the reasons are not difficult to comprehend. These theorists were only dimly – if at all – aware of the complications introduced by the economies of scale brought by high technologies. In their economic world these problems were scarcely visible. Later in the century, however, applications of new technologies to large-scale production bred industrial concentrations which eroded the basis of their natural competitive order. John Stuart Mill caught the scent of this problem, though he did not pursue it far.

Similarly, a careful analysis of the nature of economic fluctuations did not then appear to be warranted. The classical economic universe, though not without disturbances, did not experience the consequences of aggregative instability in acute form or for sustained periods. Malthus sensed that something was lacking in the orthodox approach to this matter, but he failed to build a convincing counter-argument. For the most part, classical writers were content to assume that this problem would take care of itself. Their antipathy toward mercantilist views on hoarding reinforced a faith in the efficacy of Say's Law.

An appreciation of the analytical priorities of classical thought, no less than of the institutional climate of the age, is crucial to an appraisal of the strengths and the limitations of this corpus of theory. Its central focus was on the problems and prospects of economic expansion over an extended time period, with special attention to the interaction between the distribution of income and changes in total output. From this point of view, a detailed examination of short-period changes – whether in individual markets or in the economy as a whole – was not directly relevant. What mattered was the long-term trend and the forces that influenced it. At the same time, the classical tradition did devote part of its attention to certain issues of a short-period character, as was the case, for example, in the extended discussion of the relationships between value and price. These matters were not, however, examined for their own sake. Instead, they drew their pertinence from their relationship to the larger questions of growth and distribution.

Notes

1. W. A. Lewis, 'Economic Development with Unlimited Supplies of Labour', *Manchester School of Economic and Social Studies*, 1954.

2. Lewis, 'Unlimited Labour: Further Notes', *Manchester School*, 1958, p. 26.

3. For an illustration of arguments along these lines dealing with the interrelationships between economic growth and distribution see Nicholas Kaldor's 'A Model of Economic Growth', *Economic Journal*, 1957.

4. See Piero Sraffa, *The Production of Commodities by Means of Commodities* (Cambridge University Press, 1960).

PART TWO

MARXIAN ECONOMICS

Introduction

KARL MARX and John Stuart Mill observed the same economic environment. It was a world in which industrialism – at least as measured by expansion in the output of manufactures – was flourishing. Factories had sprung up on a scale that would have astonished Adam Smith. If the first wave of industrialism were to be assessed in terms of the growth of total production, of the volume of international trade, and of the accumulation of productive capital, it would have to be judged an unqualified success.

But this was only part of the story. These impressive changes had brought little conspicuous benefit to the bulk of the population. On the contrary, the new working class was herded into urban slums where its members were exposed to miserable conditions of life. In all too many cases even the most elementary provision for sanitation had lagged behind the build-up of the urban working population and such massive menaces to health as typhus and cholera recurred with alarming frequency. Marx's colleague, Engels, drew attention to the contrasts of the age when he wrote in 1844:

One day I walked with one of these middle-class gentlemen into Manchester. I spoke to him about the disgraceful unhealthy slums and drew his attention to the disgusting condition of that part of town in which the factory workers lived. I declared that I had never seen so badly built a town in my life. He listened patiently and at the corner of the street at which we parted company, he remarked: 'And yet there is a great deal of money made here. Good morning, Sir!'[1]

117

If there was little to brighten the life of working people off the job there was still less during the time they spent earning a livelihood. Working hours were long – a fourteen-hour work day was not uncommon in the factories of the 1840s. Even after the public conscience had been stirred (as it had been in England with the beginnings of effective factory legislation in the 1830s), statutory restrictions on the length of the work day and week were aimed primarily as protections for minors and women; ceilings on the working hours of adult males were much later in coming.

These conditions were combined with wage payments at levels that left little scope for more than the bare necessities of life. These terms were still superior to the alternative of no work at all. As industrialism proceeded, uncertainties about employment for wages multiplied. A period of slack trade could easily strip sizeable groups of a means of support. In this environment, it was small wonder that concern about lawlessness mounted.

In England particularly, socially sensitive men perceived that all was not well and sought to learn more about the economic problems of their day. Marx paid high tribute to this manifestation of British empiricism when he observed that other countries would be 'appalled at the state of things' if, as in England, their 'governments and parliaments appointed periodically commissions of inquiry into economic conditions; if these commissions were armed with the same plenary powers to get at the truth; if it was possible to find for this purpose men as competent, as free from partisanship and respect of persons as are the English factory-inspectors, her medical reporters on public health, her commissioners of inquiry into the exploitation of women and children, into housing and food'.[2]

If the British economic scene had changed dramatically over the course of the first half of the nineteenth century, so also had the political climate. With the Reform Bill of 1832 the rising business and industrial community had overcome the earlier political supremacy of the landed aristocracy and – benefited by an atmosphere conditioned by Ricardian arguments – had later exercised its political power in the repeal of the Corn Laws in 1846. Meanwhile the working class, though still largely unenfranchised, showed fresh signs of political stirrings, hesitant and poorly organized though they were.

Both Marx and Mill sensed that the theoretical apparatus they had inherited was no longer fully adequate to the tasks at hand. The growth of large-scale industry showed signs of undercutting presuppositions around which classical *laissez-faire* doctrine had been organized. Moreover, this stage of industrial expansion appeared to be associated with increasing economic instability, marked by the recurrence of booms and panics. But, most important, the distributional system of an expanding economy – which Smith at least had expected would bring benefits to all – seemed not to be working smoothly.

John Stuart Mill addressed these problems by untying the classical package of laws and by arguing that the distribution of income was susceptible to human manipulation. His opposition opened new space for policies designed to promote the general welfare (and that of the labouring class particularly) and pointed the way towards a future of enlightenment and uplift.

At this point Marx dissented. In his view Mill was the 'best representative' of a 'shallow syncretism' and 'tried to harmonize the Political Economy of capital with the claims, no longer to be ignored, of the proletariat'; he regarded the result as 'a declaration of bankruptcy by bourgeois economy'.[3] Marx reasserted the inevitability of natural laws, but with a quite different interpretative twist. The laws he sought to uncover were neither universal nor eternal, but unique to particular stages of history. The failure of economists in the classical tradition to appreciate this point was, he maintained, a fundamental source of their error:

Economists have a singular method of procedure. There are only two kinds of institutions for them, artificial and natural. ... In this they resemble the theologians, who likewise establish two kinds of religion. Every religion which is not theirs is an invention of men, while their own is an emanation from God. When the economists say that present-day relations – the relations of bourgeois production – are natural, they imply that these are the relations in which wealth is created and productive forces developed in conformity with the laws of nature. These relations therefore are themselves natural laws independent of the influence of time. They are eternal laws which must always govern society. Thus there has been history, but there is no longer any.[4]

Marx's critique did not rest solely on the assertion that economic laws were specific to particular stages in history. No less important was his claim to the discovery of laws governing the unfolding of history itself. In his analysis economic circumstances were the fundamental determinants of all social relationships and even of human consciousness itself. The economic environment, in this interpretation, cast men in particular roles – roles which, in turn, governed their behaviour and their thought. All human activities – not simply those performed in the course of acquiring a livelihood, but religious, artistic, and philosophical expressions as well – were fundamentally conditioned by class positions in the economic system.

When this view is described in technical terms – i.e. as a materialist view of history or as economic determinism – the overtones of these words are likely to prejudice serious consideration of the point Marx wished to establish. If the nomenclature is neglected, few would deny that a man's job and its demands leave a significant imprint on his attitudes. The case may have been stronger in Marx's day – when, on the average, most men were obliged to spend the larger proportion of their waking hours in the struggle for a livelihood – than in ours. But even now, only an unreflective observer would maintain that a man's economic role, his behaviour off-the-job, and the attitudes he holds bear no connexion with one another. The modern discussion of the 'organization man' – whose job calls for certain consumption patterns, the public expression of certain attitudes, membership in acceptable organizations, etc. – is not too far removed from what Marx had in mind. Even those of us who work in less structured situations are not altogether immune from society's standards of the 'done' thing. Marx was the first to insist forcefully on a systematic connexion between economic roles and attitudes and he gave thereby a tremendous stimulus to the development of serious sociological study. That some such relationship exists can hardly be challenged; what is questionable is the absolute status Marx accorded to one simple relationship.

Marx's presuppositions about the nature of history and of society gave his economics a unique character that differentiates it sharply from other 'master models' in the history of economic ideas. His analytical system, while built around economic phenomena, was by no means restricted to economic issues as commonly construed. Instead, it offered a comprehensive view of society in which all events were seen as intimately inter-related. This approach is capable of offering an account of everything, but runs the risk of explaining nothing. Marx, for example, could maintain that the abstract systems of classical economists derived from their 'class interests' and that their works were apologies for capitalism. But his scheme of determinism was placed under some strain when called upon to explain the specific content of their teaching. After all, classical writers with identical class interests did not make the same reading of events and some whom fortune had blessed were markedly unsympathetic toward unregulated capitalism.

Marx was aware of this diversity and he tried to accommodate it with the aid of his interpretation of historical change. Within his frame of reference, conflicts between divergent economic interests were inevitable.

Discord among economists was itself symptomatic of the antagonisms latent within capitalism. He maintained that:

The more the antagonistic character comes to light, the more the economists, the scientific representatives of bourgeois production, find themselves in conflict with their own theory; and different schools arise.[5]

Some of these schools might genuinely lament the miseries of the proletariat and propose measures to ameliorate distress. Such sentiments, however admirable, were naïve. Marx insisted that those who held them failed to understand that conflict was inherent in capitalism and that tensions were the engines of historical change. Moreover, they failed to comprehend that the causes of distress were rooted in the very nature of the system and could only be eliminated through the destruction of the system itself.

This line of argument gave to Marxian economic thought another distinctive attribute. All of the other 'master models' have been constructed for the purpose of throwing light on the types of policy most likely to improve economic performance. Even early classicism, despite its appeal to the natural order, was reformist in orientation with its appeals for amendments in existing legislation and in prevailing administrative practice. The Marxian approach could not stand more sharply in contrast.[6] Within its historical framework, policies intended to remedy economic ills are useless and constructive reforms impossible. The function of economic analysis is thus restricted to laying bare the laws of historical change which foredoom the destruction of capitalism, and to demonstrating the futility of policies designed to relieve its ills.

Notes

1. F. Engels, *Condition of the Working Class in England* (as quoted by E. J. Hobsbawm, *The Age of Revolution: 1798–1848*, Mentor, New York, 1964, p. 218).

2. Karl Marx, *Capital*, vol. 1, author's preface to the first edition in 1867 (Charles H. Kerr and Co., Chicago, 1912), p. 14.

3. ibid., preface to the second edition in 1872, p. 19.

4. Marx, *The Poverty of Philosophy* (International Publishers, New York, 1963), pp. 120–21.

5. ibid., p. 123.

6. The early Marx, as revealed in the Economic and Philosophical Manuscripts of 1844, was much closer to the reformist tradition in social thought. By the time *Das Kapital* was produced, however, he asserted economic determination with little qualification.

CHAPTER 5

Karl Marx and the Economics of Das Kapital

DESPITE the central position occupied by an interpretation of historical change in Marx's thought, his economic writing was focused primarily on only one stage of historical evolution. The objective of his major work, as he described it, was to 'lay bare the economic law of motion of modern society' [1] – i.e. of the capitalist mode of production. Though his scheme did provide the basis for an interpretation of pre-capitalistic productive arrangements, he made no systematic analysis of the economic system that would replace capitalism following the collapse he held to be inevitable.

1. KARL MARX (1818–83)

Marx's career blended the retirement of the philosopher and scholar with the active life of the organizer and propagandist. In one role, he was a student of the dynamics of society; in the other, he was an interventionist who sought to hasten social change. These diverse facets of the man and his activities were closely associated. It was through a process of detached intellectual inquiry that he first identified the causes he sought to promote and he carried over much of the manner of the scholar to his role in public affairs. For a political organizer his style was remarkably austere.

Born to an upper middle-class Rhineland family that had forsaken Judaism in favour of the established church, his early years were largely conventional. He entered the university to study law, but changed his plans after the lively debates on Hegelian philosophy in Berlin in the

1830s captured his imagination. He identified himself with the Young Hegelians who sought to transform Hegelian orthodoxy into a radical social doctrine. With this cause in mind, Marx in his mid-twenties aspired to a university post as a philosopher. This dream soon died when the Prussian Minister of Education proscribed the Hegelian Left.

Obliged by the death of his father to find a means of supporting himself, he turned to journalism, writing for a newly-founded anti-government journal published in Cologne. He flourished in this enterprise, which afforded him an opportunity to agitate for political reform and to sharpen his skills in writing trenchant prose. Within a year, he had risen to the post of editor. This episode was short-lived. In 1843, the government censor banned the publication and Marx set off for Paris to assist in the editing of another journal.

During the next two years, the framework of ideas with which he worked began to take clear shape. While in Paris, he devoured the major literature of economic theory. Life there also brought him into contact with most of the leading members of the Continental Left and it was then that his partnership with Friedrich Engels began. This phase ended in 1845 when the French government, prompted by official Prussian protests against the contents of the publication with which he had been associated, expelled him.

In 1849 – after a period of hectic political activity that included collaboration with Engels in the drafting of the Communist Manifesto – he went into exile in London where he was to spend the remainder of his days. During these years, he passed the bulk of the daylight hours in the reading rooms of the British Museum. The materials he gathered were woven into his major contribution to economic theory – the three volumes of *Das Kapital*.

Few serious students of social problems can have worked under hardships comparable to those Marx endured. The small sums he could eke out from free-lance journalism (plus the charity of the devoted Engels) were insufficient to keep creditors from the door. Even when living in the most miserable housing conditions – conditions that a Prussian spy assigned to check on his activities reported on with horror – Marx was unable to afford adequate nutritional and medical attention for his family. When he wrote of poverty, it was not an exercise of the imagination.

2. MARX AND THE CLASSICAL TRADITION

Much of Marx's sharpest polemical writing was directed against the classical tradition of economic thought. He attacked the analytical procedures employed by classical writers as well as the conclusions they had reached. Nevertheless, his relationship to the classical tradition must be described as ambivalent. Despite his hostility towards classical economics, he made much of its analytical framework his own. Though he embellished, modified, and poured new meaning into the classical categories, he inherited the core of his system from the classical economists.

In Marx's hands the familiar classical questions were re-opened: in particular, what are the laws governing the distribution of income and how do they affect the economy's long-period prospects? He also appropriated classical insights on many points of detail. As had the mainstream of the classical tradition, he approached the problem of value in terms of labour and regarded only physical objects as embodiments of value. In addition, his scheme of income distribution was organized around a set of social class categories and his theory of accumulation was linked to the behaviour of profits.

Marx's philosophical presuppositions about history and his claim to have discovered its inner logic both gave established categories a different significance and supplied the springboard for fresh departures. His general *modus operandi* can be instructively observed in his critique of

Malthus. This polemic, moreover, is of particular interest in its own right: Malthus's population principle, which had been interpreted as demonstrating that members of the working class had only themselves to blame for their misery, had to be demolished before Marx's alternative explanation of poverty could stand.[2]

The manner in which Marx invoked his view of historical stages to undercut Malthusian population doctrine can be seen in the following passage:

The labouring population ... produces, along with the accumulation of capital produced by it, the means by which itself is made relatively superfluous, is turned into a relative surplus population, and it does this to an always increasing extent. This is a law of population peculiar to the capitalist mode of production; and in fact every special historic mode of production has its own special laws of population, historically valid within its limits alone. An abstract law of population exists for plants and animals only, and only in so far as man has not interfered with them.[3]

In short, capitalism did, in fact, create the appearance of a redundant population. But, contrary to Malthusian teaching, such population pressures were not universal throughout time and space. A change in productive arrangements could readily convert an apparent surplus of population into a shortage.

Marx's reasoning on this point rested on his distinction between various 'modes of production', each with unique characteristics. In the pre-capitalistic mode private ownership of the means of production was far from universal and, to the extent that private property was recognized, it was qualified by a reciprocal pattern of rights and obligations along feudal lines. Moreover, production for exchange was far from ubiquitous. The emergence of capitalism led to the rapid breakdown of these patterns. Most importantly, the use of machine techniques created a sharp cleavage within society. Those who owned the means of production and those who worked with them were divided into distinct groups. No longer was it possible for the worker to possess the tools with which he gained a livelihood; instead he became dependent on others to supply them. Meanwhile the widening of the market called for higher and higher degrees of specialization which heightened the interdependence between various components of the economic system. Hence arose one of the ironies ('contradictions' in Marx's terms) within the capitalist mode of production. On the one hand, it was organized on the basis of property relationships that were private; on the other, its production processes involved social relationships that were co-operative in character. Marx maintained that this situation inevitably bred tensions – tensions which would lead to the violent collapse of capitalism and which could not otherwise be resolved. Under a later socialist arrangement conflict would be replaced by harmony. The means of production would be owned collectively and both the mode of production and the productive relationships would be social in character. Class conflict could no longer occur because the very basis of class divisions – private ownership of the means of production – had been eliminated.

It might be thought that Marx's discussion of stages of economic evolution had been anticipated by some of the early classical writers. Smith, for example, had written about earlier types of economic arrangements in his consideration of an 'early and rude' stage of society. Marx's approach, however, was profoundly different. Classical writers had in mind a hypothetical state in which transactions were conducted by barter and which, in turn, could be used as a benchmark for analysing production and exchange under the simplest conditions conceivable. Marx, on the other hand, was concerned with specific historical epochs, rather than hypothetical cases, and he looked at history as a succession of stages governed by immutable laws.

It was against this background that Marx accused the classical economists of propagating gross error. Their findings, he maintained, failed to take into account the full significance of the inner dynamics of the historical process. In addition, classical writers did not comprehend that each stage of history was governed by economic laws peculiar to itself. A universal law of population was thus out of the question. Each mode of production produced its own social conditioning in forms which affected all human behaviour, including man's reproductive activities.[4]

Apart from his quarrel with classicism on method, Marx's philosophical premises also called for an important amendment in a basic set of classical categories. To the classicists, the social groupings important to the analysis of income distribution involved three classes: capitalists, landlords, and labourers. Marx insisted, on the other hand, that under capitalism this scheme would be compressed into a two-fold division based on legally-recognized rights to property. In his analysis the essential class groupings of capitalism separated those who owned the means of production from those who did not. As owners, capitalists and landlords were thus a common genus. In Marx's view it was a 'Physiocratic illusion' to hold that 'rents grow out of the soil and not out of society'.[5]

3. THE ANALYSIS OF VALUE

Marx's debts to his classical forerunners were particularly marked in the framework he adopted for the analysis of value. Here he appropriated the essentials of the Ricardian labour-input approach. Labour was held to be the only productive agent and the source of all value. Following Ricardo, capital goods were regarded as stored-up labour. Land, however, virtually disappeared as a separate element in the production scheme. Anything economically interesting about land could be dissolved into labour inputs.

Marx's version of the labour-input approach to value, however, involved a number of modifications to Ricardian procedure. His amendments did not alter the substance of the argument appreciably but they considerably advanced its sophistication. His treatment of the familiar problem presented by the lack of homogeneity in the labour force provides an interesting case in point. The standard classical escape from this difficulty had rested on an appeal to wage differentials established in the market as a basis for weighting the economic contribution of members of the labour force. This technique, it will be recalled, was not strictly admissible on classical premises: if market prices were acceptable as measures of the value of labour, why were they not adequate in the market for commodities? Marx cannot be faulted on this score. In his view the value of labour-power was itself established by labour-inputs. 'The value of labour-power is determined,' he asserted, 'as in the case of every other commodity, by the labour-time necessary for the production, and consequently also the reproduction, of this special article.' [6] In other words, the labour-time necessary to provide the means of subsistence for the work force and to permit its replacement in the next generation governed the value of unskilled labour. This amounted to a subsistence interpretation of the standard wage, though Marx was at pains to point out that the composition of the 'subsistence' bundle was not inflexible; instead it was subject to adaptation with changes in the social environment.[7]

Labour-input requirements for 'necessaries' thus established the floor beneath which wages could not sink. But differentials in the remuneration of wage earners were regulated by another type of labour input: the labour-time involved in equipping workers with skills. Here Marx picked up a thread Mill had left dangling when the latter, in his protests against the earlier classical usage of the term 'productive', insisted that the training of workers (though not an activity directly involving the production of material objects) should normally be treated as 'productive'.

Marx tightened the concept of labour-input further by stating explicitly the conditions under which inputs of labour were to count as creating value. The fact that labour time had been poured into the production of useful tangible commodities was not, he maintained, a sufficient test. Only 'socially necessary' inputs of labour time – by which he meant 'that required to produce an article under the normal conditions of production, and with the average degree of skill and intensity prevalent at the time' [8] – could qualify. Marx illustrated the force of this restriction in an example dealing with the manufacture of textiles:

The introduction of power looms into England probably reduced by one-half the labour required to weave a given quantity of yarn into cloth. The hand-loom weavers, as a matter of fact, continued to require the same time as before: but for all that, the product of one hour of their labour represented after the change only half an hour's social labour, and consequently fell to one-half its former value. [9]

In his attitude toward the displacement of labour produced by the competition between advanced and traditional techniques of production, Marx sharply differentiated his position from that of many contemporary critics of industrialism. Marx had no patience for the sentimentalism of those who called for a return to rustic simplicity and who sought to turn their backs on technological progress. He insisted that the advance of mechanization in the capitalist system, however unhappy its consequences in some respects, at least had the not inconsiderable merit of adding enormously to productive capacity.

Marx attached another restriction to his analysis of value – one that further reflected his preoccupation with the study of the capitalistic mode of production. Production for exchange, he asserted, was a prerequisite of value. Pre-capitalistic arrangements could produce outputs, but by Marxian definitions, they could produce neither commodities nor value. [10]

Once these conditions had been added there was no

question in Marx's mind that exchange values (or relative prices) were regulated unequivocally by the labour inputs required in the production of commodities. Under capitalism, exchange ratios between commodities would be expressed in money terms, but this was possible only 'because all commodities, as values, are realized human labour, and therefore commensurable, that their values can be measured by one and the same special commodity, and the latter converted into the common measure of their values, i.e. into money'.[11] At this stage in the argument the Ricardian puzzles about unequal durability of the components of fixed capital and the absence of uniformity in the proportions of fixed and circulating capital dropped out of the picture, though Marx later addressed himself to them in other contexts.

4. THE CONCEPTS OF SURPLUS VALUE, VARIABLE CAPITAL, AND CONSTANT CAPITAL

While Marx appropriated many of the building blocks of the classical labour-input version of the theory of value, he put them to work for another set of purposes. With the aid of his argument that the value of labour and the value of commodities were governed by the same principles, he was equipped to provide an alternative interpretation of the mechanisms of production and distribution in capitalist societies. The position he adopted was reinforced subsequently by his analysis of the consequences of the accumulation of capital. The initial steps, however, grew directly out of his theory of value.

This extension of the argument involved the re-assertion of the conclusion that the value of labour-power was based on labour inputs required for its subsistence and training. In a capitalistic system, workers would be obliged – simply as a condition of survival – to sell enough of their labour time to acquire the means of subsistence. But, in the conditions of capitalist production, more labour time would be demanded from labourers than was necessary to produce values equivalent to their subsistence requirements. In the absence of alternative sources of a livelihood, labourers would not only have to sell their time to capitalists but to accept the terms and conditions set by their employers. Workers, for example, might be able to produce enough to cover subsistence requirements in a six-hour working day, but employers could insist on labour inputs of longer duration. The working day was thus divided into two components: the 'necessary'[12] labour time required for the production of values equal to maintenance requirements and 'surplus' labour time.

In Marx's view the commanding position in the power hierarchy attached to the ownership of the means of production enabled capitalists to demand a working day in excess of necessary labour time and to appropriate the value created during surplus labour time for themselves. Indeed, Marx insisted, the creation of surplus value was the whole point of hiring workers in the first instance. From the employer's point of view the power of labour to create more value than was passed on to it in wages was a pre-condition of employment. This 'circumstance', as Marx described it, 'is, without doubt, a piece of good luck for the buyer [of labour], but by no means an injury to the seller.'[13]

The special power of labour to generate surplus value provided the rationale for Marx's designation of wage payments as 'variable capital'. This usage, though puzzling to those schooled exclusively in modern terminology, was clearly in the classical lineage. For Marx (as for the classical economists) the general term 'capital' was used to refer to the resources available for initiating and sustaining production. These resources could be allocated in varying proportions between the required productive inputs – e.g. labour, raw materials, and plant and equipment. In the mainstream of the classical tradition, two categories of capital – fixed and circulating – were distinguished. The line of demarcation was generally drawn on the basis of the length of the time periods before the values contained in these components of capital could be realized through sale.

Marx modified this procedure by dividing capital into a 'variable' component (the wage bill) and a 'constant' component (raw materials and depreciation allowances for plant and equipment). These distinctions turned on his concept of the surplus-generating capacity of direct labour inputs. Active labour, he maintained, had the unique property of 'being a source not only of value, but of more value than it has itself'.[14] Indeed, the circumstances of capitalist production were such that labour would be hired only when surplus value could be appropriated. By contrast, the items of constant capital were embodiments of past labour inputs and thus inert. Their contribution to the productive process, though important, was passive; they could impart no more value to the final product than they themselves contained. In Marx's words: 'However useful a given kind of raw material, or a machine, or other means of production may be, though it may cost £150, or say, 500 days' labour, yet it cannot, under any circumstances, add to the value of the product more than £150.'[15]

These definitions, occupied a strategic position in the unfolding of Marx's analysis. Three important ratios were built around them. The first $\left(\frac{s}{v}\right)$ related the capitalist's surplus to the wage bill and was described both as the 'rate of surplus value' and as the 'rate of exploitation'. The two components of capital could also be expressed in a ratio form $\left(\frac{c}{v}\right)$; this relationship, labelled the 'organic composition of capital', provided a convenient device for expressing variations in the proportions of constant to variable capital. All three variables entered into the 'rate of profit' $\left(\frac{s}{v+c}\right)$. This notion was clearly allied to the classical tradition in which the rate of profit was treated as the percentage return on the outlays advanced to labour as well as on the current costs of raw materials and fixed capital. The bulk of Marx's dynamic analysis was organized around the expected behaviour of these ratios.

5. THE ANALYSIS OF ACCUMULATION

Like the contributors to the classical tradition before him, Marx held that accumulation arose from the income shares received by property owners. But his general view of the economic process yielded a different insight into the nature of this 'net' revenue. Within Marx's framework of analysis, it could be maintained that the generation of surplus value was indeed the defining structural characteristic of the capitalist system. Given the property relationships of capitalism, workers were obliged to put themselves at the mercy of capitalists in their struggle to gain subsistence and they were, in turn, bound to contribute surplus labour time.

The consequences of the creation of surplus value under capitalism were powerfully influenced by the use of machinery. Machine techniques meant that the ranks of the eligible participants in the capitalist process were swollen. Positions in the labour force were now created, for example, for women and children (who could be employed more cheaply than men in a large number of newly-created repetitive tasks) At the same time, the advance of machine techniques augmented the leverage of capitalists by placing new instruments of control over the duration and intensity of labour input at their disposal. No longer could the productivity of the labour force be significantly influenced by the skills and initiative of workers themselves. Instead, the rhythm of the machine established the pace of work. However unhappy the consequence might be for the dignity of workers, these procedures nevertheless increased productivity enormously. It is interesting to note that in some modern discussions of the problems of underdeveloped countries, a similar argument is now invoked to support the introduction of highly capital-intensive techniques, despite the fact that a large potential labour force might be available at low wages. Where a tradition of industrial discipline is lacking, an industrial build-up based on highly mechanized techniques has the not unimportant recommendation of insuring automatic checks on labour efficiency. Machine-dominated processes must usually be operated in accordance with a scheduled pace if they are to function at all.

The extended use of machinery had other significant effects. By virtue of the fact that higher techniques increased the productivity of labour – i.e. labour inputs per unit of output were reduced – the value of commodities was depressed. At the same time, Marx maintained that the rate of surplus value would tend to rise because the cheapening of commodities would shorten the number of working hours required to produce the means of subsistence. The latter effect, of course, was at odds with the outcome expected by writers in the mainstream of classicism. Most theorists in this tradition held that the 'progress of improvement' would tend to increase the quantity of labour input required to produce necessaries. This conclusion had been based on the special conditions governing the production of food. As they saw the problem, larger national food requirements would necessarily tend to shrink the capitalist's surplus by raising the cost of the main component of subsistence. Marx rejected this analysis, arguing that the dividing line between commercialized agriculture and industry was not as sharp as the classical tradition had supposed. Instead, he maintained that capitalist production, by its nature, spread its tentacles throughout the economic structure. The industrial segment of the economy might be the dynamic engine of change. But the mere growth of capitalism would tend to homogenize conditions of production throughout the economy. In fact, he insisted:

In the sphere of agriculture, modern industry has a more revolutionary effect than elsewhere, for this reason, that it annihilates the peasant, that bulwark of the old society, and replaces him by the wage labourer. Thus the desire for social changes, and the class antagonisms are brought to the same level in the country as in the towns. The irrational, old fashioned methods of agriculture are replaced by scientific ones.[16]

This view reflected Marx's rejection of classical definitions of profits and rents. From his perspective, what counted was ownership of the means of production: nothing of substance distinguished the capitalist from the landlord. Both were in a position to exploit labour and to extract surplus value from it. Similarly, the physical constraints on the rapid expansion of agricultural output (to which writers of a classical persuasion had given so much attention) were de-emphasized. The application of new techniques to agricultural production promised to raise productivity sufficiently to satisfy the food requirements generated by industrial expansion. This did not mean that rents disappeared completely from the Marxian vocabulary. They remained, but were no longer unique to land. They might arise as the result of qualitative differentials in any of the productive agents. With this set of arguments Marx disposed of the other support to the Malthusian fear that population would tend to outstrip the availability of food.

The appropriation of surplus value by capitalists also permitted accumulation – indeed it was pre-requisite to accumulation on a substantial scale. It afforded the command over labour that Smith had written about; Marx merely added the qualification that it was 'essentially the command over unpaid labour'.[17] Nor did he entertain any doubt that a significant share of the surplus value claimed by capitalists would be used for the purpose of extending their capitals and, most particularly, for the acquisition of machinery. Further, the application of higher technologies meant that the value of commodities – measured in labour inputs – would be reduced. Commodities were thus 'cheapened'. This process would snowball because capitalists would be obliged to join in the race of competitive cheapening of commodities. Their own survival depended on their ability to acquire and use machinery for the purpose of raising the productivity of labour; otherwise, they would be killed off in the competitive struggle. The system itself thus compelled capitalists to accumulate and to introduce labour-saving innovations. Marx described the process in the following language:

Only as personified capital is the capitalist respectable. As such, he shares with the miser the passion for wealth as wealth. But that which in the miser is a mere idiosyncrasy is, in the capitalist, the effect of the social mechanism, of which he is but one of the wheels. Moreover, the development of capitalist production makes it constantly necessary to keep increasing the amount of capital laid out in a given industrial undertaking, and competition makes the immanent laws of capitalist production to be felt by each individual capitalist, as external coercive laws. It compels him to keep constantly extending his capital, in order to preserve it, but extend it he cannot except by means of progressive accumulation.[18]

And again:

Accumulate, accumulate! That is Moses and the prophets! ... Therefore, save, save, i.e. reconvert the greatest possible portion of surplus-value, or surplus-product into capital! Accumulation for accumulation's sake, production for production's sake ...[19]

This explanation of the incessant drive of capitalists had wide implications. Within Marx's system the capitalist was often described as a ruthless exploiter. Even so, Marx held it to be inappropriate to attach blame to the capitalist as a person, a point he made clear in the preface to the first edition of *Capital:*

I paint the capitalist and the landlord in no sense *couleur de rose*. But here individuals are dealt with only in so far as they are the personification of economic categories, embodiments of particular class-relations and class interests. My standpoint, from which the evolution of the economic formation of society is viewed as a process of natural history, can less than any other make the individual responsible for relations whose creature he socially remains, however much he may subjectively raise himself above them.[20]

In short, energies devoted to condemning the behaviour of capitalists were misplaced. As Marx observed in another context: 'What avails lamentation in the face of historical necessity?'[21]

Clear limits, however, were attached to the amount of accumulation undertaken at any one time. Marx stated these limits in terms that flowed directly from his labour-input analysis of value. Investment in machinery, he maintained, would be worthwhile only when it resulted in the displacement of labour. The value of a commodity could be reduced only to the extent that the labour content of the final output had shrunk. From the capitalist's point of view it would be worthwhile to acquire additional machinery only when the sum of direct and indirect labour inputs would subsequently be lower than had formerly been the case. In Marx's words, 'the limit to his using a machine is fixed by the difference between the value of the machine and the value of the labour-power displaced by it'.[22]

This line of argument, virtually by definition, made the substitution of machinery for labour a precondition for the acquisition of capital goods. This proposition was crucial to the embellishment of Marx's model. Ricardo had anticipated the conclusion in the chapter 'On Machinery' in the third and final edition of his *Principles*. He then amended his earlier support for the position that the immediate competition between machinery and employment would be offset by releases of funds which could be used to engage more labour.[23] The mainstream of classicism, it will be recalled, rested its case on the argument that this compensating effect would shortly neutralize – by swelling profits and thereby increasing the subsequent demand for labour – any short-term appearances of technological unemployment. This view, Marx insisted,

was fallacious in that it presupposed that all of the ensuing gains to the capitalist would be 'destined to support
labour'. Marx, on the contrary, maintained that the laws
of motion of capitalism demanded that part of the expanded surplus be allocated to the acquisition of machinery. Moreover, when this occurred, the total demand for
labour would necessarily diminish. Marx, of course,
recognized that the introduction of higher techniques
might be associated with reductions in costs and with
growth in the volume of output. To this extent, mechanization might generate additional demand for labour in
industries producing machines and supplying raw
materials. Such gains in employment he held to be temporary and soon to be neutralized by the accumulation of
machinery by capitalists engaged in supplying these inputs.

But even this short-lived stimulus to the demand for
labour might be swamped by forces moving in a counter
direction. Among its other consequences, the increased
use of machinery would have the effect of killing off the
jobs of those who worked with older and inferior techniques. Handicraft workers would be among the first to
feel the sting of the spread of industrialism; much of their
labour time would become 'socially unnecessary'. Later,
as the application of industrial techniques gained
momentum, the weaker and smaller capitalists would be
destroyed. In this phase, the battle of competition, Marx
maintained, 'always ends in the ruin of many small
capitalists, whose capitals partly pass into the hand of
their conquerors, partly vanish'.[24] This combination of
forces would produce a situation in which the total demand for labour would expand less rapidly than the
numbers eligible for employment. In Marx's words:

Since the demand for labour is determined not by the
amount of capital as a whole, but by its variable constituent
alone, that demand falls progressively with the increase of the
total capital, instead of . . . rising in proportion to it. It falls
relatively to the magnitude of the total capital, and at an

accelerated rate, as this magnitude increases. With the growth of the total capital, its variable constituent or the labour incorporated in it, also does increase, but in a constantly diminishing proportion.[25]

The problem to which Marx was here directing attention has by no means lost its pertinence in the modern world. It is still a widely held view that labour-saving technological improvements should be welcomed on the grounds that, whatever their short-term effects on the labour market, their long-term effects must necessarily be favourable to the economy at large. In the history of Western industrial countries there is a substantial basis for this view. In a number of underdeveloped countries, however, it has become increasingly apparent that the adoption of modern techniques of manufacture may have unfortunate 'backwash' effects on established lines of employment. The consequences of this situation are especially serious in underdeveloped economies nowadays where, in most cases, the population of working age is growing at considerably faster rates than was the case in Western countries at comparable periods in their industrial emergence. Some governments – perhaps most notably the government of India – have attempted to minimize the risks of job displacements from the introduction of modern technologies by restricting their use to product lines which do not compete with established manufacturing enterprises.[26] This approach to policy builds on an insight that was initially Marxian, though Marx himself would have rejected it. Within his perspective, policy measures designed to alter the course of history were inevitably fruitless and vain.[27]

As Marx saw it, the mechanism of accumulation under capitalism could be explained in the first instance by the creation of surplus value and by the pressures on the capitalists to re-invest a substantial part of that surplus. The significance of the process he was describing extended well beyond the domain of economic causes and effects as narrowly construed. By its very nature, capitalism was bound to produce an ever-widening cleavage within the social stucture. Increasingly labourers would be debased in skill and reduced to the status of operatives performing routine and repetitive tasks. This debasement of skill, it may be noted in passing, had the analytical consequence of simplifying the measurement of output in labour units, for the dynamics of the capitalist system itself tended to standardize the labour force. Meanwhile, the displacement of labour by machines would increase the number of jobless and swell the ranks of the 'reserve army of unemployed'. The capitalist mode of production, Marx maintained, required this outcome both to maintain the power position of capitalists and to ensure that an abundant labour supply would be available at subsistence wages. Increasing misery among the proletariat was a necessary by-product of these mechanisms. As Marx saw the outcome of this phase of capitalism: '... in proportion as the productiveness of labour increases, capital increases its supply of labour more quickly than its demand for labourers. The overwork of the employed part of the working class swells the ranks of the reserve, whilst conversely the greater pressure that the latter by its competition exerts on the former, forces these to submit to overwork and the subjugation under the dictates of capital.'[28]

Meanwhile, at the other end of the social spectrum, the situation of capitalists – or at least of those who retained a position as owners of the means of production – would be improved. They could now afford to indulge themselves in luxuries and economic inequalities would be widened. The number of successful capitalists, however, was likely to shrink. With the spread of machinery, only the strong could survive; the weak would be ground under. This proposition applied to capitalists fully as much as to the proletarian class. Caught up in the dynamics of the system, many of the smaller capitalists would find themselves pushed down the social scale to become, like the workers they had formerly employed, dependent on property owners for an opportunity to gain a liveli-

hood. Concentration and centralization of the ownership
of the means of production thus marched hand in hand
with increasing misery and inequality.

6. THE ANALYSIS OF DISTRIBUTION

Marx had enough in common with the classical tradition
to give a prominent place in his model to the mechanisms
of income distribution. Indeed, the laws governing distribution were crucial to his account of the dynamics of
the capitalist mode of production. At the same time, he re-
defined the categories of distributive shares. No longer
was the dividing line one which distinguished the roles of
the capitalist, landowner, and labourer. For Marx, a two-
fold class *schema* was sufficient. What mattered was the
separation of those who had a legally recognized stake in
the ownership of the means of production from those who
did not. On this basis the distinction between agriculture
and industry – to which the classical tradition had
attached so much importance – largely evaporated.

Nevertheless, Marx appropriated from the mainstream
of classicism two of its main conclusions about the behaviour of distributive shares during a period of dynamic
change. In both models the real wage was expected to
gravitate around a subsistence norm and the rate of profit
was expected to fall. Marx's solution, however, was distinctive in that he offered an entirely different explanation
for these phenomena.

The classical account of the behaviour of real wages,
it will be recalled, was organized around Malthusian
population postulates. Marx, for reasons indicated earlier,
was determined to demolish the Malthusian approach to
this matter. In his view the basic explanation for the
perpetuation of subsistence wages was rooted in the
mechanics of the capitalistic system. The process of technological displacement – which followed as an inevitable
consequence of accumulation – meant that the reserve
army of unemployed was swollen. On this point he asserted

that '... it is capitalist accumulation itself that constantly produces and produces in the direct ratio of its own energy and extent, a relatively redundant population of labourers, i.e. a population of greater extent than suffices for the average needs of the self-expansion of capital, and therefore a surplus-population'.[29]

The existence of this reserve army was sufficient to explain the tendency for real wages to be tied to subsistence. As long as capitalists could tap unemployed workers to replace any among those employed who sought higher pay, there was no reason to expect the circumstances of the poor to improve. On this point Marx directly challenged the classical view that workers should be encouraged to limit their reproductive rates in the interests of restricting the labour supply and of enhancing their bargaining prospects. He described as 'folly' that 'economic wisdom that preaches to the labourers the accommodation of their number to the requirements of capital. The mechanism of capitalist production and accumulation constantly effects this adjustment. The first work of this adaptation is the creation of a relative surplus-population, or industrial reserve-army.'[30]

It did not follow, however, that the real wage would never deviate from the subsistence level. For short periods it was at least conceivable that unusually intense demand for labour might bid wage rates beyond the tolerable minimum. Even Malthus had recognized that this might occur. In both the Marxian and classical traditions it was held that any tendency in this direction would soon be offset by forces inherent within the economic system — forces that would depress wages back toward their 'natural' level. But quite different explanations of this phenomenon were offered by the classical and the Marxian analyses. Malthus saw the adjustment occurring on the supply side of the labour market; improvements in the real wage, he had argued, would lead to increases in the labour force which would compete wage rates downward. Marx, on the other hand, saw the adjustment as occurring in the de-

mand for labour. He described the path toward the rest-
oration of the subsistence norm as follows:

If the quantity of unpaid labour supplied by the working
class, and accumulated by the capitalist class, increases so
rapidly that its conversion into capital requires an extraordinary addition of paid labour, then wages rise, and, all other
circumstances remaining equal, the unpaid labour diminishes
in proportion. But as soon as this diminution touches the
point at which the surplus-labour that nourishes capital is no
longer supplied in normal quantity, a reaction sets in: a
smaller part of revenue is capitalized, accumulation lags, and
the movement of rise in wages receives a check.[31]

Marx thus arrived at the classical conclusion about the
behaviour of real wages during a period of economic expansion via a different route. By the same token he offered
an alternative explanation of another classical phenomenon: the long-term tendency for the rate of profit to fall.
Within the classical tradition, the behaviour of profits
was analysed primarily in terms of the redistribution of
income between the shares of profits and rent. Productive
conditions in agriculture, it had been argued, led to rising
rents and to increases in the price of subsistence goods.
Higher money wage payments would thus be required in
order to maintain the subsistence wage. Capitalist employers, by virtue of rising wage costs, would be obliged to
accept lower rates of return on their capital outlays.

This line of explanation was obviously closed to Marx.
Having eliminated the classical concept of rent from his
analysis and having denied the existence of significant
differences in the productive conditions of industry and
agriculture, he could not invoke rising food costs in his
account of the behaviour of profits. Instead he chose to
develop the argument around changes in the values of his
three fundamental ratios: the rate of surplus value (or of
exploitation) $\left(\frac{s}{v}\right)$; the organic composition of capital
$\left(\frac{c}{v}\right)$; and the rate of profit $\left(\frac{s}{c+v}\right)$.[32]

The analysis of the behaviour of one of these ratios – that of the organic composition of capital – presented no complications. The bulk of the Marxian model had already been developed around the view that the pressure on capitalists to accumulate would mean that outlays for constant capital would grow faster than expenditures on variable capital. If Marxian propositions on the technological unemployment supposedly generated by the accumulation of capital were accepted, it then necessarily followed that the organic composition of capital would rise.

The behaviour of the rate of surplus value (or the rate of exploitation) was less straightforward. In the bulk of his numerical illustrations Marx suggested that this rate was 100 per cent; i.e. that the wage bill and surplus of the capitalist were equal. Marx nowhere argued explicitly that the rate of surplus value should be regarded as a constant, nor did he demonstrate that it should be 100 per cent. He did maintain, however, that the inner mechanics of the capitalist system prevented more than temporary reduction in the established rate of surplus value on the ground that any tendency for wages to rise would be countered by increased investment in labour-displacing machinery.[33]

An increase in the rate of exploitation, however, was not precluded. Reductions in the labour-inputs required to produce the commodities entering into the subsistence wage would make it possible to extend surplus labour time at the expense of necessary labour time. Nevertheless, Marx appeared to have assumed that the rate of exploitation was, in fact, constant.

If the assumption of a constant rate of exploitation is combined with a rising organic composition of capital it follows that the rate of profit $\left(\dfrac{s}{c + v}\right)$ must fall. When s and v are equal and c is growing at a faster rate than either s or v, the value of the denominator in this expression increases more rapidly than the value of the numerator. In this fashion Marx could reach a conclusion similar to the one arrived at by classical economists on the long-term behaviour of the rate of profit.[34]

This line of argument was not without pitfalls. In particular, one of its conclusions contradicted a vital piece of Marx's earlier argument on the course of real wages. Presumably the process of capital accumulation raises the productivity of labour and increases the size of the net product $(v + s)$. When the proportion of s to v remains constant, growth in the size of the net product would imply that total wage payments (v) increased – and quite probably at a faster rate than the volume of employment was likely to grow. Mechanization, after all, was expected to suppress the rate of growth in the demand for labour. This outcome, however, would imply that the portion of the labour force remaining in employment would enjoy improvements in real earnings. The prospect that sustained increases in real wages might occur under capitalism cannot be reconciled with the main thrust of Marxian argument, nor can this conclusion be reconciled analytically with the existence of a reserve army of unemployed. Marx appeared to have been unaware of this inconsistency in his analysis.

7. THE MARXIAN THEORY OF CRISIS

Both the main-stream of classicism and of Marxian analysis contained a type of teleological reasoning; i.e. they saw the natural laws of economic dynamics as propelling the system toward a predestined end. In the case of classical writers the economic system was interpreted as set on a course toward the stationary state. For Marx, on the other hand, the *telos* of capitalism was an inevitable and violent collapse. But whereas classical writers held that appropriate economic policies could postpone the onset of the stationary state, Marx maintained that no human contrivance could alter the destiny of the capitalist system.

Marx offered two distinct explanations of the crisis in which the capitalist order would be destroyed. He regarded these explanations as interdependent and mutually reinforcing. They can, however, be examined separately. In fact, his conclusions follow from only one of the two sets of arguments.

His first account of the capitalist crisis was built around an elaboration of distinctions he had drawn in his portrait of the capitalist system. The essential concept in this context was the division of the economy into two 'departments': one producing the means of production, the other producing the means of consumption. The relationships between these departments were then examined under differing sets of assumptions. In the simplest case (which he described as 'simple reproduction') neither net saving nor net investment occurred and output would be unchanged from one time period to the next. His analysis of the matter took the following form. In Department I (producing the means of production) the gross value of output would be equal to labour inputs and could be represented as the sum of $C_1 + V_1 + S_1$. Similarly, in Department II (in which the means of consumption were produced) the gross value of output could be stated as the sum of $C_2 + V_2 + S_2$. In both departments, of course, means of production were employed and used up in the process of creating output. For this reason, if production was to be continued on the same basis in the succeeding period, the supply of replacements forthcoming from current outputs of producer goods had to cover the current utilization of constant capital. By the same token the output of Department II had to equal the requirements for consumption goods generated in both departments.[35] Even in this simplest of cases the maintenance of a self-perpetuating equilibrium required a delicate balance between the two departments.

As a practical matter Marx saw that the task of achieving this balance was complicated by a number of factors. Realism demanded that a third department – one producing luxuries to satisfy part of the consumption demands of capitalists – be added. In addition, account had to be taken of the fact that a portion of the capitalist's surplus was allocated to net accumulation. The maintenance of the self-sustaining equilibrium thus became an increasingly intricate operation and could easily be disturbed by nothing more unusual than the acquisition of assets of unequal durability – a situation which would later lead to an uneven timing of replacement requirements and to fluctuations in the demand for producer goods. Marx's treatment of this point carried overtones of Ricardo's analysis of the consequences of inequalities in the life of capital goods. But, whereas Ricardo was concerned with the implications of this problem for a labour-input theory of value, Marx attached more importance to it as a threat to the stability of capitalism. Any departure from the conditions necessary to sustain the system on an even keel during the course of the normal process of capital accumulation would frustrate producers in one of the departments, give rise to the accumulation of unwanted stocks, and provoke a price-cutting panic (or in Marx's terms, a 'realization' crisis).

Marx's analysis of the chronic instability of capitalism contained the germs of a theory of the business cycle. Though he could argue that the intricacy of the network of production and exchange made the system both vulnerable and highly sensitive to disturbances, he was too closely wedded to the classical tradition of Say's Law to provide a systematic demonstration of cyclical fluctuations. Within his system there could be no deficiency in total demand: only capitalists were in a position to save; and what they saved went into investment expenditure. At the same time he could invoke the classical conclusion on long-term reductions in the rate of profit in support of the argument that each malfunctioning of the system was likely to intensify the aggressiveness of capitalists.

Marx was correct – and ahead of his time – in emphasizing that tendencies toward instability were inherent in industrial capitalism. But it did not follow from this phase of his analysis that fluctuations would necessarily culminate in a breakdown of the system. More was required for such a demonstration. Marx thought he supplied the additional ingredients in a second theory of crisis with arguments that rested more on his philosophical presuppositions than on his economic analysis.

The process he saw at work can be summarized as follows: capitalism bred heavy accumulations of fixed capital; as these accumulations mounted in volume, the size of the reserve army of unemployed was swollen. For the working class, misery and distress were intensified. Meanwhile the ranks of the proletariat were further enlarged by recruits from the capitalist class, primarily by small entrepreneurs who had been crushed in the war of industrial giants. As Marx described these aspects of the unfolding of the system:

> Along with the constantly diminishing number of magnates of capital, who usurp and monopolize all advantages of this process of transformation, grows the mass of misery, oppression, slavery, degradation, exploitation; but with this too grows the revolt of the working class, a class always increasing in numbers, and disciplined, united, organized by the very mechanism of the process of capitalist production itself. The monopoly of capital becomes a fetter upon the mode of production, which has sprung up and flourished along with, and under it. Centralization of the means of production and socialization of labour at last reach a point where they become incompatible with their capitalist integument. This integument is burst asunder. The knell of capitalist private property sounds. The expropriators are expropriated.[36]

But this very process also was expected to lay the foundations for a new economic order in which the inner contradictions between the mode of production and the productive relations of capitalism would be resolved. As Marx saw this matter:

> Modern Industry, on the other hand, through its catastrophes imposes the necessity of recognising, as a fundamental

law of production, variation of work, consequently fitness of the labourer for varied work, consequently the greatest possible development of his varied aptitudes. It becomes a question of life and death for society to adapt the mode of production to the normal functioning of this law. Modern Industry, indeed, compels society, under penalties of death to replace the detail-worker of today, crippled by life-long repetition of one and the same trivial operation, and thus reduced to the mere fragment of a man, by the fully developed individual fit for a variety of labours, ready to face any change of production, and to whom the different social functions he performs, are but so many modes of giving free scope to his own natural and acquired powers.[37]

The social tensions bred by capitalism were too intense for the transition to be accomplished peacefully. Revolution was an essential part of the Marxian theory of crisis. The violent overthrow of the capitalist order, however, cannot be explained on technical economic grounds. Marx's view of the dynamics of history was an essential prop to this conclusion.

Notes

1. Marx, *Capital*, vol. 1, preface to the edition of 1867 (Charles H. Kerr and Co., Chicago, 1912), p. 14.
2. The attack on Malthus was especially venomous. In his *Theories of Surplus Value*, Marx asserted:

The hatred of the English working class against Malthus – the 'mountebank-parson,' as Cobbett rudely calls him – is therefore entirely justified. The people were right here in sensing instinctively that they were confronted not with a *man of science* but with a *bought advocate*, a pleader on behalf of their enemies, a shameless sycophant of the ruling classes. (As reprinted in *Marx and Engels on Malthus*, Ronald L. Meek, ed., International Publishers, 1954, p. 123.)

3. Marx, *Capital*, vol. 1, pp. 692–3.
4. As we shall see later, Marx also challenged the other prop to Malthusian reasoning – the necessity of diminishing returns. Land, and diminishing returns to labour inputs applied to it,

were erroneously construed, he maintained, within the classical tradition.

5. ibid., vol. 1, p. 95.
6. ibid., vol. 1, p. 189.
7. In this connexion, Marx observed:

... the number and extent of his so-called necessary wants, as also the modes of satisfying them, are themselves the product of historical development, and depend therefore to a great extent on the degree of civilization of a country, more particularly on the conditions under which, and consequently on the habits and degree of comfort in which, the class of free labourers has been formed. In contradistinction therefore to the case of other commodities, there enters into the determination of the value of labour-power a historical and moral element. Nevertheless, in a given country, at a given period, the average quantity of the means of subsistence necessary for the labourer is practically known. (ibid., vol. 1, p. 190.)

8. ibid., vol. 1, p. 46.
9. ibid., vol. 1, p. 46.
10. As Marx stated the point:

Whoever directly satisfies his wants with the produce of his own labour, creates, indeed, use-values, but not commodities. In order to produce the latter, he must not only produce use-values, but use-values for others, social use-values. (ibid., vol. 1, p. 48.)

11. ibid., vol. 1, p. 106.
12. Marx maintained that the necessity attached to 'necessary' labour time did not refer exclusively to the interests of the labourer. The minimal amount of labour input, he maintained, was also necessary to 'the world of capitalists, because on the continued existence of the labourer depends their existence also'. (ibid., vol. 1, p. 240.)

13. ibid., vol. 1, p. 216.
14. ibid., vol. 1, p. 216.
15. ibid., vol. 1, p. 229.
16. ibid., vol. 1, p. 554.
17. ibid., vol. 1, p. 585.
18. ibid., vol. 1, p. 649.
19. ibid., vol. 1, p. 652.
20. ibid., Preface to the edition of 1867, p. 15.
21. ibid., vol. 1, p. 652.
22. ibid., vol. 1, p. 429.
23. Marx paid Ricardo high tribute for his preparedness to discard his earlier opinion, noting that he 'expressly dis-

claimed it with the scientific impartiality and love of truth characteristic of him'. (ibid., vol. 1, p. 478n.)

24. ibid., vol. 1, p. 687.

25. ibid., vol. 1, p. 690.

26. The wisdom of this policy has also been endorsed on theoretical grounds by a leading analyst of development problems, Albert Hirschman; see his *Strategy of Economic Development*.

27. He enunciated this position forcefully, for example, in his essays on *British Rule in India*. Machine manufacturing, he observed, was destroying the traditional crafts; but sympathy for those thereby distressed was pointless. The outcome was inevitable.

28. ibid., vol. 1, pp. 697–8.

29. ibid., vol. 1, p. 691.

30. ibid., vol. 1, p. 707.

31. ibid., vol. 1, p. 680.

32. Some later Marxist commentators have expressed the organic composition of capital as $\frac{c}{c+v}$. Marx himself used the more abbreviated expression. The same conclusions are yielded by either notation.

33. On this point, he observed: 'The law of capitalistic accumulation ... in reality merely states that the very nature of accumulation excludes every diminution in the degree of exploitation of labour, and every rise in the price of labour, which could seriously imperil the continual reproduction, on an ever enlarging scale, of the capitalistic relation'. (ibid., vol. 1, p. 680.)

34. Strictly speaking, a falling rate of profit could be deduced from these premises even if the rate of exploitation increased, so long as any rise in surplus value was more than offset by the combined expansion of constant capital and variable capital.

35. The required conditions can be reduced as follows:

(1) $C_1 + C_2 = C_1 + V_1 + S_1$ or

(2) $C_2 = V_1 + S_1$

36. ibid., vol. 1, pp. 836–7.

37. ibid., vol. 1, p. 534.

Postscript to Marxian Economics

As a body of technical argument Marx's contribution to economic analysis was, in the first instance, a highly ingenious extension and modification of the work of the classical school. In Marx's hands, however, classical tools were reformulated in a manner that yielded sharper insights into some problems – in particular, those of monopoly and instability – than had the works of his predecessors and contemporaries.

Marx's unique place in the history of economic ideas rests on more than the re-orientation he gave to classical theoretical categories. From his perspective economic reality and society at large were inseparable. The task of the economic analyst was to interpret the social process as a whole, rather than to extract only those aspects which could be treated unambiguously as economic. Moreover, this interpretation depended on a grasp of the whole sweep of human history and was by no means limited to the subject matter observable at any single moment in time.

Whatever the deficiencies of Marx's single-minded deterministic account of the economic and social process, it had the clear merit of shaking the mood of confidence and self-congratulation about the consequences of economic progress that had settled over much Western thought by the middle of the nineteenth century. Marx's doctrines became the rallying point of political forces which have left an indelible imprint on subsequent history, but they also aroused and reinforced the social concerns of many who did not share his philosophical presuppositions. After all, Marx had at least alerted men to an awareness that the consequences of the economic process under capitalism might be more brutish than benevolent.

Postscript

No less important is the stamp Marxian analysis has left on the subsequent development of other traditions in economic thought. Marx insisted that economic events could not be understood in isolation from their historical and sociological dimensions. The very sweep of his claims has meant that those who have rejected his conclusions and have wished to give economics a 'purer' and more restricted interpretation have been obliged to define their positions more precisely than would otherwise have been the case. In fact, much of the analytical shape of neo-classical economics was conditioned by an attempt to divert economic discourse from Marxian channels.

Later refinements within the Marxian tradition itself have been influenced, in large measure, by two questions that Marx himself did not address systematically: (1) how was the remarkable survival power of the capitalist system (combined with its ability to generate rising levels of real wages, rather than immiserization) to be explained? and (2) how could the categories of Marxian analysis be adapted to the problems of economic planning and administration in a post-capitalist society? The first of these questions was raised late in the nineteenth century when the revolutions expected in capitalist countries failed to materialize. The second became urgent after the Soviet government acquired power in 1917.

Within the latter-day Marxist tradition a position approaching doctrinal unanimity has been developed to account for the unexpected longevity of capitalism. Lenin's theory of imperialism – which built on foundations laid by the British socialist, Hobson, and by two Marxian revisionists, Hilferding and Rosa Luxemburg – provided the framework for the orthodox solution to this problem. Capitalist countries, it was maintained, had managed to postpone (though not permanently to escape) violent destruction through investment in colonies. The expected fall in the rate of profit was thus arrested. Further, colonial outlets for the capitalist's accumulations meant that labour displacements proceeded at a slower pace and that the size of the reserve army of unemployed was substantially smaller than would otherwise have been the case. But the economic significance of empire did not end there. Inasmuch as imperial countries were interpreted as casting colonies in the role of suppliers of low-cost raw materials and foodstuffs, it was possible that the real income of the proletarian class in the imperial countries might actually improve with the resulting reduction in the cost of the components of subsistence.

This interpretation yielded conclusions somewhat different from the ones Marx had reached, but it could be readily assimilated into the original Marxian system. Indeed, hints of Lenin's argument can be found in Volume I of *Das Kapital* as well as in Mill's *Principles*. The Leninist modifications merely extended Marx's basic analysis from the case of an economy closed to international trade and investment to that of an open system. Capitalism was not, however, reprieved; the scope of class struggle had been widened and internationalized. Imperialism subjected colonies as a group to the process of exploitation and immiserization that the proletariat had earlier experienced in industrial countries. Ultimately, the revolutionary ferment among the exploited would rise to the point that the imperial chains would be thrown off. Contradictions and rivalries within the imperial system would hasten this day of doom. Imperial countries, though united as exploiters of backward peoples, were deeply divided on other issues. Each sought to swell its share of the imperial loot at the expense of its rivals – a situation calculated to breed hostility and war. This view, it may be noted, was not at all implausible at the time of the First World War.

More recently an alternative explanation of the remarkable survival power of capitalism led a brief but illustrious life. It was offered by Eugene Varga, a Hungarian by birth, who had compiled a distinguished record of contributions to Soviet economics – among them, a revised edition of Lenin's *Imperialism* in which the original thesis was buttressed with updated materials. The work for which history is most likely to remember Varga, however, was entitled *Changes in the Economy of Capitalism Resulting from World War II*. In this study he maintained that Marxist theoreticians would be well advised to revise their expectations about the downfall of capitalism on the grounds that the Second World War had changed the character of capitalist systems. The successful conduct of the war effort, he argued, had demanded extensive state intervention in economic life and, though the role of the state would diminish with the return to more normal circumstances, the lessons learned in war-time economic planning would not be completely forgotten. In his view, an active role for governments as regulators and stabilizers had come to stay and the day of unregulated capitalistic 'anarchy' had passed. For these reasons Western capitalism could be expected to be more stable than Marxian theory had been prepared to allow. At the same time, the events of the war had altered the relationships between the imperial countries and their overseas colonies. A movement towards the non-violent transition to national independence had been set in tow and was likely to continue.

These views, though promulgated by a writer whose credentials in the Marxist tradition were well established, conflicted sharply with official Soviet doctrine. Following an extraordinary session of the Soviet Academy of Sciences in 1947, Varga was sharply censured and relieved of his official positions. From the perspective of orthodoxy he was guilty of the cardinal error of imputing to the state in a capitalist society both the will and the ability to act in the general social interest, even when its intervention ran counter to the interests of capitalists. He had exposed himself to the charge of committing another methodological sin when asserting that imperial connexions could be severed peacefully. In the era of high Stalinism, such heresies could not be tolerated.

In orthodox Marxian circles confidence in the ultimate crisis of capitalism has not been abandoned. To many the experience of the American economy in the late 1950s and again in the late 1960s and early 1970s – with a high-level 'stagnation' characterized by slow and uneven growth rates, upward pressures on the price level, and a persistent unemployment problem – bears witness to the chronic and unresolvable contradictions within capitalism. In addition, it has been maintained that during this period other symptoms of decay expected by a Marxist diagnostician have been manifested: an intensification of industrial concentration and a widening gap in the distribution of incomes between the property and labour shares. In the view of one able American Marxist, economists schooled in other traditions of analysis have been blinded to these aspects of contemporary problems because 'no genuine trends – in Marxian terminology, no "laws of motion" – are conceded to exist, still less subjected to analysis'.[1]

With respect to the second outstanding item of business on the latter-day Marxist agenda – the organization of a post-capitalist economy – Marx himself offered very little guidance. From his sketchy comments on this matter it would appear that he expected the state (at least in the period immediately following the collapse of capitalism) to make several deductions from the social product – deductions not unlike the constant capital and surplus value shares under capitalism. It would be a part of the state's task to ensure that resources were set aside for replacement purposes and as reserves against contingencies. In addition, part of the social product would have to be earmarked for capital accumulation. He also recommended deductions to cover the general costs of administration as well as to provide for such community needs as education, public health, and the support of those unable to work. Ultimately, in the highest stage of social evolution – that of the communist society – economic life could be governed by the rule 'from each according to his abilities, to each according to his needs' and the state would then wither away.

These comments fell far short of providing a systematic

blueprint useful to a planner confronted with practical problems on choices of priorities. In the light of this analytical vacuum, it is not altogether surprising that one modern Marxist commentator should describe Marxian economics as the 'economics of capitalism' and capitalist economics as the 'economics of socialism'. This judgement both draws attention to Marx's preoccupation with the analysis of the 'laws of motion' within a capitalist framework and suggests that, once private ownership of the means of production has been supplanted by social ownership, most of the impediments to an efficient allocation of resources through the price system would be removed. The market as a guideline for resource allocation could then come back into its own. Though this solution was rejected by those who initially held power in the Soviet state,[2] no alternative theoretical rationale was readily available. Lenin, for example, seemed to have viewed problems of economic planning primarily as an organizational matter. The state in the new society, he argued, would replace the 'governance of men with the administration of things'. Managers trained under capitalism – at least those who could adjust themselves to the demands of the new order – could continue to perform the same functions and, on the production and distribution side, the economic system could more or less take care of itelf.

A clearer direction for Soviet planning was ultimately set during the Stalin period when top priority was assigned to the build-up of heavy industrial capacity. Marxian economic theory provided no obvious justification for this choice, though an independent theoretical rationale for it could be developed – and was by an obscure Soviet economist named Fel'dman – with the aid of Marxian analytical categories. The basic insight of his argument can be summarized as follows: in a poor society in which economic expansion is an overriding concern, the capacity to suppress consumption in order to speed capital accumulation is limited. The risk that too much of the social product will be consumed can, however, be averted by directing a substantial share of an economy's resources and energies into producing outputs that literally cannot be eaten: i.e. into the production of capital goods. The physical form of these outputs precludes consumption and ensures capital accumulation.

The success of the Soviet economy in building a powerful industrial base from small beginnings has, quite naturally, attracted the attention of many underdeveloped nations. The formula for growth now offered to the underdeveloped world by Soviet advisers and Marxian theorists largely calls for the imitation of Soviet experience and recommends that the initial steps toward industrialization should give priority to the capital goods industries. One illustration of the application of modified Marxist analytical categories in the context of the underdeveloped world can be found in the planning framework developed by Professor Mahalanobis for the Indian economy. His model breaks the economy into 'departments' much as Marx did and argues that the growth of the economy as a whole is largely governed by the share of national output allocated to the department producing capital goods. Though similar conclusions about the desirable course for the Indian economy could be reached by other routes, Mahalanobis's analysis owes much to Marxian analytical categories and has much in common with the argument worked out in the 1920s by Fel'dman.

In two important respects, however, Marxian doctrine is inappropriate for the analysis of the current problems of the underdeveloped world. From the outset Marxian analytical categories were shaped to deal with the circumstances of industrial societies. Marx himself had little comprehension of the problems of agriculture, and particularly of traditional agrarian societies; as one critic has observed, Marx treated peasants as a 'bag of potatoes'. Yet the central fact about the underdeveloped world is the dominance of an agrarian structure. It is one of the ironies of history that Marxist doctrine has enjoyed its greatest political success in predominantly agrarian societies, even though the Marxian mode of analysis is not well suited to such environments.

For the purposes of understanding the problems of underdeveloped countries, the Marxian analytical scheme is further handicapped for another reason. Orthodox Marxism – from the days of Marx's vehement assaults on Malthusian teaching to the present – has refused to entertain seriously the possibility that population growth may present a formidable obstacle to economic improvement. The problems presented by the unprecedented growth of the populations of underdeveloped countries deserve hard-headed analysis. Though by no means the only distraction to clear thinking on demographic questions, Marxian teaching has undoubtedly impeded an adequate comprehension of these important issues.

An assessment of the place of Marxian economics within the family of 'master models' should also recognize that, in a number of important respects, Marx inherited both the strengths and weaknesses of his classical forerunners. In both theoretical systems, the central analytical categories were moulded to illuminate the causes and consequences of long-period economic change and the relationships between economic growth and income distribution. The tools useful for these purposes were not, however, well adapted (nor were they intended to be) to a systematic inspection of other matters: e.g. the process through which market prices are formed and the implications of short-period economic fluctuations.

Marx's analysis, however, presents several puzzles that are peculiar to his mode of procedure. The first involves a problem in epistemology. On what basis, it may be asked, was Marx entitled to claim an infallible insight into the forces governing the economic system? Economic determinism, strictly interpreted, meant that all thought and all action were shaped by economic circumstances. If this position were consistently maintained, would it not follow that the views of the author of *Das Kapital* were no less class-conditioned – and held no higher claim to the status of objective truth – than those of the owners of the steel industry? Within the Marxian frame of reference, no satisfactory answer to this question can be offered. But another difficulty – one concerned with the propagation of ideas – also surrounds the premises of economic determinism. If human action is always socially determined, no place remains for individual decision and volition. Why then, if the decay and collapse of capitalism are inevitable, should it be necessary to form organizations and discipline cadres to hasten its downfall? What purpose would be served by revolutionary agitation if the historical outcome would be no different? Orthodox Marxists have normally hedged this question, arguing that militant organization acts as a midwife to hasten social change. This rejoinder, however, fails to dispose of the methodological problem. On these points rests the larger historical irony of Marxian teaching. As Marx's most distinguished intellectual biographer has observed:

It [Marxian theory] set out to refute the proposition that ideas govern the course of history, but the very extent of its own influence on human affairs has weakened the force of its thesis. For in altering the hitherto prevailing view of the relation of the individual to his environment and to his fellows, it has palpably altered that relation itself; and in consequence remains the most powerful among the intellectual forces which are today transforming the ways in which men think and act.[3]

Notes

1. Paul M. Sweezy, in *Keynes' General Theory: Report of Three Decades*, Robert Lekachman, ed. (St Martin's Press, Macmillan and Co. New York, 1964), p. 311.

2. More recently, planners in East European countries (most notably in Poland) have attempted to adapt neo-classical techniques of marginal calculation to planning requirements in a socialist country. Similarly, the Soviet Union in the 1960s appears to be giving greater scope to the market in the allocation of economic resources.

3. Isaiah Berlin, *Karl Marx: His Life and Environment* (Galaxy ed., Oxford University Press, New York, 1959), p. 274.

PART THREE

NEO-CLASSICAL ECONOMICS

Introduction

In the world of neo-classical economics, the focus of analytical attention was directed to the process through which a market system allocates an economy's resources. This theme, though not altogether absent from the classical and Marxian traditions, had been far overshadowed in these theoretical systems by the paramount concern with inter-relationships between long-period dynamic change and the distribution of income among the various orders of society. The approach to economic analysis developed by neo-classical theorists reversed the earlier orderings of analytical priorities. In their type of theoretical structure, market behaviour within carefully delimited spans of time supplied the organizing principle of thought. Meanwhile, the grand themes of long-period development faded far into the background.

The re-orientation in economic thinking brought by neo-classicists was connected with changes in the economic environment of Western societies. Men of the high Victorian age could, with considerable justification in events, hold that de-emphasis of the problems with which the classical tradition had been preoccupied was appropriate. Western economies had enjoyed prosperity in unprecedented measure and without the checks anticipated by the classical and Marxian traditions. Continued economic expansion, though not unimportant, appeared to be capable of taking care of itself. Moreover, in the face of observable improvements in real wages, the Cassandra calls of Marx and his classical forerunners about the likely consequences of growth for the condition of the working class appeared to be misplaced.

From the point of view of the neo-classical economists the problem deserving study was the functioning of the market system and its role as an allocator of resources. Clearly a re-thinking of this issue was timely. In the years since the classicists had written about the economy's natural order the economic structure had altered signicantly. Industrial concentrations had grown in size and in capacity to wield unchecked economic power. Trade unions, though still in their infancy, were beginning to claim a voice in wage setting. In the language of classical writers, it could no longer be taken for granted that the normal operation of the economy would tend to make 'natural' and 'market' prices converge.

Changes in the economic environment, however, could go only part way towards accounting for the re-orientation in thought represented by neo-classical economics. Intellectual currents of the time also influenced the choice of theoretical issues and the manner in which they were treated. In the main, neo-classical writers absorbed the late nineteenth-century faith in progress and in the benevolence of its consequences. Their conclusions pointed to the existence of certain 'imperfections' in the economic system that called for policy remedies. Nevertheless, they restored a temper of optimism to economic discourse that – with only a few exceptions – had been suppressed since Malthus. Progress, they could hold, appeared to resolve social tensions rather than to aggravate them.

These influences converged to direct the attention of economic theorists to an analysis of economic behaviour focusing on its decision-making units – households, firms, and industries – and on the ways in which choices made by their economic agents were converted into an orderly process. The answers supplied at least purported to demonstrate that the market system was essentially an instrument of integration through which the resources at the disposal of the economy could be allocated to the most socially beneficial uses. With this concentration on the behaviour of small units of the system (as opposed to the dominant concern of earlier theoretical traditions with aggregate income and its share-out between profits, wages, and rents), micro-economics – i.e. the study of economic behaviour of households, firms, and industries – was brought to the centre of the stage.

This adjustment of analytical priorities was to have sweeping implications for the organization of economic thought and for the selection of issues deemed worthy of attention. One of its immediate consequences was to elevate the status of the theory of market price. For the purposes of analysing the behaviour of a market system, an understanding of the factors shaping the prices of both outputs and inputs took on a paramount importance. No longer was the discussion of price subordinated to concerns about natural 'value' and its long-period determinants. It became instead the lynch-pin of the whole network of micro-economic relationships. The elaborate embellishments to the analysis of market price formation worked out by the neo-classical economists opened up analytical horizons undreamed of by the John Stuart Mill of 1848, who had declared the theory of value to be complete.

The primacy of price-theory, however, necessarily implied a downgrading of other themes – and particularly of the long-period growth and distribution concerns of the classical and Marxian traditions. Even so, most major neo-classical theorists felt obliged to offer a few comments in passing about the longer-term prospects of the economy. This matter, however, was not close to their hearts and was, in the main, treated rather cursorily. From their standpoint the important issues were more immediate in time. One commentator has described this shift in emphasis as a displacement of the big classical questions of growth and distribution by such little ones as 'why does an egg cost more than a cup of tea?' *

It was not simply by chance that neo-classical modes of reasoning should have been so far removed from those

* Joan Robinson, *On Re-reading Marx*, (Cambridge, 1953), p. 22.

adopted in earlier theoretical traditions. Indeed, some of the pioneer formulators of neo-classical theory consciously designed their categories of analysis as refutations to Marx. In their hands economics was effectively removed from historical time and detached from the 'laws' of history. The search for the laws of motion of society was largely abandoned to be replaced by the investigation of market processes and their allocative properties. Human behaviour (or at least a stylized interpretation of its economic mainsprings) became the point of departure. On this basis neo-classical writers addressed their attention to the decisions reached by producers and consumers in market situations and to the analysis of their consequences. Worlds separated this approach from Marx's conviction that human behaviour was driven by impersonal forces beyond challenge or control. Within a neo-classical perspective the scope for conscious choice and policy initiative was enormously widened. Though many who worked within this theoretical framework opposed governmental intervention in economic life, they were still prepared to argue that policies of the state could alter the course of economic affairs.

While neo-classical analysts shunned the fatalistic overtones of earlier traditions (and of Marxism in particular) they continued to look to the natural scientists for inspiration. The images and vocabulary of the natural sciences emerged most clearly in the propensity of neo-classical economists to construct much of their argument around 'pure' cases. Economic investigation, they maintained, should proceed in a manner analogous to research in a scientific laboratory. Some allowance had to be made for the fact that economic events could not be studied under controlled experimental conditions. The ideal situation could be simulated, however, through the formulation of abstract models of the economy's behaviour in which the frictions and untidiness of the real world were neglected. Admittedly, such formal systems could claim to be no more than approximations. Nevertheless, they were defended on two principal grounds: first, they isolated for inspection the central nerves of the economic process; and secondly, they provided a benchmark against which the performance of the flesh-and-blood economy could be measured.

This *modus operandi* lent itself readily to the use of mathematics in economic analysis and particularly to the application of the differential calculus. Even so, the widespread adoption of mathematical notation in economic debate did not altogether satisfy Malthus's appeal in the early decades of the century for a standardized set of definitions in the discipline. Each theorist exercised his prerogative to define symbols in a manner of his own choosing. Nevertheless, findings that could be reported in mathematical notation did lend an aura of universality to the subject. Moreover, this manner of argument both elevated the rigour of economic discussion and placed a premium on logically tight and consistent argument – even if, at times, the price of consistency was detachment from close contact with real problems.

The era of neo-classical economics differed from that of its predecessors in yet another respect. For the first time, economic theorizing at a high level became a thoroughly international activity. By contrast with classicism – the overwhelming bulk of the contributors to which were British – insights of fundamental significance to the formal treatment of neo-classical problems were generated by nationals of many countries. While the fertility of the English tradition was undiminished, important schools of neo-classicism emerged in Vienna, Lausanne, Sweden, and in the United States. Each played its own variations on the common neo-classical theme: the analysis of the allocative properties of a market system.

In the world of neo-classicism, economics became more universal and more scientific in its claims – and less dismal in its conclusions.

CHAPTER 6

Alfred Marshall and the Framework of Neo-Classical Economics

AMONG the Anglo-Saxon neo-classical pioneers, Alfred Marshall was a giant without rival. An examination of his analysis – despite noteworthy distinctive features – is appropriate for the purposes of setting out the central properties of neo-classicism. Though his thought was organized around a tight theoretical core, he chose to present it in a deceptively simple style. He held economics to be the study of man 'in the ordinary business of life' and that its findings should be accessible to a wide public audience. This attitude largely explains the consignment of his subtler contributions to theory to the obscurity of footnotes and appendices. Unlike most of his neo-classical contemporaries he maintained that mathematical expositions, though invaluable aids to the economist in the clarification of his own thought, were unnecessary to – and might even hinder – the communication of his findings.[1]

1. ALFRED MARSHALL (1842–1924)

Throughout his adult life, Marshall occupied academic positions. Apart from four years as the Principal of the University College of Bristol and a brief period as a Fellow of Balliol College, Oxford (where he taught political economy to candidates for the Indian Civil Service), he was associated with the University of Cambridge. From the chair of Political Economy (to which he was elected in 1885) he exercised a formidable influence on one of the most fertile generations of students in modern history. His inspiration and stimulus were instrumental in bringing the Cambridge economics school to a position of eminence.

The main corpus of Marshall's teachcing was contained in one book – *Principles of Economics*. Published originally in 1890, this work went through eight editions during his lifetime. If not a prolific writer, he was an infinitely painstaking one. Marshall – to the considerable annoyance of his ablest pupil – was reluctant to commit his insights to print before they had been fully polished and before their relevance to practical problems had been established. On this trait of his master, John Maynard Keynes later commented:

> Economists must leave to Adam Smith alone the glory of the Quarto, must pluck the day, fling pamphlets into the wind, write always *sub specie temporis*, and achieve immortality by accident, if at all.
> Moreover, did not Marshall, by keeping his wisdom at home until he could produce it fully clothed, mistake, perhaps, the true nature of his own special gift? 'Economics,' he said ... 'is not a body of concrete truth, but an engine for the discovery of concrete truth.' This engine, as we employ it today, is largely Marshall's creation. He put it in the hands of his pupils long before he offered it to the world. ... Yet he hankered greatly after the 'concrete' truth which he had disclaimed and for the discovery of which he was not specially qualified.[2]

Whatever the costs of delayed publication may have been, Marshall's interest in and affection for his students later paid handsome dividends. His influence extended well beyond his role in equipping them with professional skills. He urged them to be engaged with the world's problems and advised a wary attitude towards popular acclaim. 'Evil', he once wrote, 'is with [students of social science] when all men speak well of them. ... It is almost impossible for a student to be a true patriot and to have the reputation of being one in his own time.'[3]

Though Marshall's place in history rests primarily on his contributions to economic theory, he insisted that the purpose of theoretical investigations was to illuminate practical problems. In his own career his social concerns found direct outlet in his participation (either as a member or as an expert witness) in the work of official commissions dealing with monetary questions, taxation, and the relief of the poor.

2. THE APPROACH TO THE ANALYSIS OF PRICE

For Marshall – as well as for other contributors to the formulation of neo-classical thought – analysis of the functioning of a market system began with the behaviour of consumers and producers. Throughout the discussion it was assumed that men acted rationally in pursuit of their own advantage. Consumers were held to seek maximum satisfactions; similarly, suppliers of productive services were expected to seek maximum rewards. It was not maintained, however, that economic motives were the only spurs to human action, nor that all men acted as *homo economicus* in the conduct of the day-to-day business of life. Most neo-classical writers – and Marshall with particular emphasis – insisted that their study was restricted to the economic aspects of human action, rather than the whole complex of man's aspirations. By the same token they did not wish to be interpreted as saying that all who participated in market transactions were rational calculators. Instead, they sought merely to establish that rationality as a behavioural postulate provided a realistic basis for the study of groups of people.

This mode of reasoning can be readily observed in Marshall's formulation of the concept of demand. As he interpreted it, 'demand' referred to the relationship between quantities demanded and prices. Normally it could be expected that buyers would be prepared to purchase more of a particular good at lower prices than at higher ones. For each good a whole range of price and quantity combinations was conceivable. These combinations could be depicted diagrammatically as a schedule (or curve) by representing price on a vertical axis and quantity on a horizontal axis.

This view, of course, contrasted sharply with the classical interpretation of 'demand'. Within a classical frame of reference this term was construed largely in a 'logistical' sense: i.e. to refer to the quantities of goods required for particular purposes. It was on this basis that classical economists could assert that population growth would increase the 'demand' for subsistence goods (or of the quantum of subsistence goods required by the economic system). The effects of consumer preferences on transactions received little attention; in the main the dominant classical assumption had been that the tastes of the bulk of the population (i.e. of the working class) were fairly rigid and the more pessimistic prognoses about the prospects for suppressing population growth rested on this presupposition. Nor had classical writers stressed the point that quantities demanded would vary in response to changes in market prices. Their sights were too closely centred on the forces influencing the 'natural price' of commodities to make this question central to their analytical programme.[4]

In neo-classical economics, the determination of market prices became *the* problem and the concept of demand as a schedule of price-quantity relationships was crucial to its solution. In Marshall's formulation, the construction of such a schedule proceeded in two stages. The first concerned individual consumers and rested on a notion labelled as 'diminishing marginal utility'. A consumer entered the market-place, it was maintained, in order to acquire satisfactions (or utilities) from his purchases. The amount of satisfaction obtainable from a unit of a commodity was closely related, however, to the number of units acquired. With the addition of each unit, it could be expected that the increment in total satisfaction (i.e. the additional or marginal utility) would decline. The rational consumer would thus be prepared to pay less for the last unit than for the preceding ones and a reduction in price would be necessary to induce him to buy more.

The full derivation of a market demand curve for a

specific commodity involved a further step. The demand schedules of individual consumers had to be consolidated. The price-quantity relationships likely to prevail in the market as a whole could then be depicted. It was important to note, however, that such a construction presupposed that a number of conditions remained unchanged: in particular, the tastes of consumers, their money incomes (through which their desires could be translated into effective demand),[5] and the prices of other goods. Variation in any of these conditions would shift the demand curve to a different position.

But this was not the end of the story. In a practical situation consumers have more than one good to choose from. If they were to maximize the utility obtainable from a given income they should adjust their spending patterns to ensure that no gain in satisfaction would be possible from an alternative allocation of their expenditures. The optimum result would be obtained when the last penny spent on any of the goods in question added an identical amount of satisfaction. Otherwise, a different allocation of expenditure would increase the consumer's total satisfaction. As Marshall expressed this proposition:

... good management is shown by so adjusting the margins of suspense on each line of expenditure that the marginal utility of a shilling's worth of goods on each line shall be the same. And this result each one will attain by constantly watching to see whether there is anything on which he is spending so much that he would gain by taking a little away from that line of expenditure and putting it on some other line.[6]

This type of argument had been latent in economic discussion since the days of Benthamite utilitarianism. The only novelty in its application to neo-classical problems lay in the explicit introduction of the concept of marginal utility. Just as the notion of diminishing returns had been hit upon simultaneously by a number of writers in the early nineteenth century, so also was the concept of marginal utility formulated independently (and at about the same time) by a number of neo-classical economists: Jevons in England, Menger in Austria, and Walras in Lausanne. Marshall, though he could legitimately claim to be among the innovators, could not support his case with published evidence. Characteristically he had chosen not to release his findings until they could be presented in a form intelligible to a lay audience.

This approach to the demand side of price formation had an important consequence: it swept under the carpet some of the organizing concepts of classicism. To most classical writers it had been axiomatic that economic value could be attributed only to tangible objects. By contrast neo-classical economists insisted that the point of an economic system was not the production of commodities, but the production of satisfactions. The measure of value was what the public would buy. Services, fully as much as material goods, could pass this test. Indeed, the whole debate about material-non-material distinctions could be dismissed. Marshall stressed this point when he wrote:

Man cannot create material things. In the mental and moral world indeed he may produce new ideas; but when he is said to produce material things, he really only produces utilities; or in other words, his efforts and sacrifices result in changing the form or arrangement of matter to adapt it better for the satisfaction of wants. ...

It is sometimes said that traders do not produce: that while the cabinet-maker produces furniture, the furniture-dealer merely sells what is already produced. But there is no scientific foundation for this distinction. They both produce utilities, and neither of them can do more. ...[7]

Similarly, classical notions of productive and unproductive labour were eliminated:

We may define *labour* as any exertion of mind or body undergone partly or wholly with a view to some good other than the pleasure derived directly from the work. And if we had to make a fresh start, it would be best to regard all labour as productive except that which failed to promote the aim towards which it was directed, and so produced no utility.[8]

Demand alone, however, provided only part of the explanation of price. No less important were the terms on which producers were prepared to make goods and services available for purchase. The neo-classical account of this aspect of the pricing process was developed in a manner analogous to the derivation of a demand curve. Just as consumers acquired utilities (though at a diminishing rate) through market transactions, producers suffered disutilities (and at an increasing rate) when making their services available. In short, production involved costs and sacrifices which, in most cases, were expected to rise as the quantity offered increased. It was recognized in passing that some persons might obtain positive satisfaction from work; nevertheless, supplies of the productive services of labour, land and capital were not likely to be forthcoming for long unless those in a position to offer them were compensated for their trouble.

This argument about the terms on which the services of land, labour and capital would be made available for production was reinforced by another consideration. In general it was presupposed that alternative uses of the various factors of production were available. Any individual buyer of these services would, therefore, be obliged to compete to acquire them. Firm X, for example, could not expect to acquire more land, labour, or capital for its purposes unless it was prepared to outbid other claimants for the same resources. The point at issue was described more formally in terms of 'opportunity costs' – i.e. costs in the form of income the supplier of services was obliged to forego when committing himself to one activity, thus precluding other options. It was not always recognized within the neo-classical tradition, however, that this argument depended on conditions of full employment; otherwise some suppliers of productive services might have no readily available options. In such a situation the 'opportunity costs' of employment would be zero.

These considerations provided the raw materials from which a market supply curve could be constructed. Inasmuch as it could normally be assumed that firms could obtain greater quantities of the necessary productive inputs (labour, land, and capital) only at increased cost, it followed that they could be expected to expand their offerings of outputs only when higher prices made this course of action worthwhile. In short, it was postulated that firms normally operated under conditions in which the addition to total costs associated with producing additional units of output (i.e. marginal costs) were rising. This conclusion was further buttressed by the view that the addition to the total product obtainable from adding a unit of one productive input (while the quantum of others was unchanged) was likely to decline. The structure of marginal costs, in turn, determined the shape of the supply curve. But, just as the demand curve was expected to shift should the conditions underlying it alter, the supply curve would also shift if costs of production changed. And, just as the market demand for a particular product was derived by aggregating the demands of individual consumers, a market supply curve could similarly be arrived at by consolidating the supply curves of firms producing identical outputs.

The treatment of costs developed in this analysis could not stand in sharper contrast with the notions employed by the classical and Marxian traditions. Exercises in reducing costs to labour inputs now vanished from the scene. Their place was taken by the general account of sacrifices incurred in the supply of any of the productive services. In the neo-classical scheme the former primacy of labour in the explanation of costs was completely eliminated.

With his twin concepts of supply and demand, Marshall had the tools he needed for his explanation of price. It was at the point of intersection between these two curves that the equilibrium price (i.e. the price towards which the market would naturally tend to gravitate) was established. A price above the equilibrium would produce a situation in which sellers would be prepared to offer more than buyers would take; the resulting disappointments of sellers would, under competitive conditions, lead to reductions in the offer price to a level at which the market could be cleared. Conversely, a sub-equilibrium price would produce frustrations for some potential buyers; the normal path of adjustment would be one in which competitive bidding would push the market price towards equilibrium. Marshall likened these two curves to the blades of a pair of scissors and observed that 'we might as reasonably dispute whether it is the upper or the under blade of a pair of scissors that cuts a piece of paper, as whether value is governed by utility or cost of production'.[9]

To modern readers acquainted with the micro-economics section of a standard textbook the Marshallian account of price formation may now appear to be too familiar – perhaps even too self-evident – to require extensive defence or justification. At the time of its formulation, however, it was a considerable innovation. Not only was it a major departure from the classical and Marxian labour-based account of value, but it was also constructed to counter over-zealous reactions against classical approaches on the part of some early neo-classicists. Jevons, for example, had asserted that utility and demand considerations alone were sufficient for an adequate explanation of price. Marshall rejected both the classical and cruder neo-classical positions. Demand (based on utility) and supply (based on costs of production) were both indispensable to the explanation of market prices.

One further analytical consequence of Marshallian procedure deserves mention. From this perspective the distinction upon which so much classical discussion had turned – that between value (the natural price) and the market price – evaporated. The search for an invariant measure of value over prolonged periods was abandoned. What mattered were prices as they were determined in a competitive market process.

3. THE THEORY OF DISTRIBUTION

For Marshall and his neo-classical contemporaries the analysis of distribution was essentially a problem in the pricing of productive services. Its solution was sought along lines analogous to those followed in explaining the pricing of products. In the case of both inputs and outputs, the interaction of supply and demand established equilibrium prices.

This approach was built around a three-fold classification of the basic productive factors – land, labour and capital – to each of which was assigned a unique distributive share. (Some writers added a fourth productive factor; Marshall suggested that organizational skill might be so regarded). In this scheme of things wages were defined as the reward for human effort. This definition, unlike the classical one, did not restrict wage payments to a working class. Salary incomes and an imputed 'wage to management' in owner-operated establishments also fell within the neo-classicist's wage classification. Interest accrued to the owners of capital as a reward for 'waiting' – i.e. for the sacrifice involved in foregoing present consumption in favour of prospective future gains. While rents were associated with the productive services supplied by land, the classical pre-occupation with agricultural land was shaded towards the background. In the neo-classical era the site values of urban land came into prominence.

In this re-definition of distributive shares the concept of profits with which the classical and Marxian traditions had worked largely disappeared. Much of the income earlier traditions assigned to profits was now absorbed as a wage to management and as interest. Though neo-classical economists did not share a common concept of profits, most (including Marshall) held that pure profits (i.e. rewards to business in excess of the normal wage of management, interest on invested capital, etc.) should be regarded as symptomatic of a temporary disequilibrium or of the existence of monopoly.

This approach to distribution represented a clear rejection of the class-oriented scheme around which classical and Marxian models had been organized. Neo-classical theory rested on a functional interpretation of distributive shares which linked income payments to the productive contribution of the various factors. These definitions provided ammunition for a further attack on Marxian analysis. Marshall drove the point home forcefully:

> It is not true that the spinning of yarn in a factory, after allowance has been made for the wear-and-tear of the machinery, is the product of the labour of the operatives. It is the product of their labour, together with that of the employer and subordinate managers, and of the capital employed; and that capital itself is the product of labour and waiting; and therefore the spinning is the product of labour of many kinds, and of waiting. If we admit that it is the product of labour alone, and not of labour and waiting, we can no doubt be compelled by inexorable logic to admit that there is no justification of interest, the reward of waiting; for the conclusion is implied in the premiss.[10]

Marshall might, of course, have added that his own conclusions followed from the premises he had chosen – premisses that imparted to property shares of income a legitimacy that Marx had not been prepared to allow.

Once these distributional categories had been defined, supply and demand forces in the market could be appealed to as the basis on which rewards to the suppliers of productive services were established. It was, of course, recognized that each of the markets in which productive factors were priced had special properties. The labour force, for example, was highly differentiated by varying skills and abilities; the market, however, could usually be relied upon to recognize differences in the productive contribution of various types of labour and to establish appropriate wage differentials. In any event, classical exercises in reducing labour to a standard unit were superfluous. The treatment of capital presented a complication of another sort. As Marshall recognized, a distinction between the accumulated stock of capital and the flow of new investments was required because the economic implications of payments to the owners of old and newly-created capital were quite different. As he saw the matter:

That which is rightly regarded as interest on 'free' or 'floating' capital, or on new investments of capital, is more properly treated as a sort of rent – a *quasi-rent* – on old investments of capital. ... And thus even the rent of land is seen, not as a thing by itself, but as the leading species of a large genus. ...[11]

All this was a far cry from the classical concern over the long-period behaviour of distributive shares. In Marshall's hands, distribution theory was primarily a special case of the pricing of productive inputs in the marketplace.

4. THE THEORY OF PRODUCTION

Neo-classical production theory adddressed itself to two principal issues. The first concerned the manner in which any producer set about combining the productive factors. The second dealt with the adjustments a producer might be expected to make when market conditions altered.

The first of these points could be handled quite straightforwardly with the aid of analytical tools already considered. Individual business men were regarded as rational calculators seeking to maximize their earnings. So long as competitive conditions prevailed they were powerless to influence the prices of their products. The objective of profit maximization thus amounted to an attempt to minimize costs. Technically, a number of possible combinations of various productive factors could produce whatever volume of output might be desired. The rational manager would naturally select the least-cost combination.

These rules were simple enough. The analysis of the producer's response to a change in market circumstances was more intricate. In particular, it presented the problem of time which Marshall described as 'a chief cause of those difficulties in economic investigation which make it necessary for man with his limited power to go step by step; breaking up a complex question, studying one bit at a time, and at last combining his partial solutions into a more or less complete solution of the whole riddle'.[12] This task of disentanglement involved an examination of the consequences of minute changes on the assumption described in Marshallian shorthand as *ceteris paribus*: i.e. that all the underlying factors remained unchanged.

For Marshall's purposes three time periods were distinguished from one another. The first he described as 'the market period', a period too short for the producer to make any adjustments in his output in response to a change in prices. The second – labelled 'the short run' – permitted output to be adjusted by changing the intensity with which a given plant was utilized. More workers might be hired (or the present labour force induced to work longer hours) and additional raw materials acquired. All of these measures would enable output to be enlarged in response to an increase in demand. These adjustments, however, would probably be associated with rising marginal costs. If an increase in demand was expected to be sustained, it might well be worth the firm's while to expand capacity in order to reduce its costs. The time period required to effect this adjustment was described as 'the long run'.

The nature of these divisions of economic time deserves a moment's reflection. At first sight it might appear that these categories bore a resemblance to the notions of time with which classical economists had worked. Any such appearances would be quite misleading. Classical writers had been interested in historical change. The time distinctions introduced by Marshall were divorced from calendar time, resting instead on logical distinctions.[13] If asked to specify the length of the 'long run', Marshall would reply that it was the time span sufficient to accomplish adjustments in the scale of plant necessary to produce a new market equilibrium after an earlier one had been disturbed. In a practical case, the length of this period would depend on the circumstances of individual firms and industries. The 'long run' for a steel fabricator and for the corner hairdressing establishment would not coincide.

These logical distinctions between moments of economic time opened the door to a new and interesting set of theoretical possibilities. After all, it was quite conceivable that in the long-run — when the scale of plant could be altered and the utilization of all productive factors varied — several outcomes with respect to levels of costs might follow. Changes in scale, for example, might be associated with rising, declining, or constant unit costs. The most interesting case was the one in which average costs declined with the enlargement in the scale of plant; this situation was described as 'increasing returns to scale'. By and large the classical economists had anticipated that 'constant returns to scale' would normally prevail; in other words, that the size of the individual production unit had no effect on average costs. They had, of course, given much attention to the gains in productivity arising from growth in the size of the economy (and the progessive sub-division of labour associated with it), but this scale effect was quite different from the neo-classical concern with individual enterprises. Mill and Marx, to be sure, had caught glimpses of the cost-reducing effects of large industrial concentrations though they had not fully worked out their implications.

For Marshall, increasing returns to scale associated with the application of high technologies presented an awkward problem. Economies of scale implied that a small number of large producers could operate with lower unit costs than could a large number of small firms producing the same quantum of output. Hence, one of the premisses of a competitive market – namely, that the number of firms producing similar products was sufficiently large to deny market power to any individual seller – was challenged. Bigness might indeed erode the basis of the competitive order and threaten its preservation. Marshall saw the issue when he wrote:

In fact when the production of a commodity conforms to the law of increasing return in such a way as to give a very great advantage to large producers, it is apt to fall almost entirely into the hands of a few large firms; and then the normal marginal supply price cannot be isolated on the plan just referred to, because that plan assumes the existence of a great many competitors with businesses of all sizes, some of them being young and some old, some in the ascending and some in the descending phase. The production of such a commodity really partakes in a great measure of the nature of a monopoly; and its price is likely to be so much influenced by the incidents of the campaign between rival producers, each struggling for an extension of territory, as scarcely to have a true normal level.[14]

The availability of scale economies had consequences both for the industrial structure of the economy and for the structure of neo-classical reasoning. At the analytical level it precluded a clear and unambiguous operational definition of a supply schedule. Marshall perceived the implications of this complication (and criticized others for their failure to do so) in the following language:

Some ... have before them what is in effect the supply schedule of an individual firm; representing that an increase in its output gives it command over so great internal economies as much to diminish its expenses of production; and they follow their mathematics boldly, but apparently without noticing that their premises lead inevitably to the conclusion that whatever firm gets a good start will obtain a monopoly of the whole business of its trade in its district. While others avoiding this horn of the dilemma, maintain that there is no equilibrium at all for commodities which obey the law of increasing return; and some again have called in question the validity of any supply schedule which represents prices diminishing as the amount produced increases.[15]

For his part, Marshall attempted to build an analysis in which the essentials of the competitive equilibrium model could be preserved despite this challenge to its realism.

5. THE PROSPECTS FOR THE COMPETITIVE ORDER

Two Marshalls – one the abstract theorist, the other the practical observer of everyday economic life – were blended in all of his writing. This duality was most conspicuous in his treatment of market structures and the competitive process.

As a formal theorist Marshall saw the potential danger to the competitive order latent in the growth of large productive units with considerable market power. But as an observer of events he argued that a number of factors tended to moderate the social and economic consequences of such concentrations. Characteristically, Marshall maintained that when analytical tidiness and descriptive realism appeared to be at odds with one another ordinary observation should claim precedence. Theory might be indispensable but it also had inherent limitations. No theoretical construction could embrace 'all the conditions of real life' for then 'the problem is too heavy to be handled'; but he feared that if only a few aspects were selected for study, then 'long-drawn-out and subtle reasonings with regard to them become scientific toys rather than engines for practical work'.[16]

At the descriptive level Marshall distinguished between two types of market structure. One he described as the 'special' market, a sphere in which individual firms could operate largely in isolation from immediate competitors. These circumstances might arise, for example, through geographical isolation or as a by-product of the existence of a special clientele served by a particular seller. But the 'special' market was also surrounded by a larger and more embracing 'general' market. Marshall invoked these distinctions in an attempt to reconcile the world of business behaviour with a model in which effective competition was an analytical requirement.

Marshall's strategy for salvaging his competitive plan from the threats implied by the technology of increasing returns also rested on presuppositions about the nature of business enterprises – and, most importantly, his view that firms could be likened to biological organisms. Both had a life cycle which included phases of expansion (and perhaps even of supremacy), and phases of decline, decay and – ultimately – death. Ownership and control of business enterprises might be handed down over the generations, but in the process the vigour of those who led it during dynamic periods was unlikely to be perpetuated. Marshall depicted the situation as follows:

Nature still presses on the private business by limiting the length of the life of its original founders, and by limiting even more narrowly that part of their lives in which their faculties retain full vigour. And so, after a while, the guidance of the business falls into the hands of people with less energy and less creative genius, if not with less active interest in its prosperity. If it is turned into a joint-stock company, it may retain the advantages of division of labour, of specialized skill and machinery: it may even increase them by a further increase of its capital; and under favourable conditions it may secure a permanent and prominent place in the work of production. But it is likely to have lost so much of its elasticity and progressive force, that the advantages are no longer exclusively on its side in its competition with younger and smaller rivals.[17]

These 'natural' factors were not the only ones checking the growth of firms and limiting the exercise of market power. Other constraints were inherent in the make-up of the 'special' markets within which firms could enjoy unique privileges. Marshall insisted that these advantages could not long be retained by an expanding firm. In this connexion he wrote:

. . . . many commodities with regard to which the tendency to increasing return acts strongly are, more or less, specialities: some of them aim at creating a new want, or at meeting an old want in a new way. Some of them are adapted to special tastes, and can never have a very large market; and some have merits that are not easily tested, and must win their way to general favour slowly. In all such cases the sales of each business are limited, more or less according to circumstances, to the particular market which it has slowly and expensively acquired; and though the production itself might be economically increased very fast the sale could not.[18]

Or, as Marshall again emphasized the point: 'There are many trades in which an individual producer could secure much increased "internal" economies by a great increase of his output; and there are many in which he could market that output easily; yet there are few in which he could do both. And this is not an accidental, but almost a necessary result.'[19] Expansion of a firm beyond the confines of its special market would also expose it to the competition of rivals. The market protection it had formerly enjoyed would be sacrificed as producers from the 'general' market checked its economic power.

These considerations led Marshall to the optimistic conclusion that economies of scale were unlikely to present a severe challenge to the maintenance of a competitive order. The same factors which enabled firms to enjoy a limited degree of market power (the existence of 'special' markets) also restrained the trend toward bigness. From purely theoretical considerations, a quite different conclusion might be drawn. Characteristically, Marshall cautioned against judgements based solely on *a priori* reasoning and recommended 'treating each important concrete case very much as an independent problem, under the guidance of staple general reasonings. Attempts so to enlarge the *direct* applications of general propositions as to enable them to supply adequate solutions of all difficulties, would make them so cumbrous as to be of little service for their main work. The "principles" of economics must aim at affording guidance to an entry on problems of life, without making claim to be a substitute for independent study and thought.' [20]

While Marshall was not prepared to buy analytical rigour at the price of contact with reality, his institutional portrait of business behaviour was not without limitations. The picture he offered of the restraints to expansion of firms might have been reasonably accurate in late nineteenth and early twentieth century England. His notion of the life cycle of firms, however, is much less plausible when applied to the modern corporation. Its institutional structure, in which management and ownership are largely divorced, creates a survival power that may approach immortality. Nor is Marshall's argument well-suited to production for mass markets. The 'special' markets he had in mind were built on Edwardian 'custom' tastes. In an era of mass consumption, in which the tastes of the public for a wide range of consumer outputs are not highly differentiated by social status, Marshall's views of the exclusiveness and selectivity of élite special markets must be considerably qualified.

Marshall's approach to the theory of the firm has left a dual legacy. Parts of his analysis have been elaborated into formal models of the equilibrium conditions generated by a régime of perfectly competitive firms. Other portions have provided a springboard for the more institutionally-oriented doctrines of workable competition in which it is held that the important results of a perfectly competitive system can be approximated even in a market structure which is not dominated by a large number of small firms.

6. THE AGGREGATIVE STRAND OF MARSHALL'S THOUGHT

Though Marshall's attention was primarily directed to micro-economic problems, aggregative themes still occupied a place in his thought. In his view, the major micro-economic question was the determination of the general price level. Short-term fluctuations in output and employment were peripheral matters; when they occurred they were expected to be temporary and slight.

His analysis of the general price level was developed around a version of the 'quantity theory' of money. Much of the earlier discussion of this point of doctrine had proceeded from the tautological statement that the quantity of money multiplied by the number of times it was spent in a given time period (the velocity of circulation) would necessarily be equal to the average price level multiplied by the total number of transactions; this expression, after all, amounted to no more than two ways of viewing total expenditure. Marshall modified this procedure by shifting the focus from the rate at which the money supply turned over to an examination of the money balances held by the community. In the hands of one of Marshall's pupils this way of viewing money was later to open up fresh analytical horizons. Marshall's own results from the use of this 'cash balance' approach, however, were essentially no different from those that had been reached via the 'velocity of circulation' route. He maintained that the amount of money held was regulated by the institutional arrangements of the economy and, on *ceteris paribus* assumptions, could be treated as a constant. In his words:

. . . whatever the state of society, there is a certain volume of their resources which people of different classes taken one with another, care to keep in the form of currency; and, if everything else remains the same, then there is this direct relation between the volume of currency and the level of prices, that, if one is increased by ten per cent, the other also will be increased by ten per cent.[21]

The effect of this procedure was to reinforce the essential requirement of Say's Law: that all income would be spent. The possibility of leakages into idle balances could, for practical purposes, be ignored. Money was interesting primarily in relation to spending and to the general price level, rather than for any connexion it might bear to the level of interest rates. This conclusion, of course, gained additional strength from Marshall's insistence — which was common to the neo-classical tradition as a whole — that interest rates would be established through the interaction of the supply of loanable funds (fed by saving) and the demand for loanable funds (stimulated by the productivity of capital). Moreover, the rate of interest could be relied upon to produce an equilibrium between decisions to save and to invest. Should the demand for loanable funds increase, the rate of interest would rise, making it more attractive for people to reduce consumption spending and to save. Conversely, should the public choose to save more, the rate of interest would fall. Investors would then be induced to increase both their borrowings and their expenditures on plant and equipment. Further, this way of looking at the matter implied that the intersection of the curves of supply and demand for loanable funds determined the equilibrium rate of interest. The position of these curves, in turn, was established by the thriftiness of the community (on the supply side) and by the productivity of capital (on the demand side).

This line of reasoning, while supporting a Say's Law interpretation of aggregative economic activity, did not preclude the possibility of economic instability. Though no disturbances of the scale experienced in the 1930s clouded the horizons of Marshall and his neo-classical contemporaries, they did observe modest cycles of boom and bust. How were these fluctuations to be explained? In Marshall's view the main answer was to be found in the psychology of the business community. Waves of optimism and pessimism seemed endemic to it. When business men were bullish the demand for loans increased. This phase might generate capital spending on many high-risk undertakings, some of which were doomed to failure. And when they did fail the bubble was pricked. Pessimism replaced optimism as the dominant mood; investment and economic activity generally would be curtailed. As Marshall described the process:

The recent history of fluctuations of general credit shows

much variety of detail, but a close uniformity of general out-
line. In the ascending phase, credit has been given somewhat
boldly, and even to men whose business capacity has not been
proved. For, at such times a man may gain a profit on nearly
every transaction, even though he has brought no special
knowledge or ability to bear on it; and his success may probably tempt others of like capacity with himself, to buy
speculatively. If he is quick to get out of his ventures, he
probably makes a profit. But his sales hasten a fall of prices,
which must have come in the course of time. Though the fall
is likely to be slight at first; yet each downward movement
impairs the confidence which had caused the rise of prices,
and is still giving them some support. The fall of a lighted
match on some thing that smoulders has often started a
disastrous panic in a crowded theatre.[22]

Credit cycles, however, were still incapable of converting
'partial' over-production into 'general' over-production.
Given time, the economic system would adjust itself to its
normal full employment level of operations. No special
action on the part of government was required to accomplish this result and, indeed, direct government intervention might make matters worse. The tendency toward
instability could, however, be moderated by anticipatory
action on the part of the monetary authorities whose
proper role was to minimize discrepancies between prevailing interest rates and the rate that would be established through the normal interplay of the supply of and
demand for loanable funds.

The main thrust of Marshall's aggregative analysis thus
buttressed faith in the capability of the economic system,
if left alone, to eradicate involuntary idleness. In the final
edition (1920) of his *Principles*, however, Marshall added
one dark hint that the analytical basis for this conclusion
might ultimately need to be revised. Following an orthodox neo-classical discussion of the relationship between
productivity, thrift, and the rate of interest, he inserted a
note of qualification:

. . . every one understands generally the causes which have
kept the supply of accumulated wealth so small relatively to

the demand for its use, that that use is on balance a source of gain, and can therefore require payment when loaned. Everyone is aware that the accumulation of wealth is held in check, and the rate of interest so far sustained, by the preference which the great mass of humanity have for present over deferred gratifications, or, in other words, by their unwillingness to wait. And indeed the true work of economic analysis in this respect is, not to emphasize this familiar truth, but to point out how much more numerous are the exceptions to this general preference than would appear at first sight.[23]

He elaborated this point in a footnote with the words:

It is a good corrective of this error to note how small a modification of the conditions of our own world would be required to bring us to another in which the mass of the people would be so anxious to provide for old age and for their families after them, and in which the new openings for the advantageous use of accumulated wealth in any form were so small, that the amount of wealth for the safe custody of which people were willing to pay would exceed that which others desired to borrow; and where in consequence even those who saw their way to make a gain out of the use of capital, would be able to exact a payment for taking charge of it; and interest would be negative all along the line.[24]

These heterodox afterthoughts did not mar the tranquillity of Marshall's grand design. They did foreshadow – far more than Marshall himself could possibly have suspected – the assault on neo-classical aggregative premisses launched by Keynes in the 1930s.

7. MARSHALL ON LONG-PERIOD ECONOMIC CHANGE

Within the framework of neo-classical theory, long-period economic change had little place. Marshall addressed himself only briefly to the subject with a discussion of 'the secular period' of the economy. In all essential respects this time dimension was identical with the one with which classical writers had been preoccupied.

From his vantage point in time Marshall could observe that the gloomier classical prognoses on the fate of the economy had not, in fact, been borne out. The stationary state had not emerged; despite increases in population, real incomes of workers had improved; capital accumulation had proceeded, but it had not been accompanied by a widespread displacement of labour. Nor had the growth in demand for foodstuffs given landlords a stranglehold over the economy. The expansion of international trade (and particularly the opening up of low cost sources of food supply) had been partially responsible for the outcome.

Despite all this, Marshall shared the general classical conclusion that rents would tend to rise during the course of sustained economic expansion. In his interpretation, however, this phenomenon was associated less with the natural limits to the fertility of the soil than with growth in demand for business and residential sites. Indeed, rising rents in urban situations had the more serious implications for the cost structure. The application of high technologies to agriculture held out prospects for productivity improvements that would forestall a re-distribution of income in favour of agricultural landowners.

Marshall's treatment of wages also departed substantially from the main classical line. He would have no part of the Malthusian 'iron laws'. On this point he followed the path charted by Mill by rejecting the view that population growth would necessarily frustrate sustained improvement in real wages. It was Marshall's expectation that workers would grow in skill, energy, and self-respect and that their productivity and their incomes would be correspondingly enhanced.[25] Similarly, Marshall dismissed Ricardian and Marxian anxieties about the effects of capital accumulation on employment. Much of any short-term competition between capital and labour, he contended, would be offset by the growth in demand for workers in the capital goods industries. Moreover, the cost-reducing effects of mechanization were clearly a blessing: competition could be relied upon to ensure that price reductions – the gains from which would be shared by all segments of the community – would follow. Marshall, of course, was on stronger ground when arguing this point than were the early classicists. The latter had assumed that real wages would always be so close to the subsistence level that there was little room in the worker's budget for goods produced by higher techniques (and thereby subject to price reduction). In Marshall's world, it could be more plausibly maintained that the benefits of lower prices would be much more widely diffused.

Another prominent contrast between Marshall's conclusions and those of the classical orthodoxy concerned the doctrine of the falling rate of profit. This proposition, which had occupied a central position in classical thought, supplied the underpinnings to fears about the ultimate emergence of the stationary state. Marshall's treatment of this question was, of course, adjusted to a different set of distributional categories. Profits could no longer be regarded in the classical sense (i.e. as the income of the capitalist class); instead the rate of interest was held to be a more appropriate measure of the return to the suppliers of capital. Marshall acknowledged that the rate of interest would tend to fall as accumulation proceeded, but only to the extent that increments to the capital stock were subject to diminishing returns. Such tendencies, however, might well be offset by technological progress. Marshall maintained that there was every reason to believe that technical improvement would proceed at faster rates than the classical economists had anticipated. In any event, the average rate of return on capital throughout the economy was not particularly pertinent to the investment decision. The carriers of economic progress were men who sought out avenues for reaping above-average returns on capital. In short, it was the result of calculations at the margin that mattered.

8. MARSHALL AND ECONOMIC POLICY

By his own account, Marshall was originally attracted to the serious study of economics by a desire to understand the causes of poverty and the means by which it could be alleviated. He emerged from his investigations convinced that:

the social and economic forces already at work are changing the distribution of wealth for the better: that they are persistent and increasing in strength; and that their influence is for the greater part cumulative; that the socio-economic organism is more delicate and complex than at first sight appears; and that large ill-considered changes might result in grave disaster.[26]

His sympathy for the sufferings of the mass of humanity had by no means diminished. But these impulses were now substantially tempered by the belief that radical measures to alter the existing economic order would be unwise. In particular, he opposed a socialistic programme on the grounds that:

the collective ownership of the means of production would deaden the energies of mankind, and arrest economic progress; unless before its introduction the whole people had acquired a power of unselfish devotion to the public good which is now relatively rare. And . . . it might probably destroy much that is most beautiful and joyful in the private and domestic relations of life. These are the main reasons which cause patient students of economics generally to anticipate little good and much evil from schemes for sudden and violent reorganization of the economic, social and political conditions of life.[27]

While the market system as portrayed by Marshall was largely benevolent, his analysis also demonstrated that in certain situations unregulated markets could not be relied upon to yield socially desirable results. Prominent among the exceptions were the cases in which – for technical reasons – competition would prove to be wasteful and inefficient, if not a practical impossibility. The 'natural monopolies' (a term which Marshall associated primarily with such public services as water supply, power generation, etc.) could not usefully be organized in accordance with the competitive plan and the case for government regulation (if not public ownership) in these instances was clear. He was reluctant, however, to recommend government intervention in those sectors of the economy in which increasing returns to scale threatened to produce industrial concentrations, even though these circumstances implied that individual firms could enjoy considerable market power and that prices would not be competitively determined. This problem, he contended, deserved continuing study. His general position on the life cycle of firms led him to the conclusion that the potential market power of large business units was unlikely to be abused for long.

Though he was disposed to view the market as a sensitive instrument through which an economy's resources could be efficiently allocated, he also recognized that its performance could be improved. For this purpose, improvements in public education were particularly important. Consumers and producers could then conduct their affairs more intelligently by enhancing the rationality of their choices. Moreover, improved economic education would do much to eradicate one of the blights of an unregulated market system – the bouts of speculation which gave rise to harmful fluctuations.

Marshall was also prepared to entertain the possibility that governments could play a useful role in improving the allocative efficiency of markets. Would not the sum of social satisfactions be increased, he asked, if the productive resources of society were shifted in favour of lines of production subject to increasing returns and away from those in which decreasing returns prevailed? Greater outputs could then be obtained from the existing stock of resources. Governments could encourage a re-allocation of resources along these lines through appropriate taxes and subsidies. He advanced this suggestion, however, with the utmost caution, pointing out that such policies could be justified only when it could be shown that the gains in satisfactions arising from expanded outputs in the subsidized sectors more than offset the losses in utility associated with higher tax levies on others. He recognized that this criterion would be difficult to apply to practical cases.

Conceivably the introduction of maximization of aggregate utility as a goal of public policy could also be used to support recommendations for a redistribution of income. If it could be assumed that the marginal utility of money was likely to be greater for a poor man than for a rich one, it followed that society's aggregate satisfactions would be enlarged through a redistribution from rich to poor. Marshall did not draw this conclusion. He did recommend a less systematic scheme of income redistribution for further study when he wrote of the possibilities of 'economic chivalry'. Such a régime would tax the rich to ameliorate the distress of those still trapped in poverty.

Notes

1. Marshall spelled out more fully his position on the uses of mathematics in economics in a letter to Bowley of 27 February 1906:

'. . . a good mathematical theorem dealing with economic hypotheses was very unlikely to be good economics: and I went more and more on the rules (1) Use mathematics as a shorthand language, rather than as an engine of inquiry. (2) Keep them till you have done. (3) Translate into English. (4) Then illustrate by examples that are important in real life. (5) Burn the mathematics. (6) If you can't succeed in 4, burn 3.' *Memorials of Alfred Marshall*, A. C. Pigou, ed. (Macmillan and Co., London, 1925), p. 427.

2. John Maynard Keynes, 'Alfred Marshall', *Essays in Biography* (Meridian Books, New York, 1956), p. 70.

3. From an unpublished manuscript by Marshall, as quoted by Pigou, loc. cit., p. 89.

4. J. S. Mill, of course, had attacked classical orthodoxy on precisely this point. The tastes of the labouring classes could be elevated, he had maintained, and the immutable laws of income distribution thereby broken. In the remainder of the classical tradition, only Malthus had offered some hints

about the importance of taste patterns in sustaining 'effectual demand'. His contribution – which was by no means systematically worked out – had been prompted by the debate on 'gluts' following the Napoleonic wars and referred largely to the expenditure patterns of landlords.

5. Some later contributors to the neo-classical tradition (as well as its critics) have found fault with Marshall's construction of a demand curve on the assumption that income is unchanged. Did Marshall intend to refer to real income or to money income? His treatment of this matter was ambiguous. Neither interpretation, however, is entirely satisfactory. Real income cannot remain constant when prices change – as indeed they do at different points on a demand schedule – for buyers can obtain differing quantities of goods with the same outlay of money. Nor is it self-evident that money income can be assumed constant at all of the price-quantity combinations on a demand curve. It must be expected that price changes may often alter the income of sellers. Only with the assumption that the demand of sellers for their own product was negligible could this position be defended.

6. Marshall, *Principles of Economics*, Ninth (variorum) edition, C. W. Guillebaud, ed. (Macmillan, London, 1961), vol. 1, p. 118.

7. ibid., p. 63.

8. ibid., p. 65.

9. ibid., p. 348.

10. ibid., p. 587.

11. ibid., p. 412.

12. ibid., p. 366.

13. A similar shift in definition can be observed in Marshall's treatment of the 'stationary state'. He handled this notion as follows:

Our first step towards studying the influences exerted by the element of time on the relations between cost of production and value may well be to consider the famous fiction of the 'Stationary State' in which those influences would be but little felt; and to contrast the results which would be found there with those in the modern world. This state obtains its name from the fact that in it the general conditions of production and consumption, of distribution and exchange remain motionless . . . . (ibid., pp. 366–7.)

14. ibid., p. 397.

15. ibid., p. 459n.

16. ibid., pp. 460–61.

17. ibid., p. 316.

18. ibid., p. 287.

19. ibid., p. 286.

20. ibid., p. 459n.

21. Marshall, *Money, Credit and Commerce* (Macmillan, London, 1923), p. 45.

22. ibid., p. 247.

23. *Principles*, pp. 581–2.

24. ibid., p. 582n.

25. Nevertheless, on a world-wide scale (as opposed to conditions in any one country), Marshall held that the essentials of Malthusian argument were still valid. Even with 'great improvements in the arts of agriculture', he wrote, 'the pressure of population on the means of subsistence may be held in check for about two hundred years, but not longer'. (ibid., p. 180n.)

26. ibid., p. 712.

27. ibid., p. 713.

CHAPTER 7

Pre-1914 Variations on Neo-Classical Themes

THE central nerve of neo-classical economics was the analysis of the behaviour of the market system and the mechanisms within it through which an equilibrium could be produced. Marshall occupied a commanding position in the development of the English tradition of neo-classicism and the sweep of his work was unmatched by other contributors to the neo-classical tradition. Variations on similar themes, however, were run elsewhere. The alternative approaches were inspired by considerations somewhat different from those that had prompted Marshall and often yielded slightly different results. The distinctive tracts of four additional strands of formative neo-classicism deserve inspection, if only in synoptic form: the contributions of the Lausanne, American, Austrian and Swedish traditions.

1. LEON WALRAS AND THE NEO-CLASSICISM OF LAUSANNE

Leon Walras (1834–1910), a Frenchman who spent his professionally most productive years in Switzerland, approached the neo-classical problem along a path quite different from the one Marshall had chosen. For Walras rigorous, formal elegance – rather than contact with the practical problems of real life – was the target appropriate for the aim of economists. His concern was with pure theory which he defined as 'the theory of determination of prices under a hypothetical régime of perfectly free competition'.[1] He aspired to give economics a scientific status comparable to that enjoyed by the physical sciences and to distil its findings into the form of mathematical propositions. Walras was equally insistent that a sharp line of demarcation should be drawn between pure and applied economics. Though not himself indifferent to policy considerations, he vigorously maintained that the status of economics as pure science should never be compromised in the interests of bringing the work of the theorist closer to the problems of practical affairs. The contrast between the Walrasian and Marshallian intellectual styles could hardly have been more marked.[2]

Walras's career was filled with disappointments. Thwarted in his original ambition to study engineering (ironically, because he failed to satisfy the admissions board of the École Polytechnique of his competence in mathematics), he meandered for more than a decade – with only meagre success – as a journalist, aspiring novelist, railway clerk, and bank employee. Meanwhile, he directed much of his leisure to the study of economics, a pursuit in which he received little encouragement in his native country. Lacking the proper credentials, he was unable to break into the French academic establishment. In 1870 fortune at last smiled. He was then appointed to the newly created chair in economics in the Faculty of Law at the University of Lausanne. While resident in Switzerland, he remained a loyal Frenchman, though he did not suppress a sense of irritation with French institutions.[3]

The prime objective of Walras's intellectual programme was to produce an exhaustive account of the implications of a régime of perfect competition. Part of the value of this exercise, as he saw it, lay in the fact that many economists had been too readily persuaded of the merits of *laissez-faire*. 'How could these economists', he asked, 'prove that the results of free competition were beneficial and advantageous if they did not know just what these results were? And how could they know these results when they had neither framed definitions nor formulated relevant laws to prove their point? . . . the fact that economists have often extended the principle of free competition beyond the limits of its true applicability is proof positive that the principle has not been demonstrated.'[4]

For his purposes, perfect competition was likened to a situation in which buyers and sellers could be brought together in a massive auction 'in such a way that the terms of every exchange are openly announced and an opportunity is given to sellers to lower their prices and to buyers to raise their bids'.[5] These conditions were admittedly divorced from reality. He defended the procedure by asking: 'What physicist would deliberately pick cloudy weather for astronomical observations instead of taking advantage of a cloudless night?'[6] In his view the case for a procedure which began with abstract general cases and took up the qualifications later was too self-evident to require further comment.

The basic problem to be solved within this hypothetical régime of pure competition concerned the manner in which the prices of the various inputs and outputs were established. Marshall had addressed the same issue by invoking supply and demand curves in various types of markets as the basis for the determination of equilibrium prices. His procedure, however, contained an awkward ambiguity. It will be recalled, for example, that his analysis of demand required the assumption that incomes were constant. Whether this condition was intended to refer to money income or real income was not entirely clear. In either case it could be objected – as Walras pointed out – that a reduction in any price (even when it could be represented as a movement from a higher to a lower point on the same demand curve) was unlikely to be accomplished without a change in someone's income. Barring the case in which the quantity sold increased by the same percentage as the price had been reduced, the income of sellers would necessarily alter. This, in turn, would imply a shift in the position of the original demand curve.

Marshall's formulation was thus too loose to meet

Walras's standards of analytical rigour. And it was also too 'partial'. Marshallian procedure called for the investigations of conditions in individual markets on terms which largely isolated them from wider influences. Walras, on the other hand, sought to trace out the manner in which an equilibrium solution could be reached in all markets simultaneously. His target was a statement of the process by means of which a 'general' equilibrium – one which took into account the inter-dependence of all economic activities – was established. A later commentator has described the Walrasian perspective on the economic system as one in which 'no blade of grass can move without altering the position of the stars'.

As a first step toward demonstrating the possibility of a general equilibrium solution, Walras examined the case of the simplest economy imaginable. It possessed only two goods to be exchanged (identified as x and y). All persons were assumed to be buyers of one good or sellers of the other. On these assumptions, it could be argued that the supply of x and the demand for y (as well as vice versa) were interdependent because the market demand for y (or x) was derived from the incomes received by sellers of x (or y). Consistent with neo-classical procedure, it was, of course, assumed that the terms on which sellers were prepared to exchange were regulated by the marginal utilities of x and y. Through competitive bidding an equilibrium price ratio would be established.

The problem became more intricate, of course, when more than two goods were involved. In the three-commodity economy (with goods x, y and z), three price ratios could be established (x: y, x: z, and y: z). One of these ratios, however, would be redundant, adding no information that could not be derived from the other two. This example illustrated a larger principle: namely, that in a multi-good economy, the number of equilibrium price ratios required was always one less than the number of goods involved in exchange. Thus in an economy with n goods, $(n-1)$ exchange ratios would have to be determined through competitive bidding. The redundant commodity could then be regarded as a standard – or a *numéraire* – in terms of which all other price ratios could be expressed. This standard commodity, whatever its identity, would possess all of the essential properties of money.

The Walrasian approach to the analysis of the competitive process had the considerable merit of lending itself neatly to presentation in the form of simultaneous equations susceptible to a determinate mathematical solution. This procedure also had an important recommendation in that it emphasized the interdependence of all prices within the economic system. At the same time, Walrasian general equilibrium dissolved the standard lines of demarcation between micro- and macro-theory. The activities of households, firms and industries could not be understood in isolation from one another or when detached from the economy as a whole.

This formal analysis of conditions required to produce an equilibrium was, of course, built on two important practical restrictions. The case of an underemployment of resources, for example, was obviously inadmissible. In fact, the whole argument rested on the assumption that full employment was the normal situation. The general equilibrium solution could be reached only when it could be supposed that all income was spent; otherwise the total interdependence between supply and demand could not be asserted. Indeed Walras's approach can be interpreted as a logical extension of the tradition Say established when he wrote that 'goods constitute the demand for other goods'.

Nor was Walras's system equipped to handle the case of increasing returns to scale. If such production conditions prevailed, a determinate set of equilibrium prices could not be reached. Walras placed too much of a premium on rigorous and tidy solutions to resort to the tactics Marshall had adopted – an appeal to the 'special' and imperfect markets of the everyday business world – when confronted with this complication.

If these cases could not be handled within his hypothetical régime of pure competition Walras's scheme could still throw some useful indirect light on practical issues. It could now be stated explicitly that *laissez-faire* would break down under conditions of increasing returns to scale. Alternative arrangements would then have to be devised. In his comments on this problem Walras provided few details beyond noting that the public services and the 'natural' monopolies could not conceivably be conducted under the rules of pure competition. He did insist, however, that additional considerations were pertinent to an assessment of the social results of competition. The outcome of the competitive process, he noted, depended on the initial distribution of income and property. For this reason it did not necessarily follow that the results produced were ideal, nor the only ones conceivable. Different distributional systems, both for income and property, were always possible. Perfect competition, though it might be a reasonably satisfactory allocative device in the existing order, could claim neither perfection nor immortality.

While recognizing the possibility of different modes of economic organization, Walras maintained that judgements on their merits were beyond the competence of economists as scientists. The economist could, of course, point to the existence of alternatives. But discussion of the options best calculated to serve the community's interest fell within the realm of art and was outside the domain of scientific discourse. As citizens, economists might still hold private views about the desirability of particular institutional arrangements. Walras personally was sympathetic to a régime of small agrarian freeholders, an institutional arrangement likely to approximate perfect competition about as closely as any system imaginable.

2. JOHN BATES CLARK AND THE
AMERICAN STRAND OF EARLY NEO-CLASSICISM

The American strand of neo-classicism was partly a grafting of two quite different European roots – that of German and Austrian thought (to which a substantial number of the early American academic economists were exposed during graduate study in German universities) and Marshallian influences which flowed easily across the Atlantic on the English language wave. But there were also distinctive indigenous elements in the approach to the neo-classical problem devised in the United States. Most of the important figures in this formative period managed to blend an ethical concern and a native-soil political radicalism into their theoretical systems. Thus the charter members of the American Economic Association – most of whom were unsympathetic to *laissez-faire* – declared in its original statutes that: 'We regard the State as an agency whose positive assistance is one of the indispensable conditions of human progress.' This language, however, was soon withdrawn on the grounds that a predisposition to a policy position was unfitting to an organization dedicated to scientific inquiry.

John Bates Clark (1847–1938) was not only a giant among American neo-classicists but he was also the first genuinely original theorist of the first rank to emerge in the New World. As a young man, he followed the course recommended for many promising students of his generation by pursuing graduate study in European universities (in Clark's case at Heidelberg and Zurich). On his return to America, he settled into an academic career which was climaxed in 1895 by his appointment to a chair in economics at Columbia University.

Clark's major original contribution to the sharpening of neo-classical analysis was his pioneering work on the theory of production and distribution. Two considerations influenced this concentration of his theoretical energies. One was a deep-seated moral concern which inspired him to search for criteria of distributive justice in an economic environment made increasingly complex by industrial concentrations and by the rise of labour unions. In addition, his dissatisfaction with a popular view that wage levels (and the distribution of income generally) were determined primarily by the real income available to labourers on rent-free land stimulated him to produce an alternative analysis of income distribution.[7]

Clark applied the tools of marginal analysis – including some of his own invention – to this task. As was characteristic of this tradition, he proceeded first on the assumption that conditions of perfect competition prevailed. The rational producer would then engage each of the three productive factors to the point at which the price of the marginal unit of each factor was equal to its marginal product. These production rules simultaneously determined the distribution of income between the various functional shares. In the absence of abnormal profits under perfectly competitive equilibrium the resulting distributional solution – as Clark was among the first to demonstrate – would exhaust the value of the total product. This conclusion holds, however, only so long as constant returns to scale prevail (i.e. the situation in which a doubling of the size of plant would produce no change in unit costs). It would be vitiated in the case of economies of scale that lowered unit costs.

Conditions in the real world, of course, were likely to depart from the perfectly competitive standard. Indeed, when employers enjoyed a bargaining advantage, they would probably exploit it by paying wages at rates less than the value of labour's marginal product. In Clark's judgement, this amounted to 'institutional robbery' which occurred in any 'plan of living that should force men to leave in their employers' hands anything that by right of creation is theirs'.[8] But it was also possible that tightly organized trade unions might exact – if only temporarily – wage rates in excess of labour's marginal product. This situation was also socially 'unjust'; Clark believed that it could be avoided by denying unions any powers to restrict the supply of labour (such as those that would be possible under closed shop arrangements).

Using marginal productivity techniques, Clark had, in effect, devised a neo-classical definition of 'exploitation' – but one which was totally alien to the Marxian use of the same expression. As Clark saw the matter, economic exploitation was a real possibility but not inherent in the capitalist process. Only when the system departed from the perfectly competitive standard did exploitation arise. Nor was the exploitation of labour by capitalists the only possible deviation from distributive justice, though it might be the most probable. At least in principle, labour could exploit capital if its claims resulted in sub-marginal product rewards to capital.

The programme for the analysis of the practical attainability of distributive justice required, of course, an inspection of the actual competitive order – and, in particular, of the implications of industrial concentrations – before it could be rounded out. Clark's initial position was quite unsympathetic to the moral ethos of industrial capitalism, an order he interpreted as being built on lust for private gain rather than the promotion of social virtue. But if unrestrained competition was socially abusive, monopoly was likely to be even more so. Personally, he supported the promotion of producer co-operative organizations.

He later modified these views substantially. The threat of monopoly no longer loomed so large in his thoughts as, under dynamic conditions, he maintained that technical innovation would constantly challenge established concentrations of market power. Size *per se* was not sufficient as a basis upon which to judge the social effects of an industrial organization. So long as there were no barriers to the entry of new competitors and so long as collusive agreements between producers were prohibited, most of the socially desirable features of perfect competition could still be obtained in a dynamic and expanding economy. On this matter Clark's views anticipated the 'workable competition' doctrines now current which maintain that industrial organization should be judged more by performance tests (e.g. technical progressiveness, restraint in price-setting, etc.) rather than by structural tests (e.g. size, share of the market, and the number of rival producers).

3. EUGEN VON BÖHM-BAWERK AND THE AUSTRIAN SCHOOL

Between 1870 and the outbreak of the First World War, Vienna was the site of one of the most flourishing schools of neo-classical teaching. Though this tradition of neo-classicism was launched by Carl Menger – who was among the first to bring marginal concepts to bear on the analysis of market equilibrium – the towering figure of this period was Eugen von Böhm-Bawerk (1851–1914).

In his professional career Böhm-Bawerk combined academic and official duties. He was first called from a university post to the Ministry of Finance in 1889 to work out a projected currency reform and rose to serve three appointments as the Austrian Minister of Finance. From this position he fought effectively for balanced budgets and a stable currency linked to the gold standard. Meanwhile, he maintained contact with university life, though he was able to devote substantial time to teaching and research only after resigning his ministerial post in 1904.

Böhm-Bawerk's theoretical writings were concentrated on the nature of capital and interest. At first glance, these problems, though important, might appear to be limited in range. In fact, as he treated them, they were all-embracing. He held that the analysis of capital and interest constituted 'the focal point about which attack and defence rally in the war in which the issue is the system under which human society shall be organized'.[9]

Indeed, as his ablest pupil has observed, the scale of the canvas on which Böhm-Bawerk painted justified describing him as a 'bourgeois Marx'.[10]

Böhm-Bawerk's procedure was heavily formal and deductive. Consistent with his view of economics as an exact science, he claimed to offer a correct and comprehensive view of the nature of capital and its role in the productive process. From his perspective, earlier traditions had provided only a partial account. The Physiocratic interpretation of the productive process, for example, had regarded only one factor of production – land – as crucial. The classical tradition, while eliminating this error, had bred another by holding that labour was the basic productive factor. Only in neo-classical thought was capital given an autonomous status. Even so, the existence of capital was not independent of other factors of production. In his view, it could arise only through the earlier cooperation of the two original factors, labour and land.

Nevertheless, in Böhm-Bawerk's scheme of things, all forms of production (with the exception of the most primitive in which no implements whatsoever were used) involved indirect and roundabout methods. They were thus 'capitalistic' in nature. In his terms the 'method of production which wisely follows an indirect course is nothing more nor less than what the economist calls *capitalist* production. . . . Capital is nothing but the sum total of intermediate products which come into existence at the individual stages of the roundabout course of production.'[11] Roundabout methods were used for the obvious reason that production assisted by capital instruments could produce more than could land and labour unaided. The effects of capital on output, however, were delayed; capital goods took time to construct and to be absorbed into the productive process. But no less important to an understanding of the nature of capital was the fact that the community was obliged to save before the capital stock could be enlarged. The basic problem in the analysis of production was thus one of reconciling two opposing considerations: the disadvantages of restraining consumption, on the one hand, against the advantages of future expansions in output, on the other. How was a solution to this problem to be reached?

Part of Böhm-Bawerk's explanation rested on the premisses of Austrian subjective value theory. It was assumed that economic man was motivated by the desire to maximize utility. But in this case the maximization problem had to be viewed over a span of time in which present and future satisfactions were weighed against one another. Böhm-Bawerk maintained that most men were likely to prefer the bird in the hand to the one in the bush – i.e. to over-value the present relative to the future and to underestimate the strength of future wants. For these reasons people had to be rewarded – through the payment of a rate of interest – for saving and parting with present satisfactions.

The other side of this coin was the willingness of those who purchased capital goods to pay for the means to acquire them. From the producer's point of view the desirability of additional capital goods was self-evident because of the additions to output their use permitted. For this reason borrowers were enabled – and prepared – to pay an interest charge. At the same time the existence of a positive rate of interest meant that the roundaboutness of the productive process would not be extended to infinity because additions to the capital stock were subject to diminishing returns. The existence of a rate of interest thus assured an equilibrium between saving and investment.

Böhm-Bawerk's analysis was clearly at one with the general neo-classical conviction that thrift and the productivity of capital determined the rate of interest and regulated decisions to save and to invest. In his hands, however, the argument did more: it became a powerful weapon in ideological combat. If his definitions were accepted, it was both pointless and an abuse of language to differentiate – as Marx had done – between various historical stages in which different rules for the conduct of economic life applied. Any tool-using society was, by definition, 'capitalistic' and subject to the same universal and timeless principles. Böhm-Bawerk, in fact, wrote a lengthy critique of Marxian analysis in which he maintained that Marx's basic error stemmed from a misguided labour theory of value that blinded him to a 'correct' view of the nature of capital. Though the assault on Marx took precedence, Böhm-Bawerk's vigorous assertion of the validity and value of universal, formal categories was also aimed at another group of intellectual adversaries – i.e. those members of the German historical school who had maintained that abstract reasoning had little to contribute to an understanding of the economic process and distracted attention from 'the facts'.

4. KNUT WICKSELL AND THE SWEDISH BRAND OF NEO-CLASSICISM

In a discipline that has been rich in eccentrics, Knut Wicksell (1851–1926) must rank near the top of any list of unforgettable characters. By his own admission he displayed a 'contrary disposition' from an early age and throughout his life he was a vigorous opponent of social conventions. When he married he spurned both church and state and simply announced that he and a remarkable woman had been 'united' through a private exchange of contracts. In his late forties he placed in jeopardy his first opportunity for professional recognition and for escape from the financial insecurity of free-lance lecturing and pamphleteering by refusing to follow the procedure prescribed for appointees at Swedish royal universities. So intense were his republican views that he could not bring himself to use the expression 'Your Majesty's most obedient servant' when petitioning the king for formal appointment to the chair of economics at the University of Lund. Victory in these battles did not diminish his delight in 'setting the cat among the pigeons' by championing unpopular causes.

In his theoretical writing Wicksell polished and refined the marginal approach to the analysis of value and distribution. He did not emerge with the conclusion (as some of his neo-classical contemporaries had done) that the allocation of resources produced by free competition would be socially optimal. He did not deny that a régime possessing the conditions required by pure competition would tend to yield an outcome in which the prices of productive factors would be equated to the value of their respective marginal products and the prices of outputs made equal to the marginal costs of production. Nor did he deny that these results suggested that no gains in output could be accomplished through a re-allocation of a given stock of productive resources. He insisted, however, that the social desirability of this outcome could not be judged in isolation from the distribution of income and wealth. On this point he once wrote:

As a matter of fact all argument in favour of free competition rests on one tacit assumption, which, however, corresponds but little to reality, namely that from the beginning all men are equal. If that were so, everyone would be equipped with the same working power, the same education and, above all, the same economic assets, and much could then be said in favour of free, unhampered competition; each person would have only himself to blame if he did not succeed.

But if all conditions are basically unequal, if some people have good hands from the beginning and others hold only low cards, free competition does nothing to stop the former from winning every trick while the latter pay the table.[12]

It did not follow, Wicksell maintained, that the means of production should be socialized. He saw little prospect that public ownership could improve on the productive performance of the free market system. He elaborated this position with arguments similar to those Böhm-Bawerk had used to demonstrate that all societies beyond the most primitive faced the same fundamental problems of 'capitalistic' production. The attention of the state, as he saw it, should be directed to reducing the handicaps suffered by the weak in the competitive struggle by making opportunities freely and universally available and by levying heavy inheritance taxes.

The most novel of Wicksell's analytical contributions lay in the area of monetary theory. Orthodox neo-classicism, it will be recalled, treated monetary questions as matters of distinctly secondary concern. Money, of course, was essential as a circulating medium in an exchange economy, but it was still only a 'veil' covering exchanges of goods. Wicksell contended to the contrary that money and credit had a crucial bearing on the level of economic activity. Moreover, these matters grew in importance and complexity with the increasing reliance on banks as creators of means of payment. The amount of credit banks supplied was, of course, determined primarily by the demand for loans which, in turn, derived from the net gains a borrower anticipated from the use of credit. But it did not necessarily follow that the interest rate charged by banks (i.e. the market rate) coincided with the normal (or real) rate of interest corresponding to the marginal productivity of capital and to an equilibrium between saving and investment. Should, for example, the market rate be less than the real rate of interest, then:

. . . saving will be discouraged and for that reason there will be an increased demand for goods and services for present consumption. In the second place, the profit opportunities for entrepreneurs will thus be increased and the demand for goods and services, as well as for raw materials already in the market for future production, will evidently increase to the same extent as it had previously been held in check by the higher rate of interest. Owing to the increased income thus accruing to the workers, landowners, and the owners of raw materials, etc., the prices of consumption goods will begin to rise, the more so as the factors of production previously available are now withdrawn for the purposes of future production. Equilibrium in the market for goods and services will therefore be disturbed. As against an increased demand in two directions there will be an unchanged or even diminished supply, which must result in an increase in wages (rent) and, directly or indirectly, in prices.[13]

In short, Wicksell's analysis pointed to the possibility that the behaviour of interest rates – rather than tending automatically to assure aggregative equilibrium – might instead generate cumulative movements away from equilibrium. Moreover, in a system with a highly elastic supply of bank credit, there was no reason to expect these fluctuations to be self-correcting without considerable dislocation. The indirect connexions Wicksell established between the monetary system and the level of economic activity via the rate of interest foreshadowed a major revolution in economic thinking which in the 1930s shook the very foundations of neo-classical economics.

Notes

1. Walras, *Elements of Pure Economics*, translated by William Jaffe (George Allen and Unwin, London, 1954), p. 40.

2. In this connexion, it is of interest to note that as early as 1873 Walras urged Marshall to publish some of his diagrammatical constructions. Marshall declined 'because he feared that if separated from all concrete study of actual conditions, they might seem to claim a more direct bearing on real problems that they in fact had'. (As quoted by Guillebaud in the Variorum edition of Marshall's *Principles*, vol. 2, p. 7.)

3. He once wrote of the French Academy (after a paper he had presented to it on mathematical economics had been given a very cool reception): 'I grieve for this learned body, and I venture to say that . . . it might, in its own interest, have profited by this opportunity to establish its competence in economics a little more brilliantly.' (Preface to the fourth edition of *Elements of Pure Economics*, Jaffe translation, p. 44.)

4. ibid., p. 256–7.

5. ibid., p. 84.

6. ibid., p. 86.

7. The view against which Clark was reacting had many notable classical features, though he was responding specifically to doctrines propagated by Henry George, the advocate of a single-tax on land.

8. Clark, *The Distribution of Wealth* (Macmillan Co., New York, 1899), pp. 8–9.

9. Böhm-Bawerk, *Capital and Interest,* vol. 1, translated by George D. Hunke and Hans F. Sennholz (Libertarian Press, South Holland, Illinois, 1959), p. 241.

10. Schumpeter, *History of Economic Analysis* (George Allen and Unwin, London, 1954), p. 846.

11. *Capital and Interest,* vol. 2, p. 14.

12. As quoted by Torsten Gardlund, *The Life of Knut Wicksell* (Almqvist and Wiksell, Stockholm, 1958), pp. 208–9.

13. Wicksell, *Lectures on Political Economy, vol. 2: Money* (Routledge and Kegan Paul, London, 1962), pp. 194–5.

Postscript to Neo-Classical Economics

THE intellectual achievement of the neo-classical economists was formidable. Without doubt, the models formulated by its contributors register high on the scales of aesthetic appeal and logical symmetry. Their work fitted the pieces of a complex system into a coherent package and stated the relationships between them in a fashion amenable to mathematical analysis. Their approach brought new standards of rigour to economic discourse and largely silenced the overtones of inevitability which, in varying degree, had been associated with classical and Marxian argumentation. Human volition was brought to the centre of the stage. Economic analysis, as construed by writers of a neo-classical persuasion, centred on the functioning of the market system and its major objective was to clarify the choices open to producers and consumers in market situations. From this perspective fears that cleavages in the economic structure might be unbridgeable were suppressed. Instead, the economic order was viewed as an organic unit, the components of which were mutually interdependent. On this basis, judgements about the welfare of the whole society (as opposed to statements about gains and losses to individual groups) were legitimate. Though the early neo-classicists did not speak with one voice on this matter, most maintained that – apart from cases in which economies of scale prevailed – the free functioning of the market would normally advance the general welfare.

These conclusions – as well as the elegant formal system from which they were derived – rested on two important assumptions. In the first place, it was necessary to hold that highly competitive conditions characterized the bulk of economic activity. It was, of course, recognized that certain lines of production (i.e. those subject to increasing returns) were inconsistent with these assumptions and that some form of government intervention to deal with them was justified. Nevertheless, it was held that, in most markets, consumers ultimately guided the allocation of resources and that producers could not exercise unilateral influence over prices. But if this outcome was to be judged as beneficent, it was also necessary to maintain that no resources would be involuntarily idle. From neo-classical premisses, confidence that 'full employment' would be the normal operating level of the economy flowed naturally. This did not mean that fluctuations in the aggregate level of economic activity could never occur. Despite occasional disturbances arising from miscalculations and malfunctionings in the monetary system, the normal operation of the market system would be sufficient to assure speedy correction of these abnormalities.

The appropriateness of the second of these assumptions was challenged by events in the 1930s and, at the analytical level, by the path-breaking work of John Maynard Keynes. The foundations of the first assumption began to erode even earlier. In manufacturing, particularly, markets dominated by a small number of large producers (rather than by the large number of sellers required by tight models of a competitive régime) became increasingly prominent. In face of these institutional changes, Marshall's assurances about the constraints to the exercise of market power imposed by the life cycle of the firms and by 'special' markets lost much of their plausibility. Economic theory, however, did not satisfactorily embrace the grey area between pure competition and pure monopoly until the late 1920s when Mrs Joan Robinson in Cambridge and Professor E. H. Chamberlin of Harvard worked out theories of 'imperfect' and 'monopolistic' competition respectively. These contributions, while modifying earlier neo-classical propositions, were still cast in the mould of neo-classical marginalist reasoning.

The apparatus of neo-classical reasoning has also been perpetuated by theorists who have abandoned any claims to realism for its premises concerning competition. They have instead asserted that the outcome described in the perfectly competitive model – in which market power is diffused and the economy's resources optimally allocated – is socially desirable. The model no longer purports to be descriptive, but is accorded a normative status. Supporters of this general position divide into two camps. One school advocates legislation to enforce competition by splintering large-scale producers into small competing firms. The other has opposed such attempts to reproduce atomistic competition and has instead used neo-classical reasoning to support a programme of socialism. In the latter view industries which fail to meet the standards of perfect competition should be nationalized. Under public ownership, managers would be directed to price their outputs at marginal cost. Such procedures, it has been maintained, would permit the optimum allocative solution of the perfectly competitive régime to be approximated.

Both of these adaptations of neo-classical theory have been challenged by writers whose roots in the neo-classical tradition are no less deep. In tones reminiscent of the later J. B. Clark, another school has contended that the essential characteristics of competition can be preserved (even in markets with a small number of sellers) so long as a high rate of technical innovation is sustained. Moreover, it has been argued that the abnormally high profits available to firms enjoying considerable market power permit heavier ploughbacks into research than would otherwise have been possible. With the introduction of these dynamic considerations, industrial concentrations have been defended.

Similar adaptations of neo-classical argument have been made for application to the problems of the under-developed world. In this setting – where the market is often far from ubiquitous – neo-classical ideas have emerged in two prominent forms. One version, for which there are a number of eminent spokesmen, maintains that the mobility of resources and their efficient allocation is thwarted by restrictions based on race, tribal affiliation, or caste. The inference drawn for policy from this reading of the situation is that such 'imperfections' should be eliminated; the extension of the market system should be encouraged as a spur to efficiency, to a faster rate of growth, and as a social levelling device. A variant of this point of view, though one with the same intellectual parentage, holds that government intervention bears a heavy responsibility for waste, inefficiency, and misallocation of economic resources. Greater freedom for the market through massive reductions in government controls is regarded as the appropriate course for policy.

A more sophisticated extension of neo-classical doctrines to the underdeveloped world is less confident about the capacity of untampered markets to produce desirable results. This version of neo-classical reasoning proceeds from the assumption that fundamental structural obstacles prevent an optimum allocation in underdeveloped economies and that government should be assigned the task of adjusting the prices of productive factors in order to come closer to the optimum solution. It is contended that wage rates are higher than is warranted by the productivity of the labour force (primarily because of minimum wage legislation and social pressures on employers) and that the price of capital is too low to reflect the real scarcity of capital (primarily because interest rates in organized capital markets are linked more closely to international lending rates than to local conditions). It is then argued that governments should redress this imbalance in a manner calculated to approximate the factor prices that would prevail in an equilibrium situation. Under the recommended system of 'accounting prices' the buyer of labour would be subsidized while the buyer of capital would be taxed. If this scheme could be effectively administered (a point about which there can be considerable legitimate doubt), it is expected that output, employment, and the rate of economic growth would be considerably enlarged.

The reformulation and extension of neo-classical ideas along these lines by no means exhaust its legacy. The counter-revolution in economic literature touched off by early neo-classicism also deserves mention. Perhaps its most colourful critic was Thorstein Veblen (1857–1929), an irrepressible pupil of J. B. Clark who challenged the presuppositions of his master's teaching. The neo-classical *modus operandi*, he maintained, was too formal, too deductive, and too static to provide leverage on the problems that mattered. Not only did it accord low priority to dynamic factors in economic life, but it was almost totally oblivious to the analysis of change. What passed for a discussion of the causal mechanics of the economic system was, in his view, only teleology. Change was not explained. Instead, neo-classical procedure worked with single assumed changes (when all other conditions were held constant) and attempted to trace the path to a new equilibrium. Even the neo-classical concept of equilibrium was alleged to be spurious. Inasmuch as it rested on the assumption of rational calculating behaviour, it clashed with Veblen's insistence that human action was more instinctive than reflective. In his interpretation two drives were particularly forceful in social conduct: the instinct of workmanship and the instinct of emulation.

From this position Veblen offered both a critique of orthodox neo-classical postulates and a competing explanation of the economic process. As he saw the matter, man's natural impulse to produce, to create, and to innovate – if allowed to express itself without restraint – would embarrass society with abundance. That this fate had been averted could be explained, in part, by the emergence of a leisure class, the social function of which was to waste the abundance that human energy had produced. At the same time, a highly organized market system had mechanisms for suppressing output built into it. In Veblen's account, the engineers (who epitomized the instinct of workmanship in societies with high technologies) sought to expand output without limit. Their creative energies, however, were frustrated by businessmen who, prompted by fears of spoiling established markets and of destroying capital values, became the agents of institutionalized waste. In search of maximum profits, big business kept outputs well below technologically feasible levels.

This account was clearly at odds with the mainstream of neo-classical thought. Veblen rejected all of the basic propositions of neo-classical economics. If advised that consumers would normally buy more of a commodity at lower than at a higher price, Veblen would object that considerations of emulation and conspicuous consumption might, in certain circumstances, yield the opposite result; luxury goods valued as status symbols, for example, might actually be purchased in reduced quantities as their prices fell. If told that labour had a disutility attached to it (an assumption underlying neo-classical distributional theory), Veblen would counter with the argument that man's workmanlike instincts meant that he obtained positive satisfactions from productive effort. If informed that the proper area of investigation for the economic theorist was the formal analysis of the market's allocative properties under static equilibrium conditions, Veblen's response would be most vehement. The real issue, he maintained, was the reverse: the investigation of the destabilizing impact of changes in tastes and technology.

Veblen did much to rekindle interest in an 'institutional' approach to economic problems – i.e. one which largely eschews notions derived from pure theory in favour of empirical inquiries into the workings of an economy's basic institutions. Some readers of recent best sellers on contemporary economics and social problems may also detect echoes of Veblenian themes. J. K. Galbraith's *The Affluent Society*, for example, is built on the thesis that the maintenance of a high level of economic activity in rich societies has required producers to become taste makers in order to dispose of their abundant product.

Perhaps the most sophisticated of the later criticisms of the structure of neo-classical reasoning has challenged the claim that economics can achieve the status of an exact science. Much of the attack has been directed at the value judgements latent in such standard neo-classical terms as 'equilibrium' and 'optimum' and the risk that their use will prescribe what ought to be. The transition from descriptive to normative statements proceeds so smoothly that it often escapes notice. Yet it is an operation of this sort which many of the latter-day practitioners of neo-classicism have performed. Even if it were logically legitimate – which it is not – to derive ethical conclusions from scientific data, difficulties would not be entirely avoided. It might still be questioned whether or not the neo-classical image of an economic system in which the interests of various groups were harmonized constituted an accurate characterization of reality. Some critics have maintained that unfortunate effects have stemmed from the neo-classical preoccupation with efficiency in production and exchange. Emphasis on these matters has diverted attention from distributional considerations and from divergences in the interests of various groups within society.

Despite these dissents there can be no doubt that the neo-classical economists attained a high standard of formal elegance. Their choice of central focus precluded a sharp inspection of two major economic issues – e.g. those of long-period growth and aggregative instability – and even the limited attention they gave to these matters was deficient. But the apparatus of reasoning cementing their ideas together has a utility which transcends the usual domain of economic problems. Indeed, the neo-classical mode of thought has been construed as providing the basis for a generalized logic of choice with much to offer to those charged with planning national defence strategies as well as to businessmen.

PART FOUR

KEYNESIAN ECONOMICS

Introduction

BETWEEN the two World Wars, the economic environment of most industrial countries was shaken by a crisis of unprecedented dimensions. Unemployment mounted to record levels and was stubbornly persistent. With it came a wave of social discontent. In England, the crisis began in 1921 and continued with little interruption through the 1930s. Severe depression conditions were later in reaching the United States, but when they arrived with the 1929 crash, their force was greater. Clearly, it was not 'normalcy' to which the Western world had returned.

The fabric of Western industrial communities was deeply rent by these events. In Britain, the general strike of 1926, which was bred in social hostility, generated still more. Later, when the bread lines and queues for the dole lengthened in the United States, unemployed veterans of the First World War marched on the national capital protesting that they were 'forgotten men'. Amid these symptoms of distress many reflective persons were led to ask whether or not the Marxian prognosis about the future of capitalism – which had been largely written off as falsified by history in the heyday of late nineteenth-century capitalism – might not have been so far wrong after all.

The orthodox tradition in economic thinking was unprepared to deal with this situation. The framework of the neo-classical mentality had been organized around the assumption that full employment was an economy's normal operating level, that departures from it would be minor, and that – when lapses did occur – the economic system itself would generate the necessary remedies. In the 1930s, this image of the functioning of an economic system seemed to be far out of touch with the realities. Not only had idleness in the labour force and in plant capacity reached unusual proportions but there was little to indicate that this distressing situation was correcting itself.

Despite the chasm separating the assumptions of neo-classical aggregative analysis from the world of events, economists schooled in the neo-classical tradition were not at a loss to offer an explanation for these abnormalities. The persistence of unemployment could be accounted for by rigidities within the economic system that stalled the mechanism for adjustment to full employment equilibrium. Two types of rigidities figured prominently in the discussion of the times. Perhaps the most important was the inflexibility of wages arising from the influence of trade unions. From this perspective the insistence of organized labour on strict adherence to negotiated minimum wage scales was held to be socially irresponsible. The system's normal response to unemployment, it was maintained, called for wage reductions which would, in turn, encourage employers to hire more workers. Were it not for the obstructionism of trade unions, the economy would begin to climb the path back to full employment.

A rigidity of a second type was also viewed as thwarting the self-adjusting properties of the economic system. In this case, the responsibility was placed at the door of the business community, or at least that portion of it which departed from the standards required by perfect competition. Many businesses – particularly large-scale industrial enterprises – had achieved a position in which they could exercise a substantial degree of control over prices. In the conditions of industrial organization of the inter-war period, fewer and fewer enterprises were price-takers accepting passively the prices established by unregulated markets, and more and more had the power to be price-makers. Elements of monopoly in the system reduced the flexibility of prices and augmented the ability of sellers to resist pressures to reduce prices when demand slackened. This line of explanation gained status in the early 1930s with the publication of the theories of imperfect and monopolistic competition worked out by Joan Robinson in England and E. H. Chamberlin in the United States.

If economists were not well equipped to deal with massive unemployment, statesmen were even less adequately prepared. Officially most of them appealed for business confidence and invoked the familiar canons of orthodox economic policy: the balanced budget and monetary soundness. In their conduct of affairs governments often departed from tradition, though not without a sense of sin. The leaders of most Western states in this period sought desperately to remedy their own country's ills by restricting international transactions. By various protective devices – from increased tariff rates to currency devaluation – home industries were sheltered in the hope that employment would be stimulated. In fact, however, these beggar-thy-neighbour policies bred retaliation by other countries that curtailed the volume of international trade but neutralized most of the hoped-for gains in employment.

Behind the scenes, most Western governments were groping for fresh approaches and new solutions. The distress around them was too obvious and too urgent to be ignored. But a carefully worked out strategy for attacking the economic malaise was lacking. Some halting steps in the right direction were taken. Britain experimented with public works programmes, though on a modest scale, as job-creating devices. In the United States the Roosevelt administration, which had come into office pledged to balance the budget at a reduced level of public expenditure, took bold initiatives in using public works programmes to stimulate the economy. These daring experiments were refreshing departures from the conventional wisdom, but they had no analytical foundations. In the absence of a solid theoretical diagnosis of the economics of unemployment no rational means were available to distinguish promising policy remedies from the panaceas offered by cranks and crackpots.

Much of the historical significance of Keynes's *General Theory of Employment, Interest and Money* stems from the fact that it offered a fresh insight into the aggregative behaviour of the economic system and provided a theoretical underpinning for a programme of government action to promote full employment. Many of the specific policies Keynes prescribed had been recommended on intuitive grounds by others. But a new theoretical scheme was required before these remedies could be communicated with conviction. Without a Keynes, the course of recent history would have been vastly different.

CHAPTER 8

The Economics of Keynes's
General Theory

WITHOUT question, the greatest advances in economic thinking in the twentieth century have been associated with the name and work of John Maynard Keynes. His most important contributions were produced in the years of the Great Depression. It was then that he formulated his *General Theory of Employment, Interest and Money*, a work that broke sharply with the orthodox neo-classical tradition. The reorientation of approaches to economic policy in the past four decades has, in large measure, been shaped by Keynesian economic analysis.

1. JOHN MAYNARD KEYNES (1883–1946)

Throughout the greater part of his adult life, Keynes was associated with King's College, Cambridge. But his career was not that of a cloistered academic. Upon completion of his undergraduate studies in 1905, he joined the Civil Service and was assigned to the India Office. His first published works in economics – dealing with monetary questions in India – were a by-product of this experience. For a brief period before the First World War, he returned to Cambridge to take up a college fellowship, but shortly thereafter he was called back to public duties as an adviser to the Treasury. In this capacity he accompanied the British delegation to the Paris Peace Conference. He resigned this post in June 1919, in protest against terms of settlement with Germany that he regarded as vindictive, immoral and impracticable. His outspoken attack on the work of the conference in a book entitled *The Economic*

Consequences of the Peace made him both an international figure and *persona non grata* in British official circles for nearly two decades.

Between the wars Keynes divided his time between studies in economics and editorship of the journal of the Royal Economic Society, participation in public debates on the leading issues of the day, and the administration of the financial affairs of his Cambridge college. His early theoretical works were concerned with monetary and financial problems. His competence in these matters was by no means confined to theoretical analysis. Both his college's resources and his personal estate were considerably enriched by his skill in portfolio management. When he wrote of the significance of speculative activity (as he did in the *General Theory*), he knew whereof he spoke.

In 1940 Keynes re-entered public service as a principal economic adviser to the government. During the darkest days his main preoccupation was with the mobilization of the British economy in support of the war effort. In this task the tools of national income analysis he had forged proved to be invaluable. Later his attention shifted to post-war reconstruction of the international economy. The establishment of two institutions – the International Monetary Fund and the International Bank for Reconstruction and Development – owes much to his inspiration and to his powers of persuasion as a negotiator.

Even the most abbreviated sketch of Keynes's life would do the man less than justice should it fail to mention another facet of his interests. A distinguished bibliophile and patron of the arts himself, he was anxious that the arts should be adequately supported and that they should be accessible to a wide audience. His initiative was instrumental in the creation of the Arts Council.

As a literary craftsman, Keynes was also an artist in his own right. The quality of his prose is alone sufficient to assure him a unique place in the economists' hall of fame. This skill has been recognized by no less competent a critic than T. S. Eliot, who wrote of him: 'In one art, certainly, he had no reason to defer to any opinion: in expository prose he had the essential style of the clear mind which thinks structurally and respects the meaning of words.' [1] This quality of the man is reflected in a toast he once offered to his fellow economists, whom he described as 'the trustees, not of civilization, but of the possibility of civilization'.[2]

2. THE ANALYTICAL PROBLEM OF THE GENERAL THEORY

Keynes's principal work focused on one central issue: the determination of levels of national income and employment in industrial economies and the cause of economic fluctuations. Earlier schools of economic thought had given little systematic attention to this problem. The classicists were too preoccupied with questions of long-period economic growth to concern themselves directly with short-period instability; in any event – apart from the post-Napoleonic war years – the matter was not of major significance in their day and age. Marx came closer to Keynesian concerns but his work was always overlaid with the pre-judgement that the downfall of capitalism was inevitable; in his view widespread fluctuations were the result of an incurable malignancy within the capitalist system. Though some neo-classical writers made reference to 'industrial fluctuations' and to the 'inconstancy of employment', they were far more interested in the forces influencing output in particular markets than in those governing the output of the economy as a whole. Moreover, they were persuaded that full employment was the long-run equilibrium position toward which the economy naturally gravitated and their analysis was built on this premiss.

Even before his doubts about neo-classical presuppositions had crystallized, Keynes was suspicious of this attitude – 'in the long run,' he observed, 'we are all dead'. As his thought took shape in the *General Theory*, economic analysis was reconstructed to bring short-period aggregative problems to the centre of the stage. The microeconomic questions around which the neo-classical tradition had been organized were pushed toward the wings. At the same time, Keynes was at pains to dissociate his position from the Marxist contention that capitalism was doomed. The essentials of the system, he maintained, could be preserved if reforms were made in time. An unregulated capitalism, however, was incompatible with the maintenance of full employment and economic stability.

Keynes had moved part way towards this conclusion in the mid-1920s with the recognition that conventional *laissez-faire* was inadequate to the increasingly complex problems of industrialized societies. But his thought was then still in the mould of Marshallian neo-classicism. The writing of the *General Theory* in the early 1930s was, as he described it, 'a struggle of escape from habitual modes of thought and expression' [3] – a struggle made more difficult because 'I myself held with conviction for many years the theories which I now attack. . . .' [4] His professional upbringing had taught him to respect the analytical strengths of the neo-classical theory and alerted him to the sources of its staying power. As an elegant logical structure, it had an unquestioned appeal. Nevertheless, the neo-classical system (which in the *General Theory* he referred to as 'classical theory') Keynes held to represent 'the way in which we should like our Economy to behave. But to assume that it actually does so is to assume our difficulties away.' [5]

While Keynes declared war on the aggregative strand of the neo-classical tradition, it was not his objective to re-write neo-classical micro-economics. Apart from expressing reservations about its postulates on the degree of competition and their relevance to the prevailing market structure, he largely by-passed this component of the neo-classical model.

3. THE ATTACK ON SAY'S LAW AND THE INTERPRETATION OF MONEY

Keynes saw clearly that the mainstay of orthodox confidence in the self-adjusting properties of a market system to a full employment equilibrium was the neo-classical version of Say's Law and he made this strand of theory a primary target of criticism. As originally formulated, Say's Law had distinguished between 'general' and 'partial' overproduction; the former was held to be impossible, while the latter – though it could occur – could not persist in an economy in which there were no significant impediments to the mobility of productive resources.

Subsequent re-interpretations of Say's Law (and particularly the version implicit in latter-day neo-classical thought) could be translated into the proposition that all income would be spent. In other words, there would be no important leakages from the income stream in the form of hoarding. In standard neo-classical reasoning this conclusion was held to be a self-evident truth. It was not, of course, denied that an occasional miser might mar the image. But this type of behaviour could be dismissed as irrational and likely to be so rare that, for all practical purposes, it could be ignored. After all, who in his right mind would accumulate idle funds in substantial volume when, by lending them, he could add to his income? Consumption expenditure was the main object of economic activity. Rational economic agents could only be induced to restrain their consumption – i.e. to save part of their income – when offered a reward in the form of a rate of interest for so doing.

Around these postulates the whole structure of neo-classical thinking about saving and investment in the aggregate had been built. The community was expected to respond positively to higher rewards for saving; an increase in the rate of interest would swell the volume of loanable funds. Borrowers, on the other hand, would adjust the quantity of loanable funds for which they were prepared to pay as the rate of interest changed; at low rates of interest the quantity of loanable funds demanded would be augmented and at higher rates, curtailed. The rate of interest was thus interpreted as a sensitive mechanism for producing an equilibrium between saving and investment. In turn, this equilibrium insured that the portion of income not spent on consumption goods would be spent on investment goods.[6]

This line of argument was further reinforced by the standard neo-classical interpretation of the role of money. In this view the primary function of money was as a medium of exchange. It was sought for the command over goods and services that it provided. But money *per se* was sterile and lacking in intrinsic value. This perspective, of course, was both consistent and closely inter-related with the judgement that hoarding was irrational. Money was economically interesting only as it was spent and circulated throughout the system. Indeed, this presupposition underlay the various versions of the quantity theory of money worked out by neo-classical economists.

Keynes's assault on the Say's Law tradition centred on this analysis of money. He set about the task by reversing the perspective from which money was viewed. Whereas neo-classical writers looked first at money in motion – i.e. when spent – Keynes chose to analyse money as it was held. The primary question to be answered was: how and for what reasons is the community induced to hold the stock of money that exists at a given moment? Obviously the community required some minimum stock of money to lubricate the wheels of commerce and to provide a reserve against contingencies. These motives for holding money were thoroughly compatible with neo-classical thinking. But Keynes insisted that there was also another reason for holding cash – the speculative motive for liquidity. This concept was essential to the opening of space for the analytical innovations of the *General Theory*.

Why should anyone wish to hold money in excess of

the amounts required for transactions and precautionary purposes when he sacrificed thereby an income he might have gained as a lender? Keynes's reply rested on the inverse relationship between interest rates and the capital values of paper assets. The essentials of the point he had in mind can most readily be conveyed through a moment's consideration of the yield and market price on a consol (a type of government debt issue familiar in Britain, though not in the United States). As a negotiable perpetual bond the consol is convenient for purposes of illustration because it permits the general principle to be established without the complications presented when debts with differing maturity dates enter the picture.

For purposes of argument, let us assume that a 3 per cent consol has been issued at a par value of £100; i.e. the holder is assured of £3 per year. Let it further be assumed that, subsequently, the rate of interest on new debt of comparable quality rises to 6 per cent. The holder of the 3 per cent consol, should he wish to sell, would be exposed to a considerable capital loss. At interest rates now prevailing those seeking an assured income of £3 per year could obtain it by placing £50 and would not be prepared to pay more for the consol originally valued at £100. Actual – as opposed to hypothetical – market situations are, of course, less tidy because of the variety of paper assets of widely differing quality available as alternatives to holding cash. Nevertheless, there will still be a tendency for interest rates and capital values on interest-bearing assets to move in opposite directions. Rising interest rates will be associated with capital losses to the holders of old issues, while falling interest rates will bring windfall gains. In the light of this relationship Keynes argued that there might be circumstances in which it would be prudent to hoard as a hedge against risks of capital loss. Indeed the speculative motive for liquidity might be forceful when the rate of interest was already low (and the sacrifice of income through hoarding was not great) and when it was thought that rates of interest in the future would probably move up (and expose the owners of debt instruments to substantial capital losses).

When this consideration was taken into account, money could no longer be interpreted exclusively as a medium of exchange. Instead it also performed an important function as a store of value. This insight undercut the line of reasoning upon which Say's Law had rested. Hoarding could no longer be ruled out by assumption, nor treated as an irrational activity. Once this link in the neo-classical analytical chain had been broken, confidence in the self-adjusting properties of the economy to a full-employment level of equilibrium could no longer be sustained. On the contrary, an underemployed economy might tend to get stuck at a level of income well below its potential if part of its income stream leaked into the build-up of idle hoards.

In developing this view of money Keynes found intellectual companions among mercantilist writers of the seventeenth and eighteenth centuries. He was prepared to argue that the mercantilist tradition contained clearer insights into the nature of money than those offered by the teachings of the classical and neo-classical schools. In doing this he associated himself with doctrines that had been viewed as heresy for more than a century and a half.

4. THE RE-INTERPRETATION OF THE RATE OF INTEREST

Both the Keynesian model and the aggregative strand of the neo-classical system manipulated the same variables: income, saving, investment, money, and the rate of interest. These pieces of analytical furniture, however, occupied quite different places on the stage. Shifting the relationships between any of them meant that new positions had to be found for them all.

It is already apparent that Keynes gave a different twist to one of the variables – money. His view of money, in turn, opened up a new perspective on the rate of interest.

He described the problem in the following manner: 'The habit of overlooking the relation of the rate of interest to hoarding may be part of the explanation why interest has been usually regarded as the reward of not-spending, whereas in fact it is the reward of not-hoarding'.[7]

But how was the level of the rate of interest determined? As Keynes saw the matter, the rate of interest was governed – not by the supply of and demand for loanable funds (as neo-classical writers had maintained) – but by the supply of and demand for money. The supply of money (consisting of currency and coin issued by governments and bank money held in the form of checking accounts) could, of course, be regulated by the government and the central bank. The demand for money, on the other hand, was established by the preferences of the community. At any moment, of course, all of the money in existence would be held by someone. But it did not necessarily follow that those who held money would wish to continue to do so. At the earliest opportunity they might prefer to exchange money for goods or for income-yielding assets. The explanation of the determination of an equilibrium between the supply and demand for money called for an answer to the question: what factors would induce the public to hold the available stock of money?

In working out a solution to this puzzle, Keynes built further on the foundation laid by his revisionist interpretation of the motives for holding money. The amount of money the public would be prepared to hold was, he maintained, governed by two factors: the level of national income and the rate of interest. The community clearly required a certain stock of money for transactions and precautionary purposes and the amounts required were likely to vary with the level of economic activity. In all probability, rising national income would swell these components of the demand for money and falling national income would diminish them. But the public might also demand money for speculative reasons. Balances held in this form amounted to hoarding and their size was likely to be influenced primarily by the rate of interest and by expectations about its future course. At high rates of interest the community was likely to prefer income-yielding assets to idle balances. At low rates of interest, on the other hand, hoarding might be preferred as a safeguard against possible capital losses.

An example may be helpful in conveying the Keynesian argument on the mechanics of this process. Let us suppose that the monetary authorities increase the supply of money (say by buying government securities held by the banks or by the public and thus increasing the money balances of those who formerly held these securities). How would a new equilibrium position be reached? In the absence of a change in national income there would be no reason to expect a change in the amount of money the public would be prepared to hold for transactions and precautionary purposes. Presumably, many of those who received increased money balances in exchange for government securities would prefer to hold income-yielding assets. As they acquired them, however, the market price of these assets would be bid up; simultaneously, the effective rate of interest would be depressed. Lower rates of interest would reduce the reward for parting with liquidity. This adjustment, in turn, would increase the willingness of the community to hold an enlarged quantity of money. Through this process of interaction between interest rates and the supply of money a new equilibrium would be established at which the increased supply of money could be absorbed into the system.

This interpretation of the determination of interest rates completely scuttled the orthodox neo-classical view that interest rates were established by the interaction of the demand for and supply of loanable funds. The Keynesian argument held that the rate of interest was primarily a monetary phenomenon – and one, moreover, detached from the real factors of thrift and the productivity of capital to which the neo-classical mind had linked it. This position further implied that the rate of interest could no

longer be invoked as the delicate mechanism for equilibrating intended saving and intended investment. These
relationships played no part in the determination of the
rate of interest itself. Saving and investment might respond
to changes in the rate of interest but they were not its
primary determinants.

In addition this analysis implied that the ability of the
monetary authorities to influence interest rates might, in
periods of depression, be severely restricted. The Central
Bank could continue to expand the money supply. But if
the increment simply swelled idle balances, no reduction
in interest rates would ensue. The economic system would
find itself locked into what Keynes described as a 'liquidity
trap'. This situation might arise for institutional reasons
quite independent of the intentions of the parties directly
involved. Banks, for example, do not exist to hold idle
balances; on the contrary, they seek to augment their
earnings by lending at interest. In the circumstances of a
deep depression, however, their ability to lend is curtailed
because the pool of eligible borrowers largely dries up.
Involuntarily banks may thus find themselves holding idle
balances in substantial volume as excess reserves. While
it is still possible for bankers to acquire earning assets
(such as government securities) with idle reserves, this
course may not be desirable if the market prices of fixed-
interest assets are already high and interest rates low.
Financial institutions, no less than the public at large,
may choose to protect themselves against capital losses by
hoarding for speculative reasons.

5. THE KEYNESIAN ANALYSIS OF SAVING AND CONSUMPTION

With his monetary theory of interest Keynes unhinged
saving and investment from their neo-classical moorings.
He was therefore obliged to supply some new connexions
to explain the determination of these two variables. Only
after this manoeuvre had been satisfactorily executed was

he equipped to present an alternative theory of the determination of national income.

In neo-classical thought, the rate of interest had been regarded as the primary regulator of the volume of saving. This is not to say that neo-classical writers entirely neglected changes in national income as an influence on saving. But this relationship was given little attention and, within the framework of their thought, for ample reason. National income, after all, was regarded as a rather stable variable, fluctuating only slightly and temporarily from the normal equilibrium of full employment. Fortified by this presupposition, it appeared to be more pertinent to concentrate attention on the rate of interest. Once Keynes had demonstrated that equilibrium at full employment was far from assured – indeed it was perhaps the least likely of a range of possibilities – the emphasis assigned to income and to the rate of interest in the interpretation of savings decisions was reversed. The level of income became the crucial determinant, while the rate of interest was cast in a secondary role.

Keynes's decision to tie the theory of savings more closely to the level of income had more than this analytical reason to recommend it. He also argued that this interpretation offered a more realistic account of the behaviour of savers than did the neo-classical explanation. Few people, he maintained, were highly sensitive to interest rate changes in their decisions to save. 'Interest to-day', he argued, 'rewards no genuine sacrifice, any more than does the rent of land.' [8] In his view, people sought first an acceptable level of consumption and undertook to save only when their income was more than sufficient to cover consumption requirements. Saving was thus a residual, varying in amount with changes in the level of income. Few people were likely to be influenced by changes in the rate of interest when allocating their income between consumption and saving.

An important corollary was attached to this part of Keynes's argument. Not only was the level of income the most forceful influence on the volume of saving but – as income rose – saving was likely to rise both absolutely and as a proportion of income. Expenditures on consumption, though still rising in absolute terms, would claim a diminishing share of total income. This point had sweeping implications for a rich society's efforts to achieve and maintain full employment. It indicated that a high and rising volume of investment expenditure would be required to bring saving and investment into equilibrium with one another at a full employment level of activity. As Keynes saw the problem:

... the richer the community, the wider will tend to be the gap between its actual and its potential production; and therefore the more obvious and outrageous the defects of the economic system. For a poor community will be prone to consume by far the greater part of its output, so that a very modest measure of investment will be sufficient to provide full employment; whereas a wealthy community will have to discover much ampler opportunities for investment if the saving propensities of its wealthier members are to be compatible with the employment of its poorer members.[9]

6. THE DETERMINATION OF INVESTMENT

In the neo-classical tradition, as we have seen, decisions to save and to invest were interpreted as determined by the same influence: the rate of interest. It could thus be argued that the economic system, by its nature, would tend to produce an automatic equilibrium between saving and investment. Keynes shattered the symmetry of this argument by severing the link between saving and the rate of interest. Decisions to save and to invest, he maintained, were largely independent of one another and often undertaken by different groups of people for quite different reasons.

If the rate of interest now largely dropped out of the account of saving it still retained an important place in investment analysis. On this point Keynes accepted much of the neo-classical approach. His argument presupposed that the volume of private investment would be governed largely by two considerations – the cost of borrowing and the anticipated rate of return. If expected net yields exceeded the cost of capital (i.e. the rate of interest) then capital expenditures would be worthwhile; on the other hand, should the rate of interest exceed expected rates of return, spending on plant, equipment, and inventories would not be undertaken.

This element of continuity between the Keynesian and neo-classical systems should not, however, conceal an important difference in their interpretations of the expected rate of return on investment (in Keynes's terminology, the marginal efficiency of capital). At first glance it might appear that Keynes worked with a concept closely allied to the neo-classical notion of the marginal productivity of capital. In part, he had this relationship in mind; as the capital stock grew (other things being equal), he expected that returns to the additional units would tend to fall. But his concept also embraced another matter relevant to the analysis of investment decisions – the expectations of entrepreneurs. Keynes insisted that 'the most important confusion concerning the meaning and significance of the marginal efficiency of capital has ensued on the failure to see that it depends on the *prospective* yield of capital, and not merely on its current yield'.[10]

Throughout his work Keynes assigned much more weight to the influence of psychological factors on the economic process than had his neo-classical predecessors. Just as expectations were crucial to his discussion of liquidity preference, so also did they lie at the core of his investment analysis. On this basis Keynes could assert that investment expenditures might not be undertaken even when conventional calculations of returns indicated them to be profitable. This might occur if entrepreneurial expectations were bearish. Fears of capital loss might then deter outlays which, on paper, appeared to be attractive.

It will be recalled that neo-classical writers commented on the waves of optimism and pessimism within the business community in their discussions of cyclical fluctuations. These disturbances, of course, were always assumed to be confined within narrow limits. No cases of extreme and stubborn unemployment had then been experienced and there was little reason to attach major importance to psychological considerations. Keynes saw the problem quite differently. Once he had established that the equilibrium level of income was subject to a wide range of variation it was possible to argue that entrepreneurial temperament was both volatile and highly important to the behaviour of the economy. Indeed the marginal efficiency of capital was so much a matter of expectations that the shifting moods of the business community might easily swamp the rate of interest's influence on investment expenditure.

This phenomenon highlighted one of the central policy concerns of Keynesian analysis. High levels of income were likely to generate savings in substantial volume. If full employment was to be achieved, investment expenditure on a scale sufficient to match a full-employment level of saving would be necessary. There was little basis for confidence, however, that investment spending in the amounts required for full employment would be undertaken on private initiative. As capital accumulated, the marginal rate of return would be expected to decline unless the offsets provided by technological progress were forceful. Moreover, it could not safely be assumed that substantial increases in investment could be induced by monetary measures designed to lower the costs of borrowing. In the circumstances of a depression, bearish entrepreneurial expectations might neutralize the effects of reductions in interest rates. An active monetary policy to push interest rates down was still desirable. But it was important to recognize the limitations of this procedure. Should the situation of the liquidity trap be approximated, monetary measures would be incapable of reducing interest rates.

In short, conventional techniques of economic policy were insufficient to remedy the deficiency of aggregate demand. A more active role for government as a spender was called for if prosperity was to be restored. Keynes maintained:

> Whilst, therefore, the enlargement of the functions of government, involved in the task of adjusting to one another the propensity to consume and the inducement to invest, would seem to a nineteenth century publicist or to a contemporary American financier to be a terrific encroachment on individualism, I defend it, on the contrary, both as the only practicable means of avoiding the destruction of existing economic forms in their entirety and as the condition of the successful functioning of individual initiative.
>
> For if effective demand is deficient, not only is the public scandal of wasted resources intolerable, but the individual enterpriser who seeks to bring these resources into action is operating with the odds loaded against him.[11]

7. KEYNESIAN ANALYSIS AND THE DETERMINATION OF AGGREGATIVE EQUILIBRIUM

Though so fundamentally different in many important respects, Keynes and the neo-classical writers spoke in unison in their definitions of aggregative equilibrium. In both traditions the necessary condition was an equilibrium between intended saving and intended investment. Neo-classical economists maintained that this equilibrium was achieved through allegedly sensitive adjustments in the rate of interest. Keynes, having severed the direct connexion between saving and the rate of interest, was obliged to offer an alternative account of the mechanisms for the determination of equilibrium.

Stated in its simplest form, Keynes's alternative solution linked the mechanism of adjustment to variations in the level of income. Neo-classical writers, of course, had largely neglected this relationship as, within the framework of their thought, national income was subject to fluctuation only within rather narrow limits. For Keynes, on the other hand, a wide spectrum of equilibrium income positions was possible. The pertinent question was: at what level would equilibrium in the national income be established?

Keynes's development of this problem drew upon the concept of the multiplier first formulated by his Cambridge colleague, R. F. Kahn. The essentials of this ingenious argument can be set out in a simple example. Let it be assumed that an initial equilibrium between intended saving and intended investment is disturbed by the decision of investors to spend more on plant and equipment. What adjustments would then follow? Clearly an increase in investment expenditure would add to total income. But the achievement of a new equilibrium would require saving to rise by as much as investment had increased. This condition could be satisfied when income had risen enough to generate the required increment in saving. How much would income have to grow before equilibrium was restored? The multiplier concept permitted a theoretically precise answer to be given. If, for example, the community saved one-third of its incremental income and consumed two-thirds, total income would grow by three times the amount of the increase in investment spending. In other words, changes in investment had a multiple effect on income.

The mechanics of this process can also be illustrated in more everyday terms. An increase in investment expenditure will generate higher total demand and call for more workers and more raw materials in the industries producing capital goods. A substantial part of the additional income paid out to workers and suppliers of raw materials is likely to be spent. Additional rounds of spending and re-spending are thus likely to follow. In this manner the stimulus of increased investment radiates throughout the economy, raising income and employment.

The magnitude and timing of the increase in national income touched off by a rise in investment expenditure would, of course, be affected by a number of factors —

among them, the lags between the receipt of income and its expenditure. Obviously a considerable time period would be required before the total process of expansion had worked itself out. The pace and magnitude of the rise in income might also be dampened by leakages from the expenditure stream. Part of the additional spending, for example, might be directed to imported rather than to home-produced goods. To that extent, the stimulus to domestic income and employment would be weakened. Though the multiplier does not operate quite as tidily in practice as it appears in theory, it highlights relationships that are vital to an understanding of economic fluctuations.

Keynes used the multiplier concept to explain the manner in which the level of income was determined and to emphasize the crucial importance of investment expenditure to recovery from depression. The same analytical argument, however, can be applied to a fully employed economy. In such circumstances, an increase in investment would still have multiplier effects but only an increase in money income would then be produced. Prices would be bid up, but real output could not be augmented to match the increase in demand.[12]

Later theoretical writing has integrated the Keynesian multiplier scheme with a concept known as the 'acceleration principle'. Whereas the multiplier is concerned with the connexion between changes in investment and subsequent spending on consumption, the acceleration principle refers to the manner in which increases in income and consumption may also stimulate investment and give rise to further rounds of income expansion. This line of analysis is perfectly compatible with the argument of the *General Theory*, though Keynes did not make use of it. J. B. Clark, writing in 1916, had spelled out the basic structure of the accelerator mechanism. Keynes may perhaps be excused for his failure to draw upon this insight in the 1930s. His concern was then with the problems of a depression economy. In such circumstances, the accelerator is unlikely to have a forceful impact until income has risen enough to wipe out idle plant capacity. So long as excess capacity exists the growth in demand generated by rising income can be satisfied without additional investment to augment productive capacity.

Keynes's analysis of the determination of aggregative equilibrium opened an entirely new vista for economic investigation and inquiry. For the first time, income was recognized as a primary variable and one, moreover, that was subject to extreme fluctuations. The prominence assigned to changes in national income in the Keynesian theoretical system gave quite a different orientation to a number of familiar analytical building blocks. The treatment of the rate of interest in the Keynesian model provides a significant case in point. Keynes denied that it had much influence on decisions to save and consume, but it did not follow from this conclusion that the rate of interest bore no connexion with saving. He maintained that:

> . . . the influence of moderate changes in the rate of interest on the *propensity* to consume is usually small. It does not mean that changes in the rate of interest have only a small influence on the amounts *actually* saved and consumed. Quite the contrary. The influence of changes in the rate of interest on the amount actually saved is of paramount importance, but is *in the opposite direction* to that usually supposed. For even if the attraction of the larger future income to be earned from a higher rate of interest has the effect of diminishing the propensity to consume, nevertheless we can be certain that a rise in the rate of interest will have the effect of reducing the amount actually saved.[13]

The resolution of this apparent paradox can be seen when one considers the nature of the Keynesian argument on the determination of aggregative equilibrium. Investment can be influenced by changes in interest rates. Thus, should a fall in rates of interest stimulate activity, national income would grow via the multiplier process. Higher levels of income, in turn, would produce a larger volume of saving. This result would follow from the establishment of a new equilibrium at increased levels of investment and income. A connexion between interest rates and saving was thus retained, but in a manner far removed from the one neo-classical economists had in mind. In the Keynesian formulation the causal linkage was indirect, running from interest rates to investment, from investment to aggregate income, and from aggregate income to actual saving.

8. THE KEYNESIAN THEORY OF EMPLOYMENT

In the discussion thus far, much has been said about the determination of national income, but nothing directly about the level of employment. As its title indicated, the *General Theory* was intended as an analysis of employment in the first instance. Quite clearly variations in the level of economic activity have a major impact on employment and unemployment. But Keynes was fully aware that the relationship between national income and the aggregate demand for labour was difficult to establish precisely. In his search for leverage on this problem he introduced the concept of the wage unit.

As an analytical device, the Keynesian wage unit has much in common with the manoeuvres performed by those classical economists who attempted to measure the value of goods in terms of labour. They were obliged to explain how various grades and skills of labour could be reduced to a common denominator. Normally, they treated an hour of unskilled labour as the basic unit. The same unit of time input on the part of members of the labour force whom the market rewarded more highly could be expressed as a multiple of the standard unit. In most classical accounts, however, this technique was not free of internal contradiction.

Keynes adopted a similar procedure for purposes of relating the volume of employment to national income. Differentiation within the labour force could be accommodated by assigning higher weights to the time inputs of persons possessing the more highly remunerated skills.[14] Keynes was on more secure logical ground in this exercise than were the classical economists. The latter were at a loss to find a basis for the weighting of skills without appealing to valuations assigned by market place. This introduced supply and demand considerations into an argument which was supposedly based exclusively on physical inputs. Keynes, who had no interest in searching for a criterion of value independent of the market, was not troubled by this complication.

This procedure, though logically sound, was still not ideal. Empirically the relationship between changes in income and changes in employment has been found to be far from tight. The relationship breaks down most conspicuously when employment is reckoned (as it commonly is in popular discussions as well as in official statistics) in terms of the number of persons at work. Employment, when calculated in Keynesian wage units, can be linked more reliably to changes in income. For practical purposes this technique of measurement – in terms of the number of standard hours of labour employed – is unwieldy. None of the employment statistics presently gathered lend themselves to a wage unit type of measurement without enormously time-consuming adjustments.

9. THE IMPLICATIONS OF THE ANALYSIS FOR ECONOMIC POLICY

Keynes's work had clearly assaulted the main props to confidence in the usual instruments of economic policy. The major policy weapon in the orthodox arsenal – i.e. monetary controls – could now be seen to be too blunt to be fully effective. As the argument of the *General Theory* had demonstrated, the power of the monetary authorities to influence the rate of interest (and thereby to affect investment spending) was limited. It was most seriously handicapped, of course, during periods of depression.

When the liquidity trap emerged, the rate of interest could be pushed no lower. While the monetary authorities could add to the supply of money, they were unable to control the demand for money.

But this was not the only point at which reliance on monetary policy was attacked. No less important was the Keynesian argument that highly volatile expectations were likely to have a forceful bearing on decisions to invest. Indeed, reductions in the rate of interest, though desirable as stimulants to investment, might be more than offset by increasing bearishness within the business community.

If full employment and economic stability were to be achieved, it was imperative to assign a much more active role to fiscal policy. By contrast with orthodox views holding that governments should operate with balanced budgets, Keynes called for deliberate deficits to swell aggregate demand. He recognized, however, that public expenditure financed by borrowing would have favourable effects on total demand only to the extent that a net increase in total spending was thereby accomplished. Should projects launched by governments merely displace those that would otherwise have been undertaken by the private sector, the intended growth in total spending would not be realized. Moreover, he was also cognizant of the political resistance his recommendations were likely to encounter. Some types of non-conventional measures might be more acceptable, though less beneficial to society, than others – a consideration which brought out the puckish quality in his style:

If the Treasury were to fill old bottles with banknotes, bury them at suitable depths in disused coal-mines which are then filled up to the surface with town rubbish, and leave it to private enterprise on well-tried principles of *laissez-faire* to dig the notes up again (the right to do so being obtained, of course, by tendering the leases of the note-bearing territory), there need be no more unemployment and, with the help of the repercussions, the real income of the community, and its capital wealth also, would probably become a good deal greater than it actually is. It would, indeed, be more sensible to build houses and the like; but if there are political and practical difficulties in the way of this, the above would be better than nothing.[15]

Keynes called for a re-thinking of the instruments of economic policy and for the rejection of the policy prescriptions associated with neo-classical analysis. Not only did he warn against excessive reliance on monetary controls, but he also attacked vigorously the view that unemployment could be cured through measures aimed at the inflexibility of wages. He regarded trade unions as legitimate bargaining agents and their role in wage-setting to be an established institutional fact. But quite independent of the existence of labour organizations he maintained that wage-cutting offered no cure for unemployment. Such tactics were more likely to aggravate the problem by curtailing effective demand still further.

The results of a programme of wage reduction would, of course, be happier if real wages did not fall – i.e. if output prices fell by at least as much as money wages. But this outcome was doubtful in view of the substantial market power exercised by many businessmen and their reluctance to reduce prices in face of declining demand. But even if the economic system approximated to perfect competition more closely than was in fact the case, price reductions might still have unfortunate consequences. Price cutting was likely to have depressing effects on expectations and would increase the real burden of outstanding debt. Investment on the scale required to restore full employment might thus be discouraged.

10. THE LARGER CONSEQUENCES

The message of the *General Theory* was sharply critical of unregulated *laissez-faire*. Most neo-classical theorists, it will be recalled, expressed reservations about the circumstances in which unchecked market arrangements could be counted on to yield socially desirable results. Their anxieties, however, were usually associated with the consequences of growth of large-scale enterprises. The usual rules of competitive behaviour could not be expected to apply to these situations and a case could be made for public regulation or ownership.

Keynes's critique of *laissez-faire* rested on quite different foundations. The burden of his argument was to demonstrate that an unregulated market system was likely to be chronically unstable and incapable of assuring the full utilization of productive resources. Not only did his analysis demonstrate the need for active government intervention in the economy, but it also proclaimed that thrift was not necessarily a social virtue. Indeed, when resources were under-employed, thrift was a social vice. To a public schooled in the puritan ethic, this insight was not easy to grasp.

It is not remarkable that these unconventional views should have been misunderstood when first expounded. Some critics regarded Keynes's doctrines as dangerously radical and as a threat to the perpetuation of a capitalist order. A considered judgement of the content of Keynes's thought supports quite the opposite conclusion. Revolutionary though the *General Theory* was in its approach to economic analysis, the policy recommendations derived from it were largely prompted by conservative considerations. Keynes hoped that the essential features of the capitalist system could be preserved. But its virtues could be safeguarded only if the social unrest generated by mass unemployment could be eliminated by appropriate reforms. *Laissez-faire*, as he had demonstrated, was essentially a fair weather system. It was capable of remarkably productive performance when conditions were favourable, but it was also inherently unstable. Governments had a major responsibility for regulating the economic climate in ways that would permit the market system to achieve its full potential.

In large measure Keynesian teaching has been absorbed

into economic thought and policy in most Western countries. Indeed, the adoption of a Keynesian approach by Western governments has not been least among the factors responsible for the high degree of stability exhibited by their economies in the years since the Second World War.

Notes

1. As quoted in *John Maynard Keynes, 1883–1946: Fellow and Bursar* (A Memoir Prepared by Direction of the Council of King's College, Cambridge, 1949), pp. 38–9.

2. R. F. Harrod, *The Life of John Maynard Keynes* (Macmillan, London, 1951), p. 194.

3. Keynes, *General Theory*, p. 8.

4. ibid., pp. v–vi.

5. ibid., p. 34.

6. Following standard neo-classical procedure, the influence of governments as spenders and taxers is not taken into account directly in the illustrations above. This line of argument does not assume governments out of existence, but rather that balanced budgets will mean that the influence of governments on total spending is neutral – i.e., what is withdrawn in taxes is replaced by government expenditure. Later analysis has demonstrated, however, that the presumed neutrality of balanced budgets is erroneous.

7. ibid., p. 174.

8. ibid., p. 376.

9. ibid., p. 31.

10. ibid., p. 141.

11. ibid., pp. 380–81.

12. The discussion above has focused on investment as the crucial variable in the multiplier process. Keynes placed the main weight of his own analysis on this aspect of the problem. Multiplier effects on income can also be produced by changes in the community's propensity to save when investment plans are constant. The analysis of the path back to a new equilibrium level of income is directly analogous.

13. ibid., p. 110.

14. '. . . in so far as different grades and kinds of labour and salaried assistance enjoy a more or less fixed relative

remuneration, the quantity of employment can be sufficiently defined for our purpose by taking an hour's employment of ordinary labour as our unit and weighting an hour's employment of special labour in proportion to its remuneration; i.e., an hour of special labour remunerated at double ordinary rates will count as two units.' (ibid., p. 41.)

15. ibid., p. 129.

Postscript to Keynesian Economics

The central focus of Keynes's pathbreaking work was on the determination of national income, with particular reference to the circumstances of deep depression. This preoccupation has prompted some commentators to challenge the accuracy of the title of the *General Theory* and to contend that Keynesian analysis is really the economics of a special case. Keynes himself lent support to this interpretation when, in the concluding pages of that work, he wrote:

> Our criticism of the accepted classical theory of economics has consisted not so much in finding logical flaws in its analysis as in pointing out that its tacit assumptions are seldom or never satisfied, with the result that it cannot solve the economic problems of the actual world. But if our central controls succeed in establishing an aggregate volume of output corresponding to full employment as nearly as is practicable, the classical theory comes into its own again from this point onwards.*

For once Keynes claimed too little. In a formal sense it is correct that circumstances of full employment reinstate the postulates of neo-classical analysis and dissolve the unique feature of the Keynesian model, i.e. the possibility of a liquidity trap based on hoarding. Nevertheless, Keynesian analysis cannot accurately be described as exclusively the economics of unemployment. The problems of a full-employed system can also be instructively analysed with the macro-economic tools he forged.

In his post-*General Theory* writings, Keynes charted directions in which his aggregative concepts could be

* Keynes, *General Theory*, p. 378.

adapted to other situations. During the war years he applied them to the problems of managing a fully employed economy. Similarly, he stimulated a substantial revision in the theory of international trade. From a Keynesian point of view, the process of balance of payments adjustment could more usefully be traced through changes in aggregate income associated with surpluses or deficits in the international accounts than through gold movements and the ancillary monetary and price changes to which the neo-classical economists had directed attention.

In at least two respects, however, there is substance to the charge that the analytical structure of the *General Theory* is more partial than general. In the first place the scope of this work was deliberately restricted to a time span of six to nine months. For this reason it was appropriate for Keynes's purposes to consider only one aspect of investment expenditure – namely its income-generating properties via the multiplier process – and to ignore the longer-term effects of investment spending on the economy's stock of productive assets. Secondly, the *General Theory*, when viewed as an analytical system, can quite rightly be regarded as less comprehensive than the other master models because of its neglect of micro-economic analysis. Though Keynes ruptured the neo-classical symmetry between micro- and macro-economics, he provided no integrated analytical reconstruction to replace it. Around both of these issues a substantial debate has subsequently revolved.

The first of these analytical omissions has largely been taken care of by the growth models developed by Professor Evsey Domar in the United States and by Sir Roy Harrod in Britain. These schemes are built on Keynesian conceptual foundations but raise a further question: once a full employment level of economic activity has been achieved, what conditions must be satisfied if it is to be sustained? This problem is addressed by examining the dual properties of investment expenditure: on the demand side it generates income through the Keynesian multiplier; on the supply side it augments productive capacity. If full employment is to be maintained through time, equilibrium between aggregate demand and aggregate supply must be achieved. With a few simplifying assumptions and a bit of algebraic manipulation, it can be demonstrated that the equilibrium rate of growth in national income equals the ratio of saving to income divided by the ratio of capital to the value of output.

These formulations – which are clearly of Keynesian parentage – have been widely used in discussions of planning for economic growth in a number of countries. In the United States this apparatus has supplied the framework of ideas underlying projections for growth in gross national product prepared by the President's Council of Economic Advisers. Similar procedures have been used by the British National Economic Development Council. Much the same type of analytical framework has also been extended to long-term planning operations in parts of the underdeveloped world. Among the countries which have devised ambitious long-term development plans – India and Nigeria are pertinent cases in point – the mould within which the economy is cast for planning purposes has owed much to the apparatus provided by post Keynesian growth models. Once a targeted rate of growth in national income and product has been established and estimates of the likely values of the capital-output ratio and of the saving-income ratio have been worked out, this type of model provides criteria against which the consistency of various components can be checked.

In a similar vein Keynes's kit of aggregative concepts has provided the point of departure for much of the discussion of inflationary tendencies exhibited by a number of advanced economies since the Second World War. While Keynesian notions of aggregate savings, investment, and consumption have been common to most of these analyses, many economists have sought to move beyond a simple explanation of inflation in terms of excessive aggregate demand. Several competing schools have emerged which attempt to link the behaviour of the aggregative variables to nodes of unchecked market power. One, for example, pins the main responsibility for upward pressures on prices to organized labour, arguing that trade union bargaining pushes up costs which are passed on to consumers through increased prices; another traces the trouble to the prevalence of monopolistic sellers who possess the ability to administer prices. On these points, Keynesian economics *per se* – by virtue of its neglect of micro-economic relationships – has nothing fresh to contribute.

Keynes's failure to provide a systematic link between macro- and micro-economics has left an opening for a neo-classical type of counter-attack. Much of the ensuing controversy has centred on the analysis of the rate of interest, the theoretical lynch-pin of Keynes's most revolutionary innovations. What is now labelled as the 'neo-classical synthesis' attempts to reinstate the rate of interest as a sensitive regulator of economic activity, though the argument is now more subtle than in the days before the *General Theory* challenged Say's Law. In the up-dated version the equilibrating tendencies of the rate of interest embrace the relationship between changes in capital values of paper assets and decisions to consume. A person who observes an appreciation in the value of his portfolio as interest rates fall, it is maintained, is likely to spend more freely than he would otherwise have done. This phenomenon, in turn, might more than offset tendencies for idle balances to accumulate (and for a liquidity trap to emerge). Keynes dealt with this line of criticism with the argument that the impact of interest rate variations on consumption was likely to be too limited and too delayed to forestall substantial fluctuations in economic activity. Moreover, when fluctuations occurred, the remedies of fiscal policy would be more effective than those of monetary policy. The neo-classical revivalists do not, of course, maintain that substantial underemployment can never exist. Instead it is asserted that the market system is sufficiently sensitive to assure full employment so long as wages and prices are perfectly flexible. In the world in which we live, this requirement would be extremely difficult to satisfy. Indeed the mere attempt to give it reality might have highly destabilizing consequences. However appealing the logical symmetry of the neo-classical system may be, its applicability to real problems is limited.

In most Western economies Keynesian theory has laid the intellectual foundations for a managed and welfare-oriented form of capitalism. Indeed, the widespread absorption of the Keynesian message has in large measure been responsible for the generally high levels of employment achieved by most Western industrial economies since the Second World War and for a significant reorientation in attitudes toward the role of the state in economic life. It is not yet clear whether the extension of a Keynesian analytical framework to the underdeveloped economies will have consequences equally as fortunate. Keynes, of course, fixed his own sights on the problems of highly organized industrial economies and, even in this setting, his central concern was with short-period stabilization at full employment. Many of the special problems of the underdeveloped parts of the world can be brought into clearer focus with other types of models. In fact, some of the extensions of the Keynesian aggregative reasoning – such as those suggesting that all important economic problems in the underdeveloped countries will solve themselves if the ratio of net investment to national income is raised above a critical minimum percentage – have detracted attention from prevalent institutional rigidities and from the long-term consequences of unprecedented rates of population growth. After all, a Keynesian aggregative framework is not ideally suited for close contact with questions dealing with efficient resource allocation or with long-period dynamic growth.

Keynesian theory has accomplished a great deal – but it is by no means the last word on the subject of aggregative

economics. In the four decades since the publication of
the *General Theory*, its findings have been embellished,
refined, and modified. The economists who have undertaken these tasks have paid to Keynes the highest tribute
any theorist can ever expect: the questions they have
attempted to answer are the ones he inspired.

Epilogue

The house of economic theory has many mansions. In this book we have considered the structure of four of them. Future generations, no doubt, will witness the building of new additions. Nevertheless, the structures already available provide ample room for adaptation to problems quite different from the ones their original designers had in mind.

The sometimes turbulent economic events of the late 1960s and 1970s bear witness to the continuing vitality and adaptability of the major 'master models'. Moreover, they have again demonstrated that no single system of economic ideas can be fully satisfying for all purposes. In this period, for example, the basic organizing framework of most macro-economic analysis has been supplied by Keynesian categories. But, while an American president of conservative stripe could proclaim that 'We are all Keynesians now', Western governments were simultaneously being reminded that the fiscal medicine to restrain inflationary pressures (i.e. tax increases and public-spending cuts) were less palatable politically than were Keynesian prescriptions for depression. These circumstances have been associated with a major revival of interest in monetarist analyses which have their intellectual roots in the classical and neo-classical formulations of the quantity theory.

Meanwhile, a variety of forces have inspired voices echoing other themes from the past. Growing concern about sources of energy and, in some parts of the world, about availabilities of basic foodstuffs have resurrected interest in the supply approach to the economic process which dominated the thought of the classical economists. The importance they attached to an understanding of the constraints imposed by nature's endowments to the prospects for uninterrupted economic expansion has acquired a new respectability. Similarly, the recurrence of 'stagflation' – with its combination of rising price levels and stubbornly persistent unemployment – has poured new content into a Marxian literature on the inherent contradictions of capitalism as well as into the institutionalists' critiques of neoclassical equilibrium models.

While the major 'master models' offer a variety of perspectives on the economic process, it is important to recall that the pioneers in each of these traditions shared a distinguished attribute. All of them took up their pens in a mood critical of established institutions or patterns of thought. It was this grand tradition that Keynes had in mind when he once described economics as a 'dangerous science'.

Index of Proper Names

Index of Concepts and Terms

Index of Concepts and Terms

MORE ABOUT PENGUINS
AND PELICANS

Penguinews, which appears every month, contains details of all the new books issued by Penguins as they are published. From time to time it is supplemented by *Penguins in Print*, which is our complete list of almost 5,000 titles.

A specimen copy of *Penguinews* will be sent to you free on request. Please write to Dept EP, Penguin Books Ltd, Harmondsworth, Middlesex, for your copy.

In the U.S.A.: For a complete list of books available from Penguins in the United States write to Dept CS, Penguin Books, 625 Madison Avenue, New York, New York 10022.

In Canada: For a complete list of books available from Penguins in Canada write to Penguin Books Canada Ltd, 41 Steelcase Road West, Markham, Ontario.

A Peregrine Book

MEDIEVAL POLITICAL THOUGHT

Walter Ullmann

Between the fifth and twelfth centuries, when vast
stretches of Europe were still uninhabited, a society
grew up which had to learn the very rudiments of
how to manipulate the ordering of public life. It was
during and just after this period that many of the
basic political concepts of today were formed.

In this new study Professor Ullmann employs the
latest medieval research — much of it his own – to
trace the origins and development of political ideas
in Western Europe – ideas as familiar as sovereignty,
parliament, citizenship, the rule of law, and the state.
He shows this development being forged out of the
conflict between the descending and ascending theses
of government, with their Roman and Germanic
sources, and explains the dominance of ecclesiastical
powers in medieval society.

From implicit belief in theocratic kingship to the
beginnings of popular sovereignty, Professor Ullmann's book provides an introduction to medieval
concepts of government which is both scholarly and
pertinent to the politics of today.

THE PELICAN ECONOMIC HISTORY
OF BRITAIN

1: The Medieval Economy and Society

M. M. Postan

In what *The Times Literary Supplement* called 'a survey of medieval English social and economic history which will surely hold the field for many years', Professor Postan has assembled for the first time in book-form his ideas on the medieval economy.

Beginning with the 'material' features – the settlement of the land and the technology available to the medieval husband-men – he goes on to relate demographic fluctuations to the occupation and use of the land. He continues by describing how the economic activities of the countryside, in particular the manor and the village, were controlled and organized. Finally the author analyses the shape of rural society, the rise and growth of towns, the work of companies and guilds, and concludes with a chapter on prices.

'For forty years Professor Postan has provoked and stimulated medievalists by his brilliant essays in the application of economic theory to the condition of medieval life. No English writer has done so much to open the eyes of historians in this field' – *Spectator*

THE PELICAN ECONOMIC HISTORY
OF BRITAIN

2 : Reformation to Industrial Revolution

Christopher Hill

The period 1530–1780 witnessed the making of modern English society. Under the Tudors England was a society of subsistence agriculture in which it was taken for granted that a fully human existence was possible only for the landed ruling class. In 1780 England was a national market on the threshold of industrial revolution, and the ideology of self-help had permeated into the middle ranks. A universal belief in original sin had been supplanted by the romanticism of 'Man is good'. And the first British Empire had already been won and lost. In this masterly study one of the great historians of the seventeenth century analyses the transformation of British society and the complex interaction of economic, cultural and political change in the period. In particular he stresses the political ferment of the seventeenth century and its influence on the revolutions in trade and agriculture, which in their turn prepared English society for the take-off into the modern industrial world.

'This formidable little book – its range of information is remarkable and it is stuffed with fruitful hypotheses – is rather a commentary than an analysis' – Peter Laslett in the *Guardian*

'There is clearly no lack of controversial matter here. Mr Hill has fulfilled an important function of a good social history' – *The Times Literary Supplement*

Also published in Penguins

THE PELICAN ECONOMIC HISTORY
OF BRITAIN

3 : Industry and Empire

E. J. Hobsbawm

KEYNES AND AFTER

Michael Stewart

Second Edition

In 1936 John Maynard Keynes published *The General Theory of Employment, Interest and Money*, widely acknowledged to be one of the most important books ever written.

Why was it so important? What did it say? How did it change things? Was Keynes's analysis applicable only to the mass unemployment of the 1930s, or is it also relevant to contemporary economic problems? Can Western governments really maintain full employment? Does full employment mean continuously rising prices and perpetual difficulties over the balance of payments? How does economic growth fit into the picture?

These are the issues discussed by Michael Stewart in this new and completely revised edition of his highly successful Pelican book.

'A first-rate popular study of Keynes's work and ideas' – *Banker*

'A delightful and fascinating volume . . . excellently written' – *New Statesman*

'This excellent introduction . . . the author has achieved a greater degree of readability in dealing with inherently difficult problems than one would have thought possible' – *Financial Times*

'Witty . . . and instructive' — *Spectator*